Big Book of Knitting

Katharina Buss

Big Book
of
Knitting

Sterling Publishing Co., Inc.
New York

Thanks to the Schachenmayr Company for their helpful support of this book, and for working the clothes and knitting patterns. The designs are by Elisabeth Kopff (1) and Barbara Schreyer (4).

Drawings: Sigrid Witzig, Hamburg
Cover design: Dirk Lieb
Translation: Ellen Riemschnieder—in loving memory of Jim

Library of Congress Cataloging-in-Publication Data

Buss, Katharina.
   [Urania-Ravensburger. English]
   Big book of knitting / by Katharina Buss.
     p. cm.
   ISBN 0-8069-6203-8
   1. Knitting. I. Title.
TT820.B97   1999
746.43'2—dc21

20 19 18 17 16 15 14 13

99-20386
CIP

Metric Equivalents			
Inches	cm	Inches	cm
⅛	0.3	10	25.4
¼	0.6	11	27.9
⅜	1.0	12	30.5
½	1.3	13	33.0
⅝	1.6	14	35.6
¾	1.9	15	38.1
1	2.5	16	40.6
1¼	3.2	17	43.2
1½	3.8	18	45.7
1¾	4.4	19	48.3
2	5.1	20	50.8
2½	6.4	21	53.3
3	7.6	22	55.9
3½	8.9	23	58.4
4	10.2	24	61.0
4½	11.4	25	63.5
5	12.7	26	66.0
6	15.2	27	68.6
7	17.8	28	71.1
8	20.3	29	73.7
9	22.9	30	76.2

First paperback edition published in 2001 by
Sterling Publishing Co., Inc.
387 Park Avenue South, New York, N.Y. 10016
Originally published in Germany by Urania-Ravensburger under the title *Das große Ravensburger Strickbuch*
© 1996 by Urania-Ravensburger in the Dornier Medienholding GmbH Berlin, Germany.
English translation © 1999 by Sterling Publishing Co., Inc.
Distributed in Canada by Sterling Publishing
c/o Canadian Manda Group, 165 Dufferin Street,
Toronto, Ontario, Canada M6K 3H6
Distributed in Great Britain by Chrysalis Books Group PLC,
The Chrysalis Building, Bramley Road, London W10 6SP, England
Distributed in Australia by Capricorn Link (Australia) Pty Ltd.
P.O. Box 704, Windsor, NSW 2756 Australia
Printed and Bound in China
All rights reserved

Sterling ISBN 0-8069-6203-8 Trade
              0-8069-6317-4 Paper

For information about custom editions, special sales, premium and corporate purchases, please contact Sterling Special Sales Department at 800-805-5489 or specialsales@sterlingpub.com

Contents

Introduction

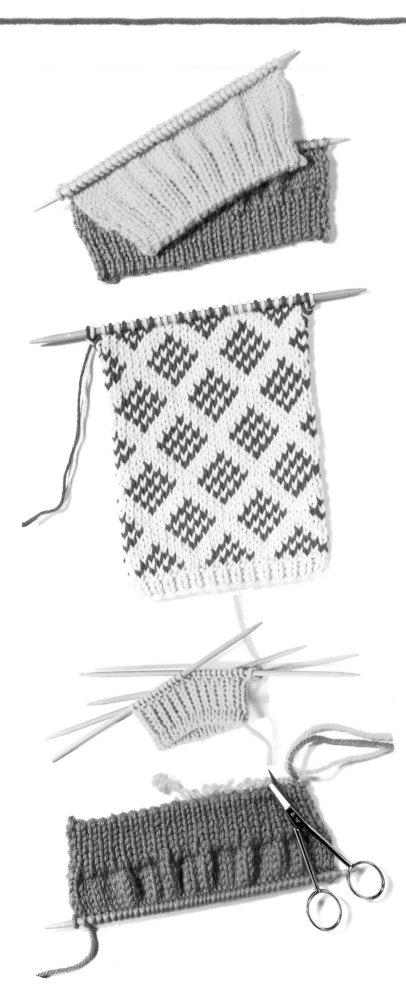

Would you like to learn how to knit? You certainly can with this book! Do you already know how to knit? Then this book is also the right one for you. It is not just a detailed, accurate, and richly illustrated book of the fundamentals, it is also a comprehensive reference work for every imaginable problem that can come up in knitting.

Knitting is one of the oldest and most popular needlecraft arts. People were knitting as far back as the Middle Ages, although at that time knitting was primarily considered "busy work" for upper-class women and girls. But it was also practiced for economic reasons. Economics played a role even later, whenever times got tough.

In today's fast-paced world, however, knitting has taken on a whole new function. Knitting is creative, fashionable, and fun. And last but not least: Knitting soothes the nerves!

Because of the enormous and constantly changing selection of yarns, there are almost no limits on your imagination. High-quality standard yarns are available in many different colors, which are constantly updated. Beginners can use fashionable specialty yarns that hide slight irregularities. For advanced knitters, there are countless patterns at all levels of difficulty.

The chapter on "Basic Techniques" explains all the fundamental steps in detail—from the various methods for casting on, to selvedge stitches, to binding off with knitting or tapestry needles.

Then there are the "Perfect Details"— bands and facings that look good from both sides. Neatly knitted neck bands for round and V-neck necklines. Polo collars and shawl collars that fit perfectly. Straight, slanted, or added pockets, buttonholes, and zippers.

There is also a detailed chapter on finishing, because how you put the parts together is what makes a piece perfect. After all, what good are neatly knitted parts if the seams are crooked! With the amount of time and attention you spent on knitting, careful sewing is the nice finishing touch.

"Special Techniques" relate to different knitting patterns, with hints and tricks for the best results. For example, double increases and decreases look better than single ones in shaker knitting. And even shortened, slanted rows are a breeze with our instructions.

Seahorses and roses are only two examples of how you can beautifully embellish a sweater. The chapter on "Decorative Details" includes not only many embroidery stitches but also bobbles, pom-poms, fringes, and tassels.

"Practical Hints" tell you how to calculate the number of stitches needed for a sweater, and how to convert patterns for different sizes and different yarns. You will find hints for designing your own sweaters, for knitting according to a pattern chart, for fixing dropped stitches, for shortening and lengthening finished pieces.

So that you can start right away and try out your knitting skills, detailed instructions are given for all the designs shown in the book as well as for knitting gloves, mittens, and socks. There is also a whole palette of beautiful patterns.

A final note: Some knitters have to "warm up" first. Many people knit relatively loosely for the first two or three rows until they get to their usual tension. So keep a small practice piece on hand—the type of yarn and needle size are unimportant. Whenever you haven't knit in a while, first knit a few rows on this practice piece before you start working on your actual project.

Materials

From knitting needles to stitch holders, from angora to viscose—here you'll learn everything you need to know about yarns, needles, and other useful knitting tools as well as important hints for taking good care of your finished pieces.

Needles and Tools

You can't do anything without knitting needles. But there are also many other useful tools that make knitting easier and more fun.

Knitting Needles

Straight knitting needles (that have the same thickness over their entire length) and interchangeable needles (that come in a set of varying sizes with interchangeable tips that are attached to the same needle shaft) are available in sizes from 0 to 15 in lengths of 10" and 14"; straight knitting needles are also available in a length of 16". They are made from aluminum, plastic, bamboo, or wood.

Circular Needles

Circular knitting needles, either nickel-plated or made of aluminum, are available in lengths of 11" to 60". and sizes from 0 to 15. Bamboo needles are available in a length of 29" and sizes 3 to 15.

Circular knitting needles can also be used in regular knitting. They are easier to handle than regular needles, especially when knitting large pieces. Also, they can be used to knit patterns in which two rows on the right side or the wrong side have to be knit one right after the other—for example, in 2-color shaker knitting. You simply push the stitches to the end where the yarn you need is located. Neck bands are knit using short circular needles.

Bamboo and wooden needles

Flex Needles

Flex needles consist of a thicker tip and a thin, round plastic strip with a length of about 20". These needles are also easier to use when knitting large pieces, such as a sweater with dolman sleeves. They are available in sizes 0 to 15.

Bamboo/Wooden Needles

Bamboo knitting needles are especially light. They have the additional advantage that persons with allergies can use them, because they are guaranteed to be free of nickel. Bamboo knitting needles are available in double-pointed sets in sizes from 0 to 11 and as straight knitting needles in sizes from 0 to 15. Wooden knitting needles, such as birch and walnut, are available in sizes 4 to 13.

Cable Needles, Needle Sets, Needle Sizer

Cable needles are available as straight or angled. The angled ones prevent stitches from accidentally slipping off the needle while you are making cables.

Needle sets or sock knitting needles consist of four or five double-pointed needles. The stitches are divided among three or four of the needles, and you knit with the fourth or fifth needle. They are available in lengths of 4" to 12". The short needles work particularly well for knitting baby booties or gloves. Needle sets are available in sizes from 0 to 15.

Needle sizers make it easier to check the size of knitting needles such as double-pointed needles. Gauges come in different varieties.

Stitch Gauge

This practical aid can be used to count stitches for knitting a gauge sample, to read off the required number of stitches, and to check the size of knitting needles.

Knitting needles

Circular needles

Flex needles

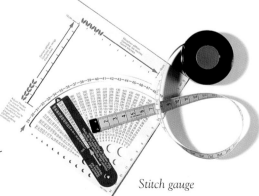

Cable needles, needle sets, needle sizer

Stitch gauge

Stitch markers, row counters, needle guards

Knitting thimbles, bobbins

Yarn boxes

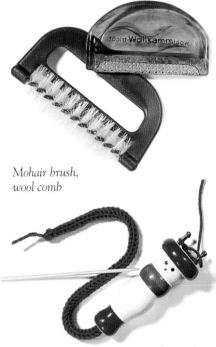

Mohair brush, wool comb

Stitch Markers, Row Counters, Needle Guards

Stitch markers are available in different colors and sizes. They make it easier to count stitches and rows, and they can be used for marking pattern sections, such as an armhole.

Row counters can be slipped onto the knitting needle. For knitting in the round, there are also row counters with open loops.

Needle guards are not intended to protect the needles but rather to keep the stitches from slipping off the needles when you are not knitting.

Yarn Guides, Bobbins

For knitting jacquard patterns, 2-eyed yarn guides are available for 2-color knitting; others with 4 notches are available for multicolor knitting.

Bobbins are available in 2 sizes. They are very helpful when knitting small areas in a different color and for intarsia knitting.

Line Marker

Using a line marker will always keep you on the correct row when you're working off a pattern chart.

Line marker

Blocking Pins, Tapestry Needles, Stitch Holders

For blocking knitted pieces, blocking pins are longer and easier to handle than normal sewing pins.

Tapestry needles or blunt needles should be used for sewing together knitted pieces, securing yarn ends, or for embroidery.

Stitch holders are extra-long safety pins. They can be used to hold stitches that will be worked later, such as those for pocket bands, or if shoulder seam stitches are going to be knit together later.

Yarn Boxes

Yarn boxes are very useful in keeping your yarn under control—and not just if you have a cat.

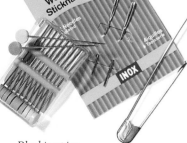

Blocking pins, tapestry needles, stitch holders

Knitting dolly

All of the products shown on pages 10 and 11 are manufactured by Inox and are available in craft stores.

Mohair Brush, Wool Comb

Mohair brushes can be used to fluff up mohair sweaters.

Wool combs remove pilled wool and fuzz.

Knitting Dolly

Knitting dollies are used to "knit" thin tubes of knitted material. For people who are impatient, there are also "knitting mills" (not shown).

Yarns

Of course, the most important thing besides knitting needles is yarn. So we'll start with a brief description of the most common kinds of yarn.

Alpaca

Alpaca wool (not to be confused with Alpakka batting) comes from alpacas, which are part of the llama family and live in South America. Alpaca wool is fine, soft, and slightly curly. You can get about 1 kg (about 2 lbs) of wool from an alpaca every 2 years.

Angora

The fur of Angora rabbits is fine and lightweight, but also relatively delicate. Angora has a very high moisture absorption capacity; it can absorb twice as much moisture as virgin wool and four times as much as cotton without feeling wet. Angora rabbits can be shorn every 3 months and each shearing yields about 250 g (about ½ lb) of wool.

Ribbon Yarn

Ribbon yarns are made primarily from cotton or viscose. They are available in knit or woven form and in different widths.

Cotton

Cotton—white gold—is the oldest known fiber in the world. It grows in tropical and subtropical climates, is a pure, natural product, and does not cause any allergies. It is breathable and can absorb a lot of moisture. It feels cool and comfortable even in hot weather.

Something new on the market is naturally colored cotton, which is grown primarily in the U.S. The earth-tone colors range from light yellow to brown, from khaki to olive.

Mercerized cotton is treated with concentrated, warm soda lye to make it shrink-proof, shiny, and stronger.

Cotton can be gas-treated to singe off the projecting fiber hairs to make the yarn even smoother.

Bouclé Yarn

Bouclé yarn is made from specialty yarns with irregular loops, twisted together with a "support thread" that is generally thinner. The denser the loops, the bulkier the knitted piece.

Angora

Ribbon yarns

Bouclé yarns are generally made from wool or wool mixed with other yarn. For light summer, bouclé yarns, cotton and linen can also be twisted together.

Cablé Yarn

For cablé yarns, two or more spinning threads are twisted together. Then several twisted threads are twisted together again. Cablé yarns are very durable, but usually they are not as soft as normal yarns.

Cotton

Bouclé yarns

Chenille Yarn

Chenille yarns can be made from cotton or synthetics. They have a plush-like and soft surface. Therefore, they are not well suited for textured patterns.

Wick Yarns

Wick yarns are open, soft yarns that are twisted together only loosely during spinning. Wick yarns with thick nubs have a real country look.

Nubby Yarns

Nubby yarns are specialty yarns with irregular, wick-like sections. Frequently, the nubs are emphasized by being a different color.

Fluffy Yarns

Fluffy yarns are high-volume yarns that look like mohair or angora, but are made from synthetic fibers.

Shorn Yarns

Shorn yarns contain a fine looped thread. The specialty yarn is added more quickly during spinning so that the excess yarn forms small loops.

Shiny or Specialty Yarns

The list of shiny yarns is endless. The natural exception is shiny silk, because most shiny yarns are produced from chemical fibers. Specialty yarns are generally used for dressy pieces or for pieces made from mixed yarns with individual "glittery" areas.

Camel Hair

Camel hair has a slightly natural shine. Pure camel hair cannot be dyed. In order to obtain fashionable colors, camel hair always has to be mixed with other fibers. Generally, high-quality virgin wool is used for this purpose, since it is very similar to camel hair.

Cashmere

Cashmere goats are not shorn; their hair is combed out when they lose their coats in the spring. A cashmere goat only gives about 100 grams (less than ¼ lb) of wool a year. That's why cashmere is very expensive. Clothing made of cashmere is very light and soft. It also provides greater warmth than any other type of yarn.

Lamb's Wool

Lamb's wool is obtained from the first shearing of a young sheep. It is particularly soft and warm.

Linen

Linen is a fiber obtained from flax plants. It feels cool, is slightly shiny, relatively stiff, but not very pliant. Linen yarn is best suited for summer clothing, since it provides little warmth and rapidly evaporates moisture. For hand knitting, linen is usually mixed with other yarns.

Metallic Polyester

These yarns are also called lamé yarns or lurex yarns. A very thin metal layer is applied to a polyester filament. Individual filaments are also twisted together with non-shiny yarns for a more quiet effect.

Chenille

Chenille specialty yarns

Wick yarns

Multicolor wick yarns

Metallic polyester yarn

Yarns

Tweed and nubby yarns

Pure wool

Mouliné and melange yarns

Melange Yarn
The French word "mélange" means mixture. For melange yarns, fibers of different colors are mixed before spinning.

Mohair/Kid Mohair
Angora goats have a long, white, curly coat. The wool obtained from young goats is called kid mohair. Since mohair dyes easily, it is available in every fashion color.

Mouliné Yarn
Mouliné, also a French word, means "twisting." For mouliné yarn, two or more different colors or different types of filaments are twisted together. If the yarn is made from different kinds of material and then dyed, each material takes on the dye in a different way.

Shetland Wool
The wool of Shetland sheep is very robust, and it is generally used to spin country tweed yarns.

Silk
Silk keeps you cool when it's hot and warm when it's cold. It is also very comfortable. But it is not easy to knit. Silk has to be knit very tightly, because finished pieces stretch the first time they are washed. Don't check the gauge until after you have washed your sample piece.

Tweed Yarns
Tweed yarns are nubby specialty yarns with the nubs dyed a different color.

Viscose
To obtain viscose, chemically pure cellulose (from wood and other plants) is treated with soda lye and carbon disulfide. Viscose is easy to knit; the finished pieces drape like cloth. The yarn can be matte or shiny. Viscose is often used as a shiny specialty yarn in mixed yarns.

Mohair

Specialty yarns

Caring for Your Finished Knit

Here's some information about how to wash and store knits so that you will enjoy the clothes you create for as long as possible.

Pay attention to the cleaning information on the yarn label. For example, if the label shows a washtub and a hand, the pieces have to be washed by hand. If there is a number in the washtub, you can wash the items at this temperature. A line under a washtub means that you should use the gentle cycle.

Yarns are often advertised as being "easy-care." But that does not necessarily mean you can wash them in a washing machine. It only means that they are easy to wash and will dry quickly.

Here's a tip: Write the most important care information onto a laundry tag with a laundry pen, and sew the tag into the back of the neckline.

Storage

Knitted clothing should always be stored lying down. Putting them on a hanger would stretch them out of shape under their own weight.

Also, wool clothing should never lie in the sun, and it definitely should not be dried in the sun. Until now, it has not been possible to dye wool so that it does not fade.

Washing and Drying

Knitted pieces should never be soaked, because that quickly causes felting. It is best to wash knitted articles in cold water with detergent for delicate items, and make sure not to rub or brush them. Also, don't wring them dry—just squeeze out the excess water. Then put the pieces between terrycloth towels, roll them up, and squeeze them dry.

If machine washing is permitted, use the gentle cycle and a slow speed for spinning.

To dry the pieces, spread them out and pull them into the correct shape. For example, cotton sweaters sometimes shrink slightly and can be stretched again while wet; on the other hand, viscose stretches, so those pieces have to be pushed together slightly. If an article is made from different colors, put cloths between the front and the back and into the sleeves to check whether the colors are still bleeding.

Use only a small amount of fabric softener (and not just to protect the environment). Don't ever use fabric softener for "superwash" yarns, unless you want to use your sweater as a dust rag when it's dry!

Most yarns will not survive being put in the dryer.

More Tips for Basic Yarns

Angora is especially delicate. Wash angora sweaters in cold water, with a mild shampoo, and rinse well many times. Then carefully squeeze the water out, roll the piece in towels, and allow it to air dry on a towel.

Pure cotton can generally be washed in a washing machine, at 140°F/60°C (see label). Use only a detergent for delicates, without a fabric brightener. Since cotton absorbs a lot of water and therefore gets very heavy, you should put the piece into a mesh laundry bag so that it can't stretch very much during washing and spinning.

Pure silk is not resilient and will stretch, particularly during the first wash. That is why you have to wash your sample before checking the gauge. Wash silk articles by themselves and move them as little as possible. Rinse with a lot of cold water. Squeeze water out carefully and allow the article to dry flat.

Viscose is similar to silk in that it tends to stretch a lot. Viscose is also not allowed to be pulled and must dry flat on a towel.

Cleaning Symbols

Symbol	Meaning
30°	Normal wash cycle
30°	Gentle wash cycle
	Hand wash
	Do not wash
	Do not use chlorine bleach
	Use cool iron
	Do not iron
P	Standard dry cleaning
P	Dry cleaning for delicate textiles
	Do not dry clean
	Dry on gentle cycle (max. 140°F)
	Do not put in dryer

Basic Techniques

Every knitted piece starts with casting on and ends with binding off. Both of these are basic techniques, along with increasing and decreasing, knit and purl, selvedges, and, last but not least, checking the gauge. All of them are explained in detail with many photographs and drawings.

Casting On

Every knitted piece starts with a cast-on row. It should not only be even, but it must also be stretchable and durable, so that the edges, not to mention the whole piece, don't lose their shape later.

Casting On with One Needle

The best-known method of casting on uses 1 needle. This Italian cast-on method gives you a strong, stretchable edge that can be used with any knitting pattern.

In order to achieve the best possible appearance, you must work very evenly. Don't cast on too tightly in order that the first row is easy to knit off. But you shouldn't cast on too loosely either; otherwise, the edge stretches out too easily. If your stitches are too tight, you can also cast on holding two needles together, and pull the second needle out before you start to knit the first row.

Before you start, measure out enough yarn for the bottom part of your piece for casting on. For every stitch you cast on, you need about ¾" of medium-weight yarn, slightly less for thinner yarn. Add another 8" to the length you have calculated. It doesn't hurt to leave the yarn a little long as you can always use it later to sew the parts together.

You don't need a slip knot or any other knot to start casting on with this method.

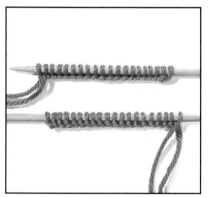

Make sure that the first row after casting on is a wrong-side row, because the loops that form on the back look like purl loops.

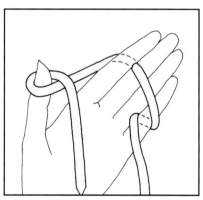

1 Wind the yarn end around the left pinkie finger, bring it to the back between your forefinger and middle finger, and forward over the forefinger. Then wrap it around your thumb from front to back.

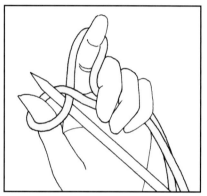

2 Hold both ends of the yarn tightly and insert the knitting needle from your right hand up into the loop around your thumb.

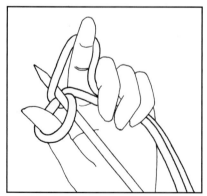

3 Bring the needle behind the yarn that comes from your forefinger...

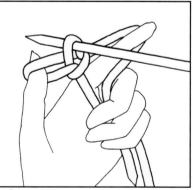

4 ...and draw this piece through the thumb loop. Let the yarn slip off your thumb.

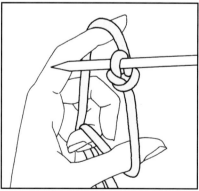

5 Pick up the bottom piece of yarn with your thumb again, from the back to the front. Pull the stitch tightly and lift your thumb up again.

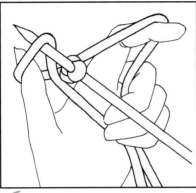

6 The first stitch is now on the needle in your right hand. Now insert the needle into the loop around your thumb...

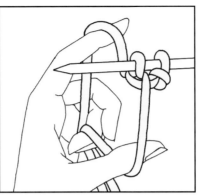

7 ...and pull the yarn through again. Tighten the loop.

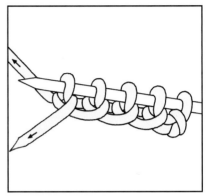

8 Repeat each of these steps for a new stitch.

Making Doubly Sure

This method of casting on produces an especially durable edge if you use double yarn for the bottom part. This is particularly important for children's sweaters as well as for socks or hats, since the cast-on edge is often stretched a lot. Place the yarn around your left hand as previously above. The end piece of yarn has to be about twice as long.

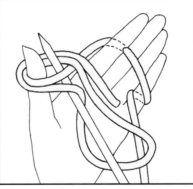

1 Place the end of the bottom piece of yarn around your thumb too and start casting on as described on page 18.

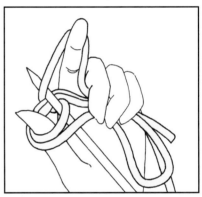

2 After you have tightened the first stitch, put the short end piece aside and keep working with the two loops of yarn on your thumb.

Casting On Wide Pieces of Sweaters

It's difficult to estimate the correct length of the bottom piece of yarn. Use a skein each for the top part and the bottom part, and knot the ends loosely together. This way, you can cast on as many stitches as you like. Cut off the bottom piece of yarn at the end of the casting-on row, and continue with the top piece.

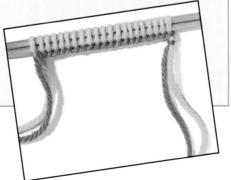

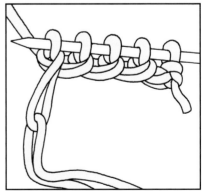

3 If you run out of yarn on the bottom, you can easily make it longer by putting an additional piece of yarn into the loop.

Open Cast On

If you want to add a ribbing or band later, use the open cast-on method. This is also a way to avoid a thick seam for pieces that are knitted crosswise.

Using yarn of a different color but approximately the same thickness, crochet a row of chain stitches. Pick up a stitch from the back, crosswise part of each crochet stitch. Make sure to pick up the stitches neatly, so that the chain stitches can be undone easily later on.

After the piece is finished, pick up the first row of stitches on a thinner needle and undo the row of chain stitches.

Now knit the first row as if it is on the right side of the work, or purl as if

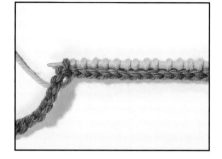

it is on the wrong side of the work, using the thinner ribbing needle. If you don't work this additional row, the stitches knit with the heavier needles can be clearly seen (see photo to the right).

Even if you knit the ribbing in the same color as the rest of the piece, you should work this additional row.

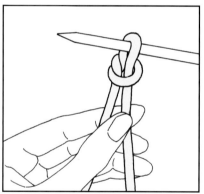

Simple Cast On

A simple cast on is not good for casting on a large number of stitches. The loops are difficult to knit from the needle, and the row of stitches does not stretch well.

A simple cast on is used for short pieces, such as the top edge of buttonholes. To start a row of simple cast on, you need a slip knot.

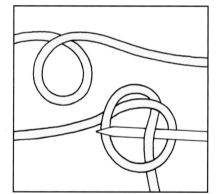

1 To make a slip knot, form a loop with the end of the yarn. Put the end of the yarn under the loop and catch it with the needle.

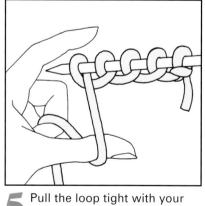

2 Pull both ends of the yarn while pushing the knot towards the needle.

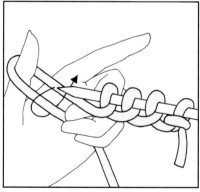

3 To cast on, place the yarn around your thumb and...

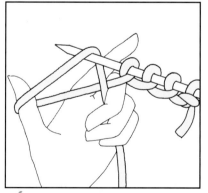

4 ...pick the front of the yarn up with the needle from below.

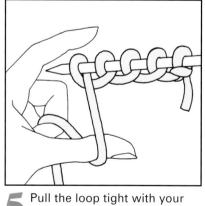

5 Pull the loop tight with your thumb.

Knitted Cast On

Used a knitted cast on whenever several stitches have to be added at a side edge, such as for sweaters knitted crosswise when you need many stitches for the side edges at the end of a sleeve.

For a knitted cast on at the beginning of your work, you need a slip knot. For a knitted cast on of stitches at the side of a started piece, always cast on at the beginning of a row.

This method of casting on is not good for ribbing, because it is too loose.

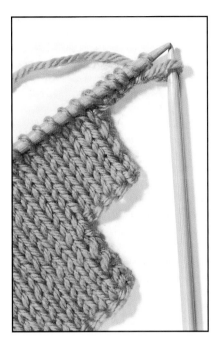

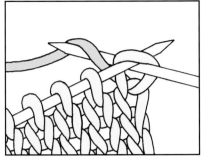

1 Draw a loop out from the first stitch of the row (or out from the slip knot, if you are starting a piece) and pull it a little longer than normal.

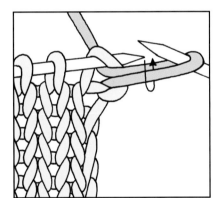

2 Now insert the left needle through the loop from the front and below.

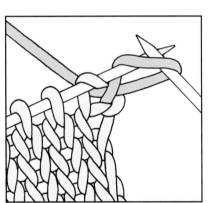

3 Put the loop onto the left needle and pull the stitch tightly.

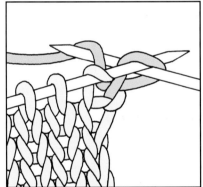

4 Don't take the right needle out. Use it to draw out another loop, which you'll lift onto the left needle again, etc.

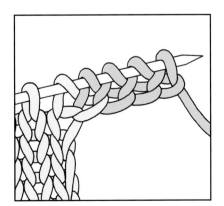

5 This results in a loose edge that is easy to knit off and easy to sew together later.

From the Middle

It's a matter of luck if you happen to find the yarn end in the center of a skein in your first try. In most cases, you will pull out too much yarn. But only if you pull the yarn out of a skein from the middle will the yarn always stay in the same place and not roll around as you knit. This is especially important when you are knitting with several skeins.

The little tangle of yarn at the beginning is easy to untangle and will soon be used up.

Casting On in Kitchener Rib

So that your hand-knit items look as professional as possible, you should try casting on in kitchener rib. This is also an "Italian method" of casting on.

To start, you can cast on with 1 needle or crochet a row of chain stitches, using a yarn of a different color in each instance, or you can start with the yarn you are going to use and cast on the number of stitches you need right away. These two ways will be described in detail on the following pages.

Kitchener rib always starts with 4 rows that are knit on needles 1 or 2 sizes smaller than the rest of the ribbing. In these rows, only the knit stitches are knit; the purl stitches are slipped. These four rows are knit exactly the same way as a double-face work (starting on page 160). If you put the knit and purl stitches on two separate needles, there will only be knit stitches on both sides.

Casting On in Kitchener Rib with a Different-colored Yarn

There are two possibilities: Crochet a row of chain stitches or cast on with 1 needle, as explained above. Choose a yarn of a different color that is equal in thickness to the yarn you intend to use and as smooth as possible. That allows you to undo the chain stitches or cast-on stitches easily after the piece is finished.

Number of Stitches
For both ways, you need to crochet or cast on half the number of stitches needed plus 1 stitch. Or you can calculate the number of stitches this way:

Except for the selvedge stitches, every stitch is doubled: 24 x 2 = 48 stitches plus two selvedge stitches. So for 80 stitches you need 41 starting stitches; for 90 stitches you need 46.

Needle Size
If you intend to knit the basic pattern of your piece using size 6

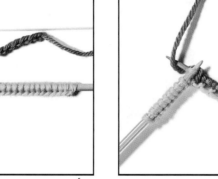

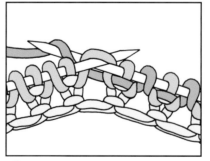

1 Cast on ½ the number of stitches needed + 1 with a different-colored yarn and largest size needle, and knot ends together (bottom). Or crochet a loose row of appropriate number of chain stitches (top).

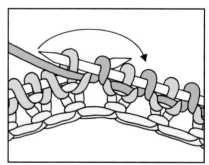

2 Then knit, or pick up from the back, the crosswise part of the crochet stitch as follows, using the smallest size needles (for example, size 2). After the selvedge stitch, alternately knit 1 stitch...

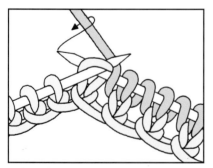

...from the next stitch or chain stitch, then bring the yarn over to end with a selvedge stitch.

3 In the next row, knit the loops formed by bringing the yarn over, and...

4 ...pick up the purl stitches purlwise, keeping the yarn in the front of your work.

needles, you should also use size 6 needles for casting on the first row. Then knit the first 4 or 5 rows with the main yarn, using size 2 needles, and the rest of the ribbing with size 4 needles.

After finishing steps 1–4, you must always knit the knit stitches and slip the purl stitches purlwise in the next 3 rows, keeping the yarn in the front of your work.

After these 4 rows, keep alternating knit and purl with the needles used for the ribbing (for example, size 4).

When you are done, cut the different-colored yarn at intervals of 3 or 4 stitches…

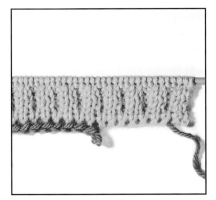

…and pull out the pieces, or undo the chain stitches.

Cross-over for 2 x 2 Rib

If you want to alternate 2 knit, 2 purl stitches for your ribbing, start the same way as for the 1 x 1 ribbing. After the first 4 rows, in which you only knit the knit stitches and slip the purl stitches purlwise, cross 2 stitches out of every 4 so that 2 knit stitches and 2 purl stitches lie next to each other.

Always choose a number of stitches that can be divided by 4, plus 2 selvedge stitches. This means that the pattern will be complete even after the seams are closed.

After the selvedge stitch, knit the next stitch, as before. Then always alternately cross 2 stitches, as described to the right, and knit 2 stitches as they appear.

You can also cross the stitches using a cable needle. To do this, place every 2nd purl stitch onto a cable needle behind the work, first knit the knit stitch from the left needle, then purl the purl stitch from the cable needle.

Casting on in kitchener rib looks good whether you alternately knit 1, purl 1, or knit 2, purl 2.

1 First knit the stitch after the next, i.e., knit stitch, passing in front of the purl stitch. Leave both stitches on the left needle for now.

2 Now bring the yarn to the front and purl the purl stitch that is in front of it. Then slip both stitches off the left needle. Knit the next two stitches "normally."

Casting On Kitchener Rib with Main Yarn

Place the yarn around your left hand as usual and then over your thumb. The end of the yarn will hang over the thumb and has to be about three times as long as the intended width of the piece—as is the case for all other types of casting on.

Hold the end of the yarn tightly between your middle finger and your ring finger. Work the casting on and the next 4 rows using needles one size smaller than the needles you will use for the ribbing.

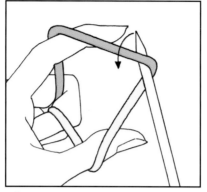

1 Bring the tip of the needle from the left to the right under the yarn, and turn it counterclockwise to the left...

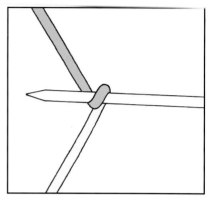

2 ...so that a loop is formed on the needle. Hold this loop, which will be the selvedge stitch, tight with your right thumb.

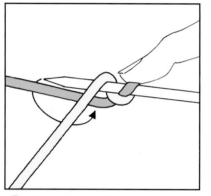

3 Bring the needle under the part of yarn that is on your thumb, take hold of the yarn with your forefinger, coming from above and going down, and draw it under the yarn on your thumb and to the front.

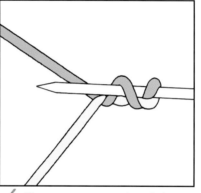

4 The yarn on your thumb is now behind the first (knit) stitch, that is, behind the needle.

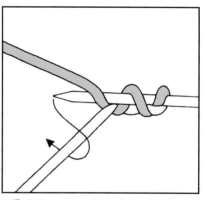

5 Bring the needle from back to front, under the yarn on your forefinger. Take the yarn on your thumb, coming from above and going down, and draw it under the yarn on your forefinger to the back.

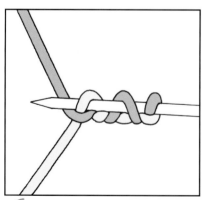

6 The forefinger yarn is in front of the (purl) stitch—in front of the needle. It is on the needle the "wrong" way and will be knitted in the first row on the right side.

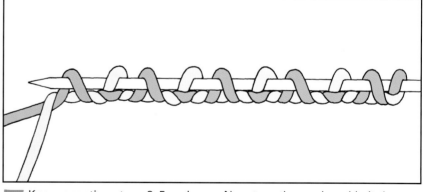

7 Keep repeating steps 3–5 and end the row with a "knit" stitch, that is, with steps 3 and 4.

Now turn the work and knit the first stitch as a selvedge stitch.

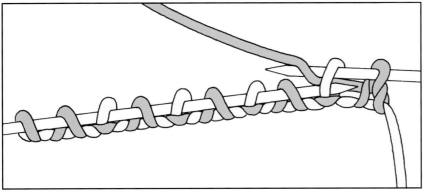

8 The next stitch is a knit stitch and is twisted on the needle. Insert the needle into the back part of the stitch, from right to left, and knit this stitch twisted.

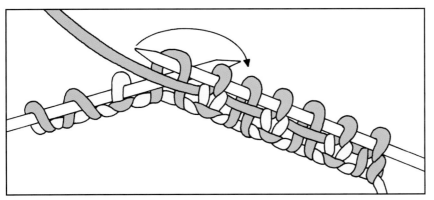

9 Place the yarn in the front of your work and slip the next stitch purlwise.

Once you have cast on the required number of stitches in steps 1–7, turn your work. From then on, you must keep repeating steps 8 and 9; this means that you must knit the knit stitches twisted, since they are on the needle the "wrong" way, slip the purl stitches purlwise, and carry the yarn along at the front of your work.

In the next 3 rows, keep on knitting the knit stitches and slipping the purl stitches purlwise using the smaller-size needles.

After these 4 rows, continue working in the ribbing pattern, using needles that are one size larger—as described for casting on with yarn of a different color.

The finished ribbing looks the same from both sides. After they are no longer on the needle, the loops formed by the yarn on your thumb (which are yellow in the drawings) form the knit stitches on one side, while the loops formed by the yarn on your forefinger (which are orange in the drawings) form the knit stitches on the other side.

To make the individual steps easier to understand, the yarn on your thumb and forefinger is shown in different colors in the drawings and in the knit example.

Selvedges

Perfect edges are an important part in knitting. They make it easier to sew the knit pieces together, and those edges that are not hidden away in a seam are supposed to look decorative.

For all knitted pieces that will be sewn together later, I recommend selvedge stitches that are knit twice, that is, in every row, rather than selvedge stitches that are knit once. This makes the stitches next to the selvedge stitches more uniform. Also, the pieces can be sewn together more attractively, because when selvedge stitches are knit only once, little holes often form at the seams.

Seam Selvedge

For seam selvedge in stockinette stitch, all the stitches are knit in the stockinette pattern—i.e., all of them are knit on the right side of the work, purled on the wrong side of the work; vice versa for reverse stockinette stitch.

This firm selvedge is good for any pieces that are going to be sewn together later. So that the seam stays flat, half stitches can be sewn together in the case of thick or bulky yarns.

Also, this is the best selvedge if you intend to knit on bands.

Garter Stitch Selvedge

In a garter stitch selvedge, the selvedge stitches are slipped knitwise at the beginning of each row, and knit at the end of each row. Or vice versa: the selvedge stitches are knit at the beginning of each row and slipped knitwise at the end of each row. However, this way of knitting has been shown to have some drawbacks. In every 2 rows, there is an offset in the knit piece, which reaches several stitches into the piece and remains visible even after the seams are sewn.

For this reason, a **knitted** or **purled** garter stitch selvedge is better. Here, the selvedge stitches are knit or purled at the beginning and end of each row.

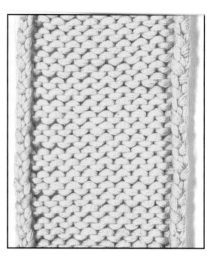

Seam selvedge

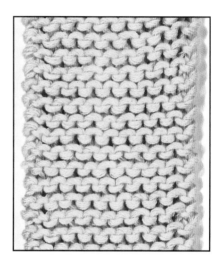

Knitted garter stitch selvedge

Purled garter stitch selvedge

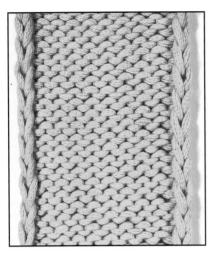
Conventional chain stitch selvedge

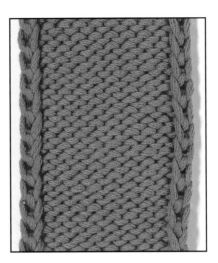
Decorative chain stitch selvedge

Selvedges in shaker knitting

A knitted garter stitch selvedge is good for any pieces worked in garter stitch, since the rows tend to contract more than in a stockinette stitch. It is also good for mohair yarn with very long fibers, because the knots can be sewn together like the parts of a zipper to allow the seam to lie flat (see seams, page 113).

With a purled garter stitch selvedge, the stitches can be pulled even tighter. For this reason, this selvedge is particularly good for shaker knitting.

Chain Stitch Selvedge

Chain stitch selvedges can be knit in two different ways: the conventional chain stitch selvedge and the decorative chain stitch selvedge.

For a conventional chain stitch selvedge, bring the yarn to the front at the beginning of every row on the right side of the work, and slip the selvedge stitch purlwise; bring the yarn to the front again in front of the last stitch and slip the last stitch purlwise. In every row on the wrong side, knit the first stitch twisted, inserting the needle into the back part of the stitch, and knit the last stitch.

For a decorative chain stitch selvedge, in every row on the right side

of the work, knit the first stitch twisted, inserting the needle into the back part of the stitch, and knit the last stitch; in every row on the wrong side, slip the first and last stitch purlwise, keeping the yarn in the front of your work.

Selvedges in Shaker Knitting

This selvedge is especially attractive for edges in shaker knitting that will not disappear into a seam later. It is worked over three stitches, in each instance, at the beginning and end of a row. You should knit these three stitches as tightly as possible so that this selvedge doesn't stretch out later.

On right side of work: Knit the selvedge stitch, slip the next stitch purlwise, placing the yarn in the front of your work, then knit 1 stitch. Now continue working in the shaker knitting pattern, beginning and ending with a purl stitch. Over the last 3 stitches, knit 1 stitch, slip 1 stitch purlwise, and, keeping the yarn in the front of your work, knit the selvedge stitch.

On wrong side of work: Slip the selvedge stitch purlwise, placing the yarn in the front of your work, knit 1 stitch, slip 1 stitch purlwise, placing the yarn in the front of your work.

Then continue working in the shaker knitting pattern, beginning and ending with a knit stitch. At the end, slip 1 stitch purlwise, placing the yarn in the front of your work, knit 1 stitch, and slip the selvedge stitch purlwise, placing the yarn in the front of your work.

> **TIP**
> In every row, knit the first 4–5 stitches tightly, this will make the edges next to the selvedges more uniform (see also page 29).

Knit and Purl

Knit and purl are the basis of all knitting. No matter whether it's a textured pattern or an openwork pattern, a cable pattern or shaker knitting, these 2 basic stitches are always used.

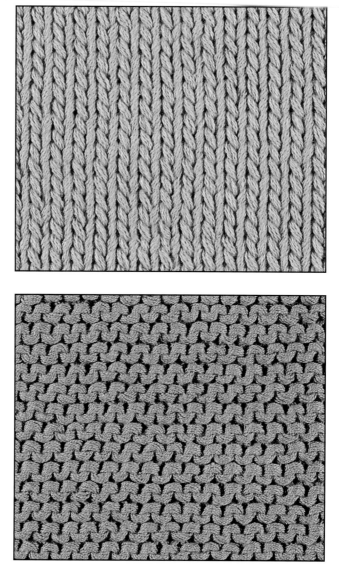

Stockinette: Knit every row on the right side of the work, purl every row on the wrong side.

Garter stitch: Knit every row, both on the right side and on the wrong side of the work.

Pieces knit in stockinette stitch have a flat, smooth surface. Pieces in reverse stockinette stitch have a grainy texture. Pieces knit in garter stitch have a rough surface.

For beginners, textured patterns composed of knit and purl stitches are best. The combination possibilities are almost infinite. If the knit and purl stitches are arranged vertically—i.e., in rib patterns—the knit stitches are more prominent. In horizontal stripes, purl stitches form a clearly marked crosswise rib. Some examples of simple knit-purl patterns are shown on page 30.

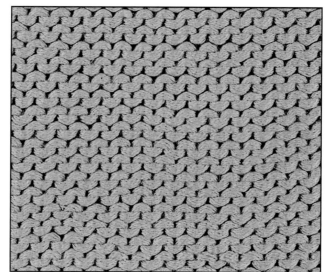

Reverse stockinette: Purl every row on the right side of the work, knit every row on the wrong side.

Knit Stitch

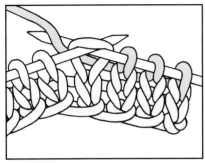 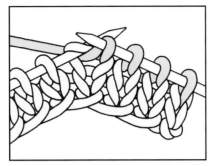 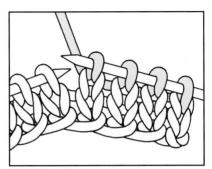

1 Insert the right needle into the first stitch of the left needle, going from front to back.

2 Pass the yarn under and up the front of the right needle. Draw it through the stitch with the right needle.

3 Drop the stitch from the left needle. The stitch on the right needle is a knit stitch.

Purl Stitch

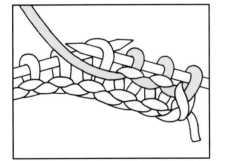 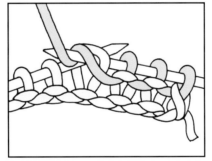 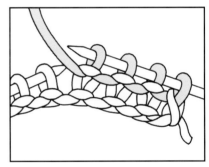

1 Place the yarn in the front of your work. Insert the right needle into the first stitch on the left needle, going from back to front.

2 Pass the yarn over, down the back, and under the right needle. Draw it through the stitch to the back.

3 Drop the stitch from the left needle. The stitch on the right needle is a purl stitch.

Attractive Edges

When knitting pieces in stockinette stitch, some stitches at the sides, directly next to the selvedge stitches, look very tight, and those in the row above them look very loose. This problem is generally even more pronounced on the left side.

The cause for this lies in the previous row! When inserting the needle into the stitch, the yarn of the previous row is generally pulled up a little too much, and then the next stitch is made. This way, a little bit of extra yarn is pushed along to the next stitch, almost invisibly, at every stitch. This is not so obvious within the row but at the end of the row— the excess yarn spreads out over the last few stitches before the selvedge stitch.

These unattractive edges can be prevented with a little bit of practice:

In every row, you have to pull the first 3–4 stitches after the selvedge stitch tightly, and knit the last 3–4 stitches more loosely.

Basic Patterns and Color Changes

You can knit lovely textured patterns using simple knit and purl stitches. Here are some examples.

Small Seed Stitch

Alternately knit 1 stitch, purl 1 stitch. In the next row, knit over the purl stitch and purl over the knit stitch. Use even number of stitches.

Large Seed Stitch

Just as in small seed stitch, alternately knit 1 stitch, purl 1 stitch, but work two rows of the same stitches before switching stitches. Use even number of stitches.

Box Stitch

For this pattern, you need an even number of stitches. Alternately knit two stitches, purl two stitches, and switch the stitches after two rows.

Ribbed Stitch

For this pattern, alternately knit two stitches, purl two stitches. So that the pattern matches at the seams, start with 1 knit stitch on the right side of the work, 1 purl stitch on the wrong side.

Crosswise Rib

After 5 rows of stockinette stitch, knit a row on the wrong side of the work. This row will form the crosswise rib on the right side.

Small seed stitch

Large seed stitch

Box stitch

Ribbed stitch

Crosswise rib

Color Changes in Reverse Stockinette Stitch and Patterned Stripes

"Lines" form when knit and purl stitches come on top of each other in horizontal stripes with textured patterns. In order to have a clear color differentiation on the right side of the work with these patterns, the stitches in the first row of a new color have to be knit on the right side and purled on the wrong side. This makes the two-color line show on the wrong side of the work.

TIP

Work color patterns with an uneven number of rows, like the box stitch pattern without a "line" (see column 3, row 2 photo on this page), on a circular knitting needle. This way, you can always push the stitches to the end of the needle where the yarn for the new color is located. You won't have to sew in all those ends after every color change.

These 4 rows in aqua and white are in reverse stockinette stitch. The line is made in the first row of the new color each time the color changes.

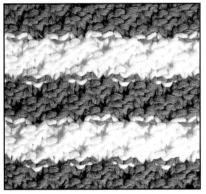

Here the pattern is alternately 2 knit, 2 purl, and after every other row—i.e., in every row on the right side of the work, the stitches are switched. A new color starts every 6 rows. In all seed or box stitch patterns, purl stitches in the new color will show up as a line.

After the first 4 rows, knit 1 row on the right side of the work and then work 3 rows in reverse stockinette stitch in every color. The colors will not mix together.

Here the box pattern is knit over 7 rows. The first row of each new color is worked as an additional row. It is knit on the right side of the work and purled on the wrong side. This additional row is hardly noticeable in the pattern. Only the stripe is a little wider.

At the bottom, the stitches between the cables are done in reverse stockinette stitch. At the top, these stitches are worked as knit stitches in the first row on the right side each time there is a color change. This allows better color definition.

Decreasing

Decreases should always be worked in such a way that they match the knitted piece as perfectly as possible. This also applies to decreases at the edges and within a piece.

When working rounded or slanted shapes at the side edges—such as armholes, V-necks, or raglan patterns—individual stitches have to be decreased at the edges. These decreases should always match the design of the piece and the knitted pattern.

If only 1 stitch has to be decreased at the armhole or the neckline, you can simply knit or purl the selvedge stitch together with the stitch next to it as needed. However, for raglan sleeves or V-necks, it looks better if you shift the decrease 1 or 2 stitches in from the edge and knit the second and third, or third and fourth stitches together. In the examples shown, the third and fourth stitches were knit together or worked together, as appropriate.

Decreases within a piece are worked the same way as at the edges. If you want to decrease symmetrically on both sides, you must knit or work two stitches together two times. You need such double decreases for V-neck edgings, picot, or openwork patterns.

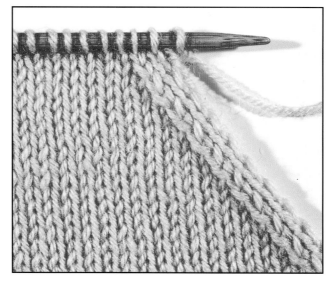

Decreases slanted to the left: Knit 1 stitch after the selvedge stitch, then work a single decrease; slip the next stitch knitwise, knit 1 stitch, and pass the slipped stitch over it.

Decreases slanted to the right: Knit to within 4 stitches from the end of the row, knit the next 2 stitches together, knit 1 stitch, then work the selvedge stitch.

On the right side, a single decrease to the left is worked with the last stitch of the stockinette rib and the next stitch. On the left side, the first stitch of the rib is knit together with the stitch in front of it.

Knit Decrease

For a 1-stitch decrease slanting to the right within a knitted piece, knit 2 stitches together.

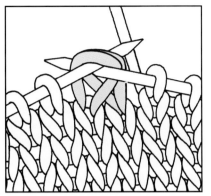

1 Insert the needle into the front of the two knit stitches from left to right.

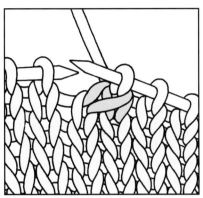

2 Draw the yarn through to the front knitwise, and drop both stitches from the needle.

Slip Decrease

Work a single decrease slanting to the left by passing 1 stitch over the other.

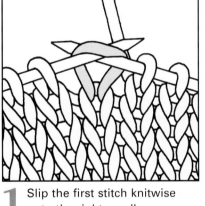

1 Slip the first stitch knitwise onto the right needle.

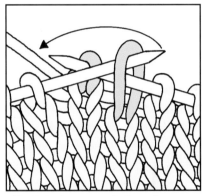

2 Knit the next stitch and pass the slipped stitch over it.

Twist Decrease

You can also work decreases slanted to the left by knitting the stitches twisted. This will cause the stitch on top to twist.

1 Insert the right needle into the back part of the 2 knit stitches, from the right to the left.

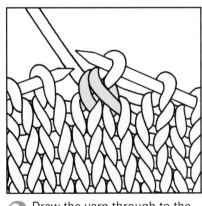

2 Draw the yarn through to the front knitwise, and drop both stitches from the needle.

Purl Decrease

In reverse stockinette stitch, you can work all the decreases by purling 2 stitches together. However, if the decrease is supposed to be symmetrical on the stockinette side, purl 2 stitches together for a decrease slanted to the right.

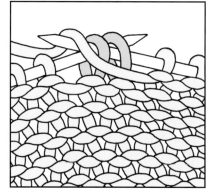

1 Insert the right needle into the front of the next 2 stitches, from right to left.

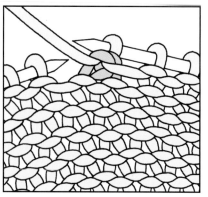

2 Draw the yarn through both stitches purlwise, and drop these stitches from the needle.

Purl Slip Decrease

Work a single decrease slanted to the left on the stockinette side by passing 1 stitch over the other.

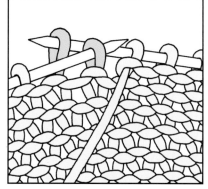

1 Carefully drop the first and second stitch off the left needle. Pick up the second stitch with the right needle and pick up the first stitch again with the left needle.

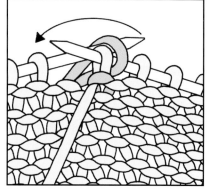

2 Now purl the first stitch (the stitch on the left needle) and then pass the second stitch over the first stitch at the back of the work.

Purl Twist Decrease

For a decrease that will be slanted to the left on the stockinette side, you can also purl 2 stitches together twisted. This causes the stitch on the right to twist, just as when knitting 2 stitches together twisted.

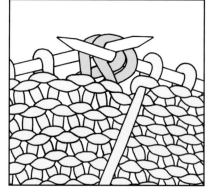

1 Insert the right needle into the back of both stitches at the back of the work, from left to right.

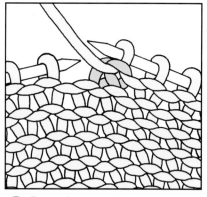

2 Draw the yarn through the stitches purlwise, and drop both stitches from the left needle.

Double Decrease Slanting to the Left or to the Right

If you want to decrease 2 stitches, you can knit 3 stitches together for a decrease slanted to the right. For a decrease slanted to the left, you can knit 3 stitches together twisted, or you can work as described on the right.

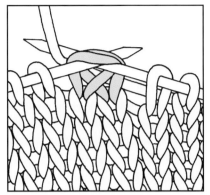

1 For a double decrease slanted to the right, slip the first stitch knitwise, knit the next 2 stitches together,...

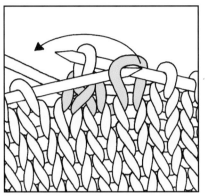

2 ...then pass the slipped stitch over the 2 knitted-together stitches.

Double Decrease with Center Stitch on Top

This decrease, also called a decrease with 2 stitches passed over, is frequently used for lacy openwork patterns. It is also the most attractive decrease for the center of V-neck neck bands that are knitted on (starting on page 80). Working a double decrease with the center stitch on top is described on the right.

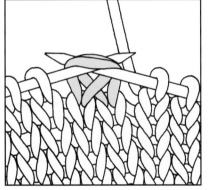

1 Slip the stitch in front of the center stitch, together with the center stitch, knitwise.

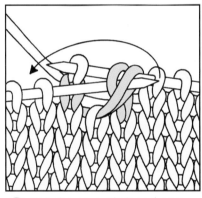

2 Knit the next stitch and pass the slipped stitches over it.

For decreases in the wrong side rows, slip 1 stitch. On the right side, knit this stitch together with the stitch in front of it. On the left side, work a decrease slanted to the right.

On both sides of the edge, purl together 2 stitches. For the band tip, knit together 2 stitches on the right side of the center, and a decrease to the right is worked on the left side.

For this band, 3 stitches are purled together 3 times. The last decrease is worked with the knit stitches slanted to the left (see above).

Increasing

For slanted edges of sleeves and sides, wider parts after ribbing, and many different textured patterns, stitches have to be added in different ways. All the various kinds of increase are explained in detail on the following pages.

Increases for Slanted Edges

These increases are generally knit into the horizontal part of the yarn between 2 stitches by twisting the strand so that no holes will form. It is best not to work the increases directly next to the selvedge stitches, but rather 2–3 stitches in from the edge. When the pieces are sewn together later, using an invisible seam, the crosswise parts of the yarn can be sewn together precisely. I recommend an increase next to the second stitch, particularly in openwork patterns, since the horizontal threads pull out of shape even more when the yarn is wound around the needle

(see also sleeve increases in open-work patterns, page 192).

Increasing Several Stitches

If several stitches have to be increased at the sides, such as for the body of a sweater knit crosswise, you can add the stitches at the beginning of a row by knitting them on or by a simple cast on (see casting on, page 20–21). However, it is better to knit them on. If you use a simple cast on, the edge will not be as stretchable, and these stitches are also more difficult to knit off.

Increases After Ribbing

Stitches also can be increased after ribbing. At the waist, a few increases are generally sufficient, but after tight wrist ribbing, the number of stitches to be added is generally greater. These increases should be distributed evenly over the entire width of the piece so that you don't get ugly "bulges." And the increases should be worked twisted so that no holes appear.

If a simple pattern is used after the ribbing, such as stockinette stitch,

the increases can be worked in the first row of the pattern. However, if the body of the piece is being worked in a complicated cable, openwork, or jacquard pattern, it is easier to work the increases in the last row of the ribbing. This gives you the right number of stitches right from the first row of the pattern.

Some patterns require double increases after the ribbing—for example, if you are going to continue to work in a ribbed pattern or in shaker knitting. Such increases are the most attractive if you work a twisted purl increase before and after the purl stitch, and knit the purl stitch.

Double Increases Within a Piece

In some patterns, double increases have to be worked within the knitted piece, i.e., a stitch is increased on both sides of one or several center stitches. If you work these increases the same way on both sides of this center stitch, the increases will both be slanted to the left and look asymmetrical.

Whenever you have to increase several stitches at the sides, such as for items that are knit crosswise, knit the stitches on (see casting on, page 21).

To make your knitting appear symmetrical when working with increases with yarn over, work the yarn over ahead of the center stitch "the wrong way." Place the yarn over the right needle from the back to the front; but after the center stitch, place the yarn over the normal way. In the next row on the wrong side of the work, purl the normal yarn over ahead of the center stitch twisted, and just purl the "wrong" yarn over after the center stitch.

For increases from the horizontal threads between stitches, pick up the horizontal thread ahead of the center stitch from back to front and knit it; after the center stitch, pick up the horizontal thread from front to back and knit it twisted.

These symmetrical increases are important for emphasized slanted edges that are knit from the top to the bottom. Here, the pattern is uniformly widened on both sides of the center stitches, and the increases recede into the background.

In the knitted examples on the following pages, the increases are worked on both sides; however, they can be worked either only on one side or on both sides.

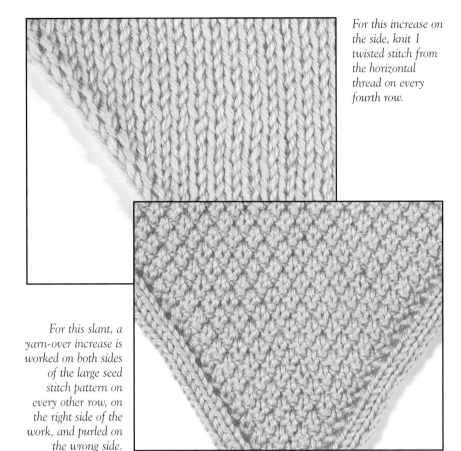

For this increase on the side, knit 1 twisted stitch from the horizontal thread on every fourth row.

For this slant, a yarn-over increase is worked on both sides of the large seed stitch pattern on every other row, on the right side of the work, and purled on the wrong side.

Patterns with Decreases and Increases

Here are two more examples of patterns in which double decreases and increases form the basis of the pattern. The increases are worked with yarn over; the double decreases are worked with the center stitch on top.

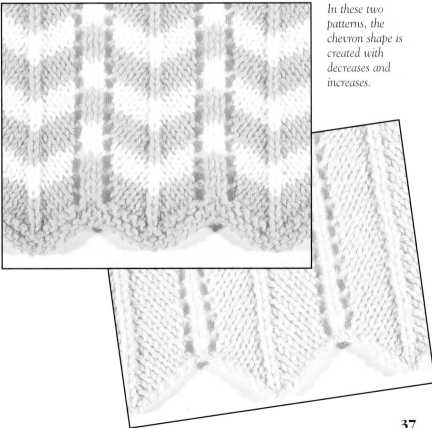

In these two patterns, the chevron shape is created with decreases and increases.

Knit Increase Without Twisting

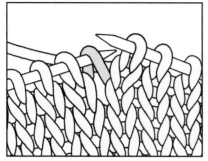

1 Using the left needle, pick up the horizontal thread between 2 stitches from front to back, and...

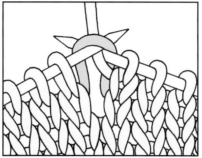

2 ...knit it. The new knit stitch is on the right needle. This increase creates a visible little hole.

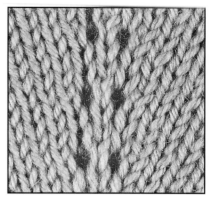

On both sides of the center stitch, 1 stitch is increased from the horizontal thread, without twisting; 2 little holes can be seen here.

Twisted Knit Increase

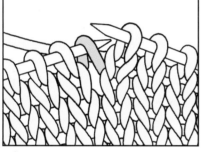

1 Using the left needle, pick up the horizontal thread between 2 stitches from front to back, and...

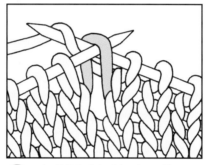

2 ...knit it twisted by inserting the needle into the back part of the loop.

On both sides of the center stitch, 1 twisted stitch is increased from the horizontal thread; there are no holes in the knitting.

Symmetrical Increases from Horizontal Thread

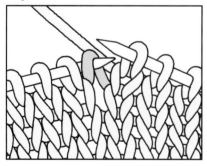

1 For symmetrical increases, pick up the horizontal thread ahead of the center stitch from back to front...

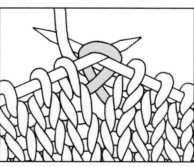

2 ...and knit it. Work the horizontal thread after the center stitch with a twisted knit increase (see above).

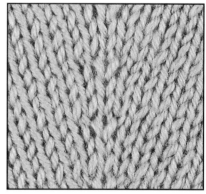

The increases are symmetrical if the horizontal thread ahead of and after the center stitch are worked as described on the left.

Purl Increase Without Twisting

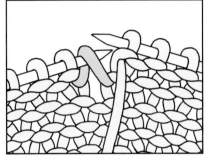

1 Using the left needle, pick up the horizontal thread between 2 stitches from front to back, and...

2 ...purl it. The new purl stitch is on the right needle. This increase creates a visible little hole.

Twisted Purl Increase

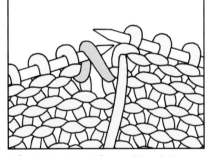

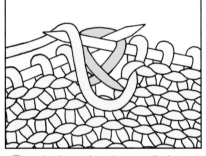

1 Using the left needle, pick up the horizontal thread between 2 stitches from front to back and purl it twisted...

2 ...by inserting the needle into the back part of the loop from left to right. This prevents holes in the knitting. On the stockinette stitch side, this increase slants to the left.

Symmetrical Twisted Purl Increase

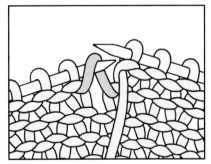

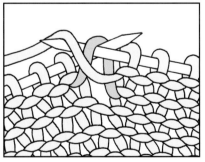

1 This increase is important for a symmetrical appearance in stockinette stitch. Using the left needle, pick up the horizontal thread between 2 stitches from the back to the front, and...

2 ...purl it by inserting the needle into the front part of the stitch from right to left. The loop will twist by itself. On the stockinette stitch side of the work, this increase is slanted to the right.

Increases in Ribbing

In 1 x 1 ribbing, you should always work double increases. To do this, increase 1 stitch with a twisted purl out of the horizontal thread after a knit stitch, then knit the next stitch (which was a purl stitch), then increase another stitch with a twisted purl out of the next horizontal thread. In this way, the ribbing is maintained even after the increases.

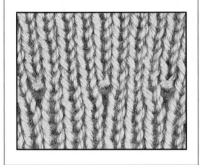

Increase with Simple Knit Yarn Over

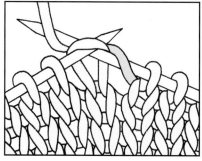

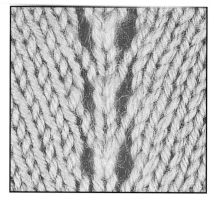

1 Place the yarn over the right needle from front to back, and continue knitting normally.

2 In the next row, on the wrong side of the work, purl the yarn over the loop.

Increase both sides of center stitch 1 stitch with a yarn over. Purl stitch the new loops on the purl row of the wrong side. This makes 2 large holes.

Increase with Twisted Knit Yarn Over

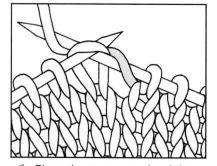

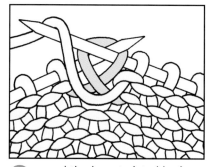

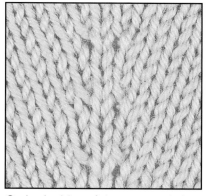

1 Place the yarn over the right needle from front to back, and continue knitting normally. In the next row,...

2 ...purl the loop twisted by inserting the needle into the back part of the loop from left to right. On the stockinette stitch side, this increase slants to the left.

On both sides of the center stitch, increase 1 stitch using a yarn over, and purl it with a twist in the next row. This makes the holes smaller.

Symmetrical Increases with Yarn Over

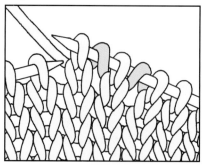

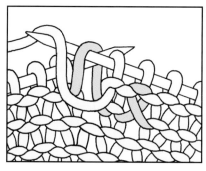

1 For symmetrical increases on both sides of the center stitch, place the yarn over "the wrong way" ahead of the center stitch, and "normally" after the center stitch.

2 In the next row, purl the "normal" yarn over twisted. Purl the "wrong way" yarn over as shown. On the right side of the work, this increase is slanted to the right.

For symmetrical increases, work the yarn overs differently before and after the center stitch.

Increase from Previous Row Stitch

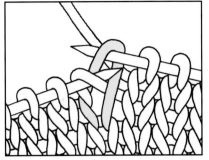 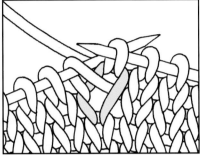 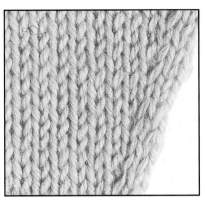

1 Using the right needle, pick up the horizontal loop of the stitch in the previous row and knit it.

2 Then knit the stitch itself.

Increasing from the previous row stitch is good for the slanted edges of sleeves. Work this increase 2–3 stitches in from the side edges (see drawing on the left).

Increase in Previous Row Stitch

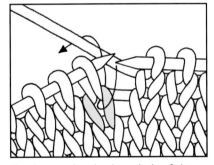 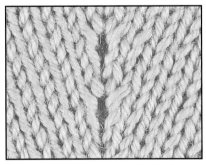 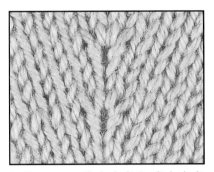

For increasing in the stitch of the previous row, don't pick up the horizontal loop, but instead insert the needle directly into the stitch in the previous row and knit it.

Over the same stitch, knit 1 stitch in the stitch of the previous row, knit 1 stitch, and knit 1 stitch in the stitch of the previous row. Don't drop the stitch from the left needle until all 3 stitches have been made.

In the same stitch, knit 1 stitch, knit 1 stitch in the previous row, and knit 1 stitch. Don't drop the stitch from the left needle until all 3 stitches have been made.

For this decorative corner, the increases are worked with yarn overs. The center stitch is slipped in the knit rows and purled in the purl rows.

Binding Off

You have to bind off stitches at the end of knitted pieces, at armholes and necklines, and also for buttonholes. You can choose from among 3 different ways: binding off by passing stitches over each other, binding off by knitting stitches together, or finishing with crochet.

Binding Off by Passing Stitches over Each Other

The stitches in the binding-off row are adapted to the pattern. For textured patterns, continue according to the pattern, bind knit stitches off knitwise, purl stitches purlwise.

The binding-off row of ribbing can be worked entirely with knit stitches; this will make the edge turn slightly forward (see knit-on bands, page 62). But an edge bound off entirely in knit stitches is less stretchable than an edge bound off in accordance

with the pattern—for example, alternately 1 knit, 1 purl.

Work as close to the tip of the needle as possible and make sure that when you are passing the stitch you are binding off over the next one and you don't pull it out too far.

In the binding-off row, keep an eye on the pattern, because this row will still show a little once the pieces are sewn together.

Binding Off by Knitting Stitches Together

When you bind off by knitting stitches together, you get a firm edge that doesn't stretch much, because the binding-off stitch is only as large as a normal stitch, since it is picked back up onto the left needle. In normal binding off, on the other hand, the stitch is usually pulled out a little when it is passed over.

Knitting the stitches together is therefore good for patterns in which the stitches tend to pull together, such as cable patterns as well as for jacket or pocket bands that are not supposed to stretch. Also, it is very good for shoulder seams, since it will keep the seams from stretching out.

Finishing with a Crochet Hook

Some knitters prefer to finish with a crochet hook. The size of the hook influences how loose the edge will be.

For a normal, relatively stretchy edge, use a crochet hook that is the same size as the knitting needles. For an especially strong edge, such as for front bands, use a smaller crochet hook. For a looser edge, such as for neck bands that will be turned in and sewn down later, use a bigger hook.

Insert the crochet hook into the stitch the same way you would knit the stitch following the pattern: for stockinette stitch from front to back; for purl stitch from back to front.

No matter how you bind off, there will always be 1 stitch left over at the end of the row. Draw the end of the yarn through this stitch and pull it very tight. Then you can sew the yarn end into the selvedge stitches or use it to sew the pieces together.

Binding off by passing stitches over each other in stockinette stitch: For patterns with knit stitches, knit the stitches and then bind them off by passing one over the other.

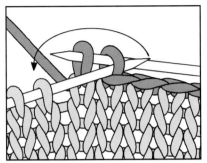

For patterns with a stockinette stitch background, knit the selvedge stitch and the next stitch, then pass the selvedge stitch over the second knit stitch. Keep knitting 1 stitch at a time and passing the previous stitch over it until all the stitches are bound off.

Binding off by passing stitches over each other in reverse stockinette stitch: For patterns with purl stitches, purl the stitches and then bind them off by passing one over the other.

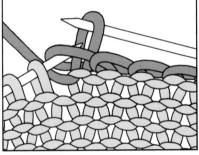

For patterns with reverse stockinette stitch background, work selvedge stitch and purl next stitch, then pass selvedge stitch over second purl stitch. Keep purling 1 stitch at a time and passing previous stitch over it until all stitches are bound off.

Binding off by knitting stitches together: This results in a firm, non-stretchable edge, which is especially good for patterns that "pull together," such as cable patterns, or for bands and buttonholes.

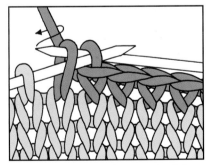

Knit the first 2 stitches on the left needle together, twisted, and put the finished stitch back onto the left needle. Keep knitting 2 stitches together until all the stitches are bound off.

Basic Techniques

Finishing with a crochet hook also produces a neat edge. The size of the crochet hook determines the stretchability of the edge.

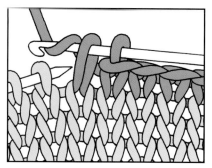

When you finish with a crochet hook, draw a loop through selvedge stitch. Pick up 1 stitch at a time from knitting needle, add it to stitch on crochet hook, and crochet both stitches together like a chain stitch, i.e., pull working yarn through with the hook.

Binding Off in Cable Patterns

When you bind off large cables, the edge usually gets very wavy if you knit and bind off all the stitches. This could easily cause problems when you sew shoulder seams together or sew sleeves in.

You can eliminate this excess width by knitting the center stitches of the cables together before you bind them off. If the cables are very wide, you can knit 2 stitches together 2 or 3 times.

When binding off cable pattern stitches, knit 2 stitches together, more than once if necessary, so that the pieces don't become too wide.

Binding Off in Shaker Knitting

In shaker knitting, the stitches are bound off the way they lie. Yarn overs are knit together with their related knit stitch, purl stitches are purled.

You will get a stronger edge if you knit the last row before binding off, not in the shaker pattern, but rather alternating knit and purl without yarn overs. Then you can bind off by knitting the stitches together.

Shaker knitting stretches out easily at points that are subject to greater stress, such as the shoulders. That is why it is especially important to bind off firmly.

If your binding off edge has become too loose or irregular, don't despair! You can pull the stitches up so that they come out perfect.

Many knitters have problems with binding off uniformly and precisely to measure. When binding off sleeve stitches, that isn't so important, since the binding-off row disappears into the seam later. But for cardigan and pocket bands, or for shoulder seams, which are not supposed to stretch too much, firm edges when binding off are very important.

Always start at the beginning of the row so that you can sew the excess yarn away when you are done. If you work in the other direction, you will end up with a loop.

If you bind off in a row on the right side of the work, turn the piece and work from left to right. One stitch at a time, pull up first the back part of the stitch (the

part that is facing the front of the work), then the front part of the stitch. Do this for every single stitch.

If you bind off in a row on the wrong side of the work, you can pull the stitches up on the right side of the work. Here again, first pull up the back part of the stitch, then the front part of the stitch, of every single stitch.

Even a band knit loosely with many stitches will fit perfectly after the stitches are pulled up. The binding-off stitches will be precise and uniform at the top edge, and in the right size.

Binding Off in Kitchener Rib

Analogous to casting on in kitchener rib, there is an especially professional-looking way of finishing your pieces; it's called binding off in kitchener rib.

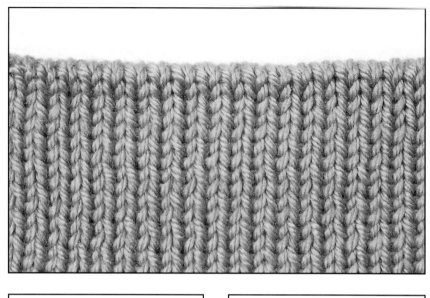

 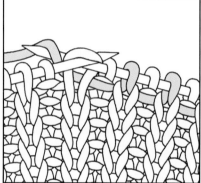

This edge is particularly stretchable if you work the last 2 rows exactly the same way you worked for casting on in kitchener rib (pages 22–25). This means that in the last row on the right side and the last row on the wrong side of the work, you only knit the knit stitches and slip the purl stitches. Work these 2 rows with a needle one size smaller. If you are using heavy yarn, depending on how you knit, you can even use a needle 2 sizes smaller. Try it out to see which works better.

You finish by sewing the edge with a heavy tapestry or blunt needle. The yarn end for sewing has to be about 3 times as long as the piece is wide. It's better if you leave it a little longer, because you can't add any yarn if you run out!

After the selvedge stitch(es), keep repeating steps 3 to 5 (page 47). Pull the yarn relatively tight after every step.

1 In the last 2 rows, knit only the knit stitches and slip the purl stitches, keeping the yarn in front of the needle.

2 Insert the tapestry needle into the selvedge stitch from front to back, i.e., from left to right. If a knit stitch is next, insert the tapes- try needle into both stitches at the same time. Allow the stitch, or 2 stitches, to come off the needle and pull the yarn relatively tight.

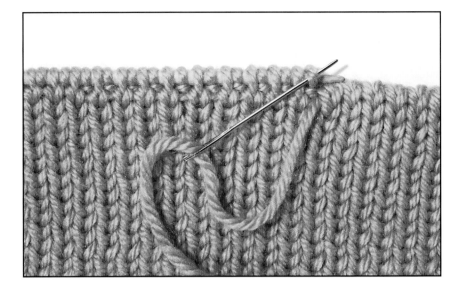

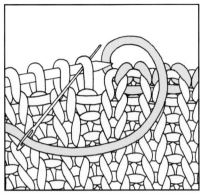

3 Now insert the tapestry needle into the purl stitch from left to right—i.e., from back to front—and pull the yarn tight. Leave the stitch on the needle for now.

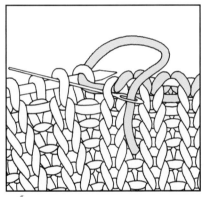

4 Insert the tapestry needle from right to left through the last knit stitch (not on the needle) and at the same time through the next knit stitch (on the needle). Pull yarn tight.

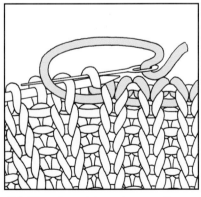

5 Then insert tapestry needle through the purl stitch again, from right to left, and pull yarn tight. Then let the 2 stitches—1 purl and 1 knit—drop off the needle.

Binding Off in Kitchener Rib for 2 x 2 Ribbing

Since binding off in kitchener rib is actually only possible with 1 x 1 ribbing, the ribbing has to be prepared properly.

In the third-to-last row, which is a row on the wrong side of the work, you "exchange" 2 stitches. If you start the ribbing in a row on the right side of the work, purl 1 stitch, knit 2 stitches, purl 2 stitches, etc. If you start the ribbing in a row on the wrong side of the work, start by purling 1 stitch.

Now, in a row on the wrong side of the work, knit the selvedge stitch and purl 1 stitch. Exchange the next 2 stitches as follows: First knit the knit stitch, which is not the next stitch but the one after it, and leave it on the needle. Then place the yarn at the front of the work, purl the purl stitch, and let both stitches drop from the needle.

Alternately, keep on working knit 1, purl 1, exchange 2.

If you tend to knit rather tightly, pull the knit stitch slightly to the front with the right needle, because this will make it easier to insert the needle from left to right as you finish an exchange. You can also use a cable needle to exchange the stitches, just as for crossing stitches. But in most cases this takes even longer and involves even more effort.

Now work 2 more rows the same way as in 1 x 1 ribbing, and then start working with the tapestry needle.

In a row on the wrong side of the work, knit 1 stitch and purl 1 stitch after the selvedge stitch. Cross the next 2 stitches: First knit the knit stitch, which comes after the next stitch. Then place the yarn at the front of the work,…

…purl the purl stitch, which is in front of it, and let both stitches drop from the left needle. Keep repeating these steps over 4 stitches. After you are done, you will end up with alternating knit and purl stitches on the right needle.

Finish by working 2 rows with slipped purl stitches and using a tapestry needle to finish as in 1 x 1 ribbing.

Binding Off in Kitchener Rib When Knitting in the Round

Tight-fitting neckline ribbing is usually worked with short circular knitting needles. This is the most attractive way to work necklines, because it avoids a seam.

Here again, the last 2 rounds have to be worked with slipped stitches. To do this, in the first round, knit all the knit stitches and slip the purl stitches with the yarn at the front of the work. In the next round, work all the purl stitches and slip all the knit stitches with the yarn at the back of the work.

After these 2 rounds, start with the tapestry needle and in a purl stitch:

Insert the tapestry needle into the purl stitch from left to right and pull the yarn tight. Leave this stitch on the knitting needle for now. Then insert the tapestry needle through the last knit stitch on the right needle, and at the same time through the next knit stitch on the left needle, from right to left, and pull the yarn tight. The stitch on the right needle stays on the needle. Now insert the tapestry needle into the purl stitch again, from right to left, and allow the first 2 stitches to drop from the left needle.

Continue working as for open ribbing until the end of the round. After the last purl stitch has been bound off, pull the yarn end in to the inside and sew it in on the back.

After having put the tapestry needle through the purl stitch and pulled the yarn tight, put the tapestry needle through the last knit stitch on the right needle and the first knit stitch on the left needle and pull the yarn tight. Then put the tapestry needle through the purl stitch again. At the end of the round, sew the yarn end in on the inside.

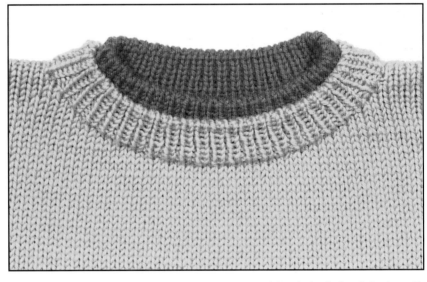

Two neck bands finished with binding off in kitchener rib. Here's how you can save a neckline that has come out too wide: Under the first neck band, knit on a second, slightly longer neck band in the same color or a contrast color (see also necklines, pages 76ff.).

TIP

Always make sure that your yarn end is long enough for binding off in kitchener rib. You need about 3 times the width of the piece. You can't add more yarn if you run out before you finish.

Gauge

Before you start knitting an article of clothing, you should always knit a sample to check your gauge! This is absolutely necessary, because everyone knits differently, and you might need more or fewer stitches and rows for the same width. Even though it takes a little time, it will save you time in the long run—not to mention money and trouble.

U se the same yarn as the one you intend to use for your sweater or cardigan. Pay attention to the information on the label.

You should always work a sample that is at least 5" x 5" square. Selvedge stitches and casting-on and binding-off rows generally don't give reliable measurements. Before you measure your sample, dampen it slightly, block it, and let it dry—in other words, treat it just like your finished piece will be treated.

Now place the sample piece on a smooth surface; you might have to pin it down.

Using a stitch gauge (available in needlework stores), you can easily count the stitches and rows. But you can use a simple tape measure, too; putting pins in at the appropriate locations will help.

If the number of stitches and rows matches the information on the label or in the instructions, you can go ahead and start knitting.

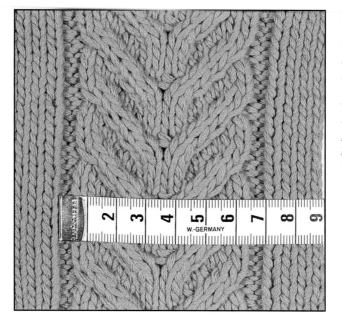

Cable patterns tend to pull together in comparison with stockinette stitch. That is why you must work a separate sample piece for each pattern and check the gauge.

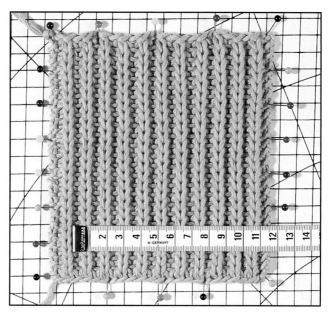

Pieces worked in shaker knitting tend to stretch when worn: Single shaker knitting tends to stretch lengthwise, Double shaker knitting tends to stretch sideways. Stretch your sample piece correctly before counting the stitches and rows.

If you counted more stitches and rows, you knit too tightly. Then use a larger-size needle. If you counted fewer stitches and rows, you knit too loosely. You should use a smaller-size needle.

Pattern Samples to Check Gauge

For the gauge of pieces in stockinette stitch or reverse stockinette stitch, the ratio of stitches to rows is about

2:3. The same holds true for textured patterns and for intarsia worked in stockinette stitch.

For jacquard patterns, the number of stitches is generally the same as for stockinette stitch, but you need fewer rows in comparison. For uniform jacquard patterns, the ratio is actually only 1:1—i.e., you need an equal number of stitches and rows for a 4" square. Some patterns have to be stretched slightly to measure them—for example, you should stretch

For jacquard patterns, the number of stitches over the width is the same as for stockinette stitch, but you need fewer rows for the same length.

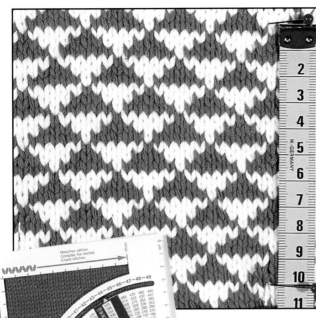

Different kinds of stitch and row counters are available in needlework stores.

ribbing out sideways slightly before measuring. Pieces worked in shaker knitting also stretch out as you wear them. You should stretch samples worked in single shaker knitting the long way slightly, while samples worked in double shaker knitting should be stretched sideways slightly, before you count the number of stitches and rows.

For cable patterns, you need more stitches than for stockinette stitch. If

you are combining cables and stockinette stitch, you must knit a sample piece for both patterns. This also holds true for all other kinds of pattern that tend to "pull together."

You can calculate the required number of stitches for the desired width of your piece using the table below. The selvedge stitches always have to be added. For a gauge of 22

TIP

Even if your sample piece has the correct gauge, check your work again once your piece is about 12″ long. Many knitters work differently when they have a lot of stitches on the needles, as compared with working a small sample piece.

---

stitches per 4″ and a desired width of 22″, you will need 66 + 55 + 2 selvedge stitches = 123 stitches in total.

Number of Stitches per 4 Inches

	10	11	12	13	14	15	16	17	18	19	20	21	22	23	24	25	26	27	28	29	30	31	32
¼″	1	1	1	1	1	1	1	1	1	1	1	1	1	2	2	2	2	2	2	2	2	2	2
½″	2	2	2	2	2	2	2	2	2	3	3	3	3	3	3	3	3	3	4	4	4	4	4
¾″	2	2	3	3	3	3	3	3	4	4	4	4	4	4	5	5	5	5	5	5	6	6	6
1″	3	3	3	4	4	4	4	4	5	5	5	5	6	6	6	6	7	7	7	7	8	8	8
2″	5	6	6	7	7	8	8	9	9	10	10	11	11	12	12	13	13	14	14	15	15	16	16
3″	8	9	9	10	11	11	12	13	14	15	15	16	17	17	18	19	20	20	21	22	23	23	24
4″	10	11	12	13	14	15	16	17	18	19	20	21	22	23	24	25	26	27	28	29	30	31	32
5″	13	14	15	17	18	19	20	21	23	24	25	26	28	29	30	31	33	34	35	36	38	39	40
6″	15	17	18	20	21	23	24	26	27	29	30	32	33	35	36	38	39	41	42	44	45	47	48
7″	18	20	21	23	25	26	28	30	32	33	35	37	39	40	42	44	46	47	49	51	53	54	56
8″	20	22	24	26	28	30	32	34	36	38	40	42	44	46	48	50	52	54	56	58	60	62	64
9″	23	25	27	30	32	34	36	38	41	43	45	47	50	52	54	56	59	61	63	65	68	70	72
10″	25	28	30	33	35	38	40	43	45	48	50	53	55	58	60	63	65	68	70	73	75	78	80
11″	28	31	33	36	39	41	44	47	50	52	55	58	61	63	66	69	72	74	77	80	83	85	88
12″	30	33	36	39	42	45	48	51	54	57	60	63	66	69	72	75	78	81	84	87	90	93	96

Perfect Details

The details are what's important! Whether it's a simple ribbing or a double facing, neckline or collar, pocket or buttonhole—perfectly worked details decide the quality of your finished piece.

Bands, Hems, Ribbing

Attractive ribbing and bands on a sweater can catch the eye. The more decorative the outside edges, the prettier the piece. No matter which method of casting on you prefer, you should match the bands to the main pattern as well as possible.

Always start the ribbing with a row on the wrong side of the work so that the purl stitches of the casting-on row are on the inside of your sweater.

Bands are the edges at the beginning of a knitted piece, whether they are wristbands on the sleeves or waistbands on the back and front. They can range from traditional ribbing—1 or 2 stitches alternately knit and purled, either worked normally or twisted—to double hems to bands that are patterns in themselves with cable patterns or openwork patterns. Everything is possible. A rolled edge worked in stockinette stitch is very simple to make but also very decorative.

Make sure that after the casting-on row (except when you are using open casting on), you always work a row on the wrong side of the work first, because the casting-on row itself forms a purl-like line that often does not match the pattern.

Ribbing should be stretchable and slightly gather the piece. That is why it is generally worked with a needle one or two sizes smaller than the rest of the piece. This holds true even for bands that are worked double.

So that the seams match too

If you are working a 2 x 2 ribbing, the number of stitches should be divisible by 4, plus 2 selvedge stitches—for example, 50 or 98 stitches. No matter whether you start with 1 or 2 knit stitches or purl stitches, the pattern is maintained even after the parts are sewn together.

In the first row on the wrong side of the work, purl 1 stitch; the row will then also end with a purl stitch and the selvedge stitch. After the pieces are sewn together with an invisible stitch (see pages 112ff.), 2 knit stitches will be right next to one another. Or start the first row on the wrong side of the work with 2 purl stitches; then you will automatically end with 2 knit stitches. Here again, the pattern is complete after the pieces are sewn together.

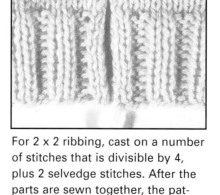

For 2 x 2 ribbing, cast on a number of stitches that is divisible by 4, plus 2 selvedge stitches. After the parts are sewn together, the pattern will also match at the seams—

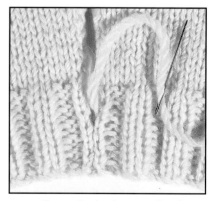

regardless of whether you begin with 1 or 2 stitches knit or purl after the selvedge stitch.

With twisted stitches

With seed stitch in the ribbing

Rolled edge

Seed stitch edge all around

Garter stitch

With Twisted Stitches

In the rows on the right side of the work, alternately knit 1 twisted stitch and purl 1 stitch. In the rows on the wrong side of the work, alternately knit 1 stitch and purl 1 twisted stitch.

With Seed Stitch in the Ribbing

After casting on, begin with a row on the wrong side of the work, alternately knit 1, purl 1. In the row on the right side of the work, knit all the stitches. Keep repeating these 2 rows.

This ribbing is less stretchable. It is good for boxy sweaters with a straight cut and for straight facings, such as for polo necklines or side slits.

Rolled Edge

For this edge, work about ¾" to 1¼" in reverse stockinette stitch, then work in stockinette stitch. Work the rows in reverse stockinette stitch with a needle one size smaller so that the edge does not become too loose.

Seed Stitch Edge All Around

Small seed stitch is good for bands and facings. But it does not stretch. Alternately knit 1, purl 1, and offset the work in the rows on the wrong side of the work.

Garter Stitch

Edges worked in garter stitch do not roll up. Knit all the rows.

Kitchener Rib Cast On and Stripes

If the ribbing includes a few stripes in a contrasting color, a sweater worked in only one color other than the additional color in the ribbing has a much fresher look. Casting on in kitchener rib is described starting on page 22.

Mini-ribbing and Jacquard Border

If you want to work a jacquard border into the band, because of the yarn carried on the back of the work, you either have to work a double hem (page 58) or start with a very narrow ribbing (in the photo, it was started by casting on in kitchener rib).

A border worked in stockinette stitch is not stretchable. It is therefore good for waist-length sweaters or long sweaters with a side slit. Work with needles one size smaller than the basic pattern requires to the end of the border.

Two-color Ribbing

Here the 2-color rows are worked using the jacquard technique (starting on page 142). The selvedge stitches always have to be worked with both yarns.

After the casting-on row, in the next row, on the wrong side of the work, alternately knit 1, purl 1, then continue in 2 colors: In the rows on the right side of the work, work the knit stitches with the first color, the purl stitches with the second color, and vice versa in the rows on the wrong side of the work. Make sure that the yarn not being used is carried at the back of the work in the rows on the right side of the work, and at the front of the work in the rows on the wrong side of the work. At the end, continue ribbing in just the first color for another 2 rows, then continue in the desired pattern.

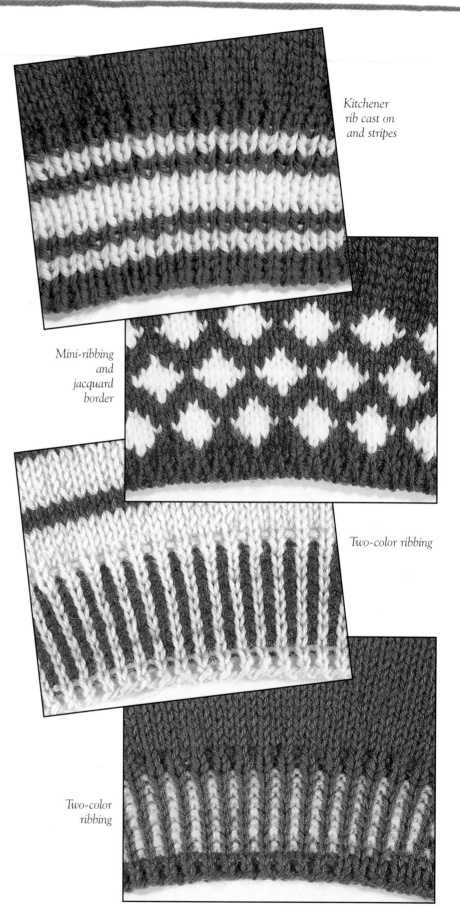

Kitchener rib cast on and stripes

Mini-ribbing and jacquard border

Two-color ribbing

Two-color ribbing

With large cables

With small cables

Openwork pattern with points

Openwork pattern with garter stitch

With Large Cables

If you want to work a sweater with ribbing and cables, this band is a nice "finish." The wide cables (worked over 8 stitches) are worked over the entire sweater; the narrow cables (worked over 4 stitches) turn into stockinette stitch ribs (see cable patterns, pages 132ff.).

With Small Cables

On the left, 2 stitches are crossed to the left every other row, and on the right every 4th row. Cables pull the stitches together a lot. If you continue in stockinette stitch after the ribbing, don't increase any more stitches; if the sweater is supposed to be boxy, you have to decrease a few stitches (see cable patterns, pages 132ff.).

Openwork Pattern with Points

Bands of openwork are also very attractive on sweaters worked in stockinette stitch. The increases and decreases usually result in a wavy edge, which does not roll up or only rolls up slightly (pattern chart on pages 218ff.).

Openwork Pattern with Garter Stitch

This pattern is also good for bands, since it does not roll up because of the garter stitch. The length of the pattern can be varied; it is always offset by half a pattern repeat (pattern chart on page 219).

Double Hems Knitted Together

Cast the stitches onto two needles (or on a needle two sizes larger), then work 6 or 8 rows in stockinette stitch using the ribbing needles, starting with a row of purl stitches on the wrong side of the work. After the 8 rows, work a row of knit stitches on the wrong side of the work, and then another 6 or 8 rows in stockinette stitch. Then pick up the stitches of the casting-on row on a thin needle, and knit 1 stitch from the main needle and 1 stitch from the cable needle together.

If you need an odd number of rows for the desired length of the hem, work 7 or 9 rows of stockinette stitch, for example, then 1 row of purl stitches on the right side of the work, and then another 7 or 9 rows of stockinette stitch. Again, the stitches are knit together with the casting-on stitches in a row on the right side of the work.

Pick the stitches of the casting-on edge up onto a thin needle.

Now always knit 1 stitch from the knitting needle and 1 stitch of the casting-on row…

…together and keep working this way to the end.

If the hem gets a little too loose, you can pull a wide elastic through it.

Picot Edge

For this decorative edge, instead of working the turning line with purl stitches, work a row with yarn overs on the right side of the work. For this, you need an even number of stitches and must work this row as follows: selvedge stitch, *knit 2 stitches together, work 1 yarn over, keep repeating from*, selvedge stitch. Afterwards, purl 1 row on the wrong side of the work and then work the same number of rows as before the row of openwork. Then knit the stitches together with the picked-up stitches of the casting-on edge.

For a row of openwork, alternately knit 2 stitches together and work 1 yarn over. Pick up the stitches of the casting-on row as for the double hem, and…

…knit them together with the stitches on the working needle. Or continue knitting and turn the hem after the piece is finished, and sew it down at the appropriate point.

Turn the hem over at the row of purl stitches, and carefully pin it down over its entire width. When you sew it down, catch every other stitch.

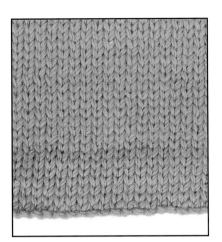

The finished hem from the right side of the work. Don't pull the yarn too tight when you are sewing the hem down, otherwise the hem tends to turn to the outside.

Increase 1 stitch every other row at the corners until you reach the desired hem length and facing width.

First sew the double hem down as described above.

Then turn the facing in to the inside and sew it down.

On the right side of the work, you see a neat, flat corner.

Double Hems Sewn Together

Instead of knitting the hem together, you can also simply continue knitting after the row of purl stitch, which creates the turning line (or after the openwork row), and at the end, turn the hem to the inside at this edge and sew it down. To do this, pin the stitches very carefully one on top of the other, because even a single stitch that is in the wrong place will make the hem look crooked. Then sew the stitches loosely to the back stitch parts of the corresponding row.

Hem and Facing with Mitered Corner

If you want to work a piece with a double hem and knit-on facings, you should use a mitered corner so that you don't have a thick bunch of material at the bottom edge.

Depending on the gauge, cast on 4–6 stitches less than you need. Then increase 1 stitch every other row at the outside edge. At the desired length for the hem, work the row of purl stitches and then continue in the pattern. Use the stitch that was increased in the purl row as the outside edge for the front facing, and slip it every other row—don't knit it. Then increase as many stitches as before for the hem, every other row.

Knit-on Facings

If you knit facings on afterwards, it is very important to pick up the correct number of stitches and to bind off correctly. The finished facing is not supposed to pull together or to be unattractively stretched out. Pay attention to the following tips and your facing will be perfect!

Single Facings

Follow this basic rule for the number of stitches to be picked up: Always work 3 stitches over 4 rows. This is almost always the case for facings in stockinette stitch or reverse stockinette stitch. For ribbing patterns that are worked as 1 x 1 or 2 x 2 ribbing, or for cable patterns, you have to try out the correct ratio of stitches to be picked up over the rows by using your sample as a gauge. If the facing is not supposed to tighten too much, more stitches are required—for example, 4 stitches

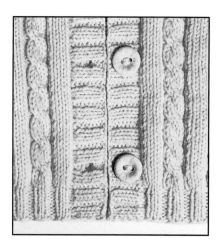

On cardigan facings, make sure that the ribbing is arranged to be symmetrical.

over 5 rows or 5 stitches over 6 rows.

If you knit very tightly, or with needles two sizes smaller, or if you want to work a small cable pattern, you may have to pick up a stitch out of every row.

When you have few stitches and rows on your gauge sample—for example, if you are knitting with size 10½ or 11 needles and only need approximately 16 rows for 4" in length—little holes might form when you pick up the stitches if you skip rows. In this case, the best thing to do is to pick up a stitch from every row and knit 2 stitches together in the first row on the wrong side of the work at regular intervals. Again, you should try this out using your sample for gauge.

For picking up the facing stitches, it is important to have the correct selvedge stitches; they should always be worked either in stockinette stitch or in reverse stockinette stitch in every row. Only then is it possible to pick the stitches up evenly. In order for the facing not to fold towards the outside later, the entire selvedge stitch also has to be picked up.

If the selvedge stitches are not knit well, or are knit too loosely, you can strengthen the edge with crocheted slip stitches. When crocheting, pay attention to how many slip stitches to work over the rows so that you can pick up a facing stitch out of every slip stitch later. You can also work the slip stitches several stitches in from the edge and then sew the edge down on the inside.

Binding off correctly is also important (see pages 42ff.). Normally, a facing bound off as the stitches lie will be very stretchable. Therefore, you should always bind off firmly. Always work as close as possible to the tip of the needle, and make sure that when you pass the binding-off stitches over, you don't pull these stitches and make them long.

You get the tightest edge if you bind off the stitches by knitting them together.

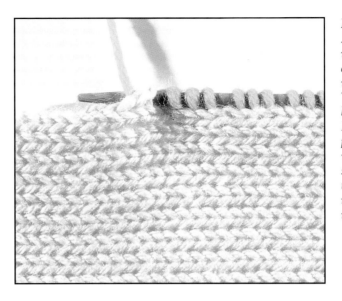

Normally, pick up 3 stitches over 4 rows for stockinette stitch or reverse stockinette. The sets of 3 can be clearly seen. For facings with patterns, including ribbing, use the sample for gauge to try out how many stitches you need to pick up.

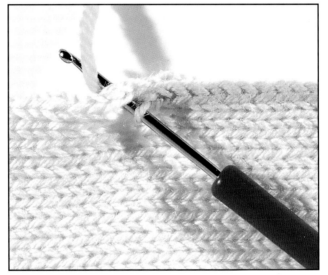

You can reinforce an edge that was worked too loosely or not done well with a row of slip stitches crocheted on (page 73).

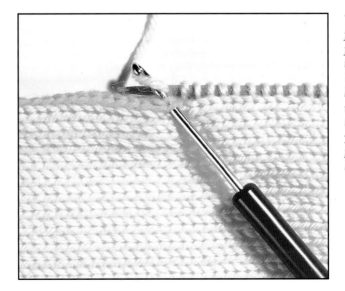

Then pick up the facing stitches from both parts of the slip stitches. Use a thinner knitting needle or use a crochet hook to pull the knitting yarn through and put the loop on the knitting needle.

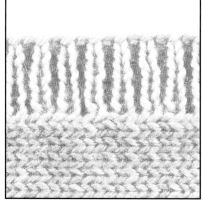

A facing in 1 x 1 ribbing is very stretchable if it is bound off as the stitches lie.

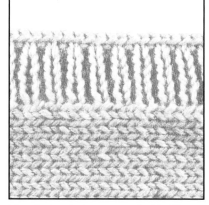

The facing is less stretchable if you bind it off entirely with knit stitches.

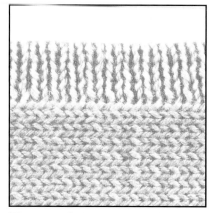

The same facing bound off in kitchener rib (see pages 46ff.).

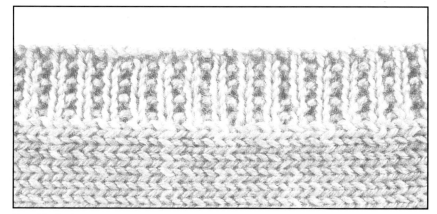

For this facing, alternately work 1 stitch in stockinette stitch and 1 stitch in seed stitch: On the right side rows, knit all the rows. On the wrong side

rows, alternately knit 1, purl 1. You can bind the facing off with knit stitches on the right side, or as they lie in a wrong side row (as shown).

For a rolled edge, add about 1₀" in reverse stockinette stitch. This will make the edge roll towards the outside.

For a facing with mini-cables, pick up 1 stitch from every row. There is a reverse stockinette stitch between every cable. Bind the

stitches off very tightly, crossing the cables even in the binding-off row.

This facing of 2 x 2 ribbing is bound off as the stitches lie, 2 knit stitches, 2 purl stitches.

For pieces knit on the diagonal, a facing is easier to work and also more attractive if you crochet a slip stitch through every row along the edge.

Then work a stitch out of every slip stitch, catching both parts of the stitch. For this facing, the stitches were picked up from the front,...

...and for this facing, they were picked up from the back. Here the slip-stitch edge makes a nice transition.

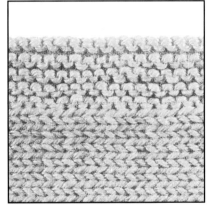

For this garter-stitch facing, the stitches are bound off in a row on the wrong side of the work as knit stitches.

Worked around the corner: If facings are supposed to be worked all around, stitches have to be increased at all the corners. These increases turn out best with yarn overs purled twisted. At every corner, knit an additional knit stitch out of the corner edge stitches. On both sides of this stitch, the increases are made alternately with

a twisted knit stitch and a twisted purl stitch. In order to get a nice angle, 2 rows with increases and 1 row without increases have to be worked alternately. For knit increases, make sure that the appearance is symmetrical (see symmetrical increases with yarn over, page 40). Bind the stitches off after the desired length is reached.

Binding off stitches that are too loose or irregular can be quickly and easily corrected (see page 45).

Double Facings

Fundamentally, double facings, such as at the front edges of a cardigan, give a piece more hold. They also look good from both sides and don't tend to fold over to the inside or outside.

Pick up the facing stitches as knit stitches, as for single facings. Now work in ribbing pattern or in stockinette stitch to the desired length, then work a row of purl stitches on the right side of the work and continue in the pattern. In order to be able to sew the facing down onto the edge at which the stitches were picked up, you need 1 row more for the back half of the facing.

When using the ribbing pattern, the facing is a little flatter if you work the pattern offset by 1 stitch in the second half.

Five rows stockinette stitch, 1 purl row, and 6 rows stockinette stitch were worked for this facing.

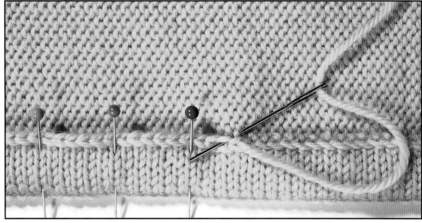

Turn the facing in to the inside and pin it down carefully so that the stitches are exactly on top of one another. As you are sewing, always catch 1 stitch of the knitting and ½ a selvedge stitch.

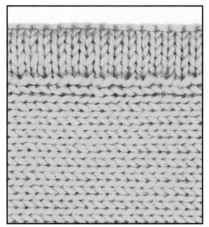

The finished facing looks good from both sides.

When you work a double facing in ribbing pattern, shift the pattern over 1 stitch for the second half...

...and sew it down the same way as for the facing in stockinette stitch.

A Special Tip for Armhole Facings on Sleeveless Sweaters and Vests

So that armhole facings don't stick out at the shoulder, knit 2 stitches together 4 times, in total, in the binding-off row before and after the shoulder. In 2 x 2 ribbing, purl 2 purl stitches together. In 1 x 1 ribbing, knit a purl stitch together with the next knit stitch.

The second way of making armhole facings slightly slanted is double decreases at the shoulder. For this, make sure there is a knit stitch at the shoulder seam. In the next-to-last and last row on the right side of the work, slip this stitch knitwise with the stitch ahead of it, knit the next stitch, and pass the slipped stitches over (see also decreasing, page 35). Bind the stitches off as they lie in the last row on the right side of the work or the next row on the wrong side of the work.

Top photo: On the orange facing, all of the stitches were bound off normally; the facing comes away straight from the shoulder.
On the yellow and light yellow facings, 2 stitches were knit together 4 times; this makes the facing fit better.

Bottom photo: 2 double decreases at the shoulder assure a good fit for an armhole facing.

A binding-off edge that is too loose…

…can be corrected afterwards: Pull the stitches of the binding-off row up, one by one, using the tip of the knitting needle (see also page 45). After they have been pulled up, the binding-off stitches lie precisely along the top edge in the correct size.

Knit-in Facings

On cardigans and vests, the front facings can be knit as you are working the piece itself. Double facings look particularly neat. They give the piece a professional touch and also make it fit better.

Double Facing in Stockinette Stitch

When you make a double facing in stockinette stitch, the half of the facing that is turned to the inside needs to be 1 stitch wider. In the example shown, the facing is 5 stitches wide on the outside, 6 stitches wide on the inside, with the selvedge stitch. In between, a slipped stitch ensures a good turning edge.

For sewing the facing together, it is also important that you work a row of reverse stockinette stitch between the cardigan piece itself and the facing. This purl stitch can hardly be seen from the outside in stockinette stitch or textured patterns, and disappears into almost all other patterns too.

The slipped stitch is only worked every other row. It is either slipped as if to purl in the rows on the right side of the work (carry the yarn along at the back of the work) and

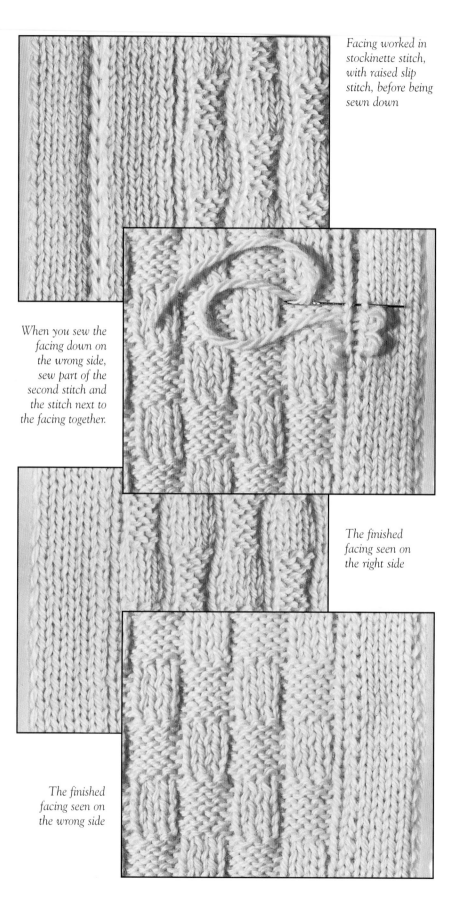

Facing worked in stockinette stitch, with raised slip stitch, before being sewn down

When you sew the facing down on the wrong side, sew part of the second stitch and the stitch next to the facing together.

The finished facing seen on the right side

The finished facing seen on the wrong side

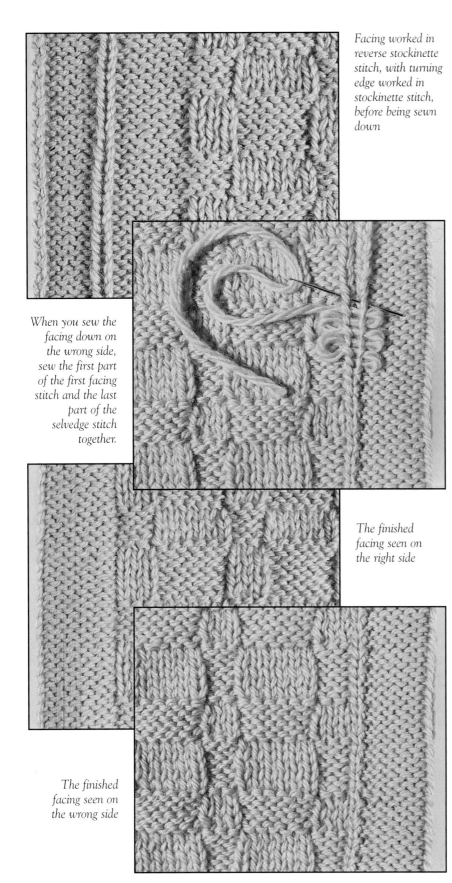

Facing worked in reverse stockinette stitch, with turning edge worked in stockinette stitch, before being sewn down

When you sew the facing down on the wrong side, sew the first part of the first facing stitch and the last part of the selvedge stitch together.

The finished facing seen on the right side

The finished facing seen on the wrong side

purled in the rows on the wrong side of the work, or it is knit in the rows on the right side of the work and slipped as if to purl in the rows on the wrong side of the work (carry the yarn along at the front of the work).

When you sew the facing down on the wrong side, sew the outer part of the stitch you worked as reverse stockinette, which appears as a knit stitch, together with the left half of the first stitch next to the selvedge stitch. Sew from side to side, alternately from left to right and from right to left. Work the sewing stitches in every row and don't pull the yarn too tight so that the knitted piece is still stretchable and the individual stitches are not pulled together. On the wrong side, the seam is almost invisible. On the right side, it can't be seen at all.

Double Facing in Reverse Stockinette Stitch

For a double facing in reverse stockinette stitch, you work the same number of stitches in reverse stockinette stitch to the right and the left of the turning edge. Here, you work 1 stitch in stockinette stitch as the turning edge. The seam edge—in other words, the selvedge stitch worked in every row—is important here for sewing the facing down later. It is purled in the rows on the right side of the work, knit in the rows on the wrong side of the work, and pulled tight.

When you sew the facing down, sew from side to side, as for a double facing in stockinette stitch. But now, on the wrong side, sew the left part of the first facing stitch together with the outside part of the selvedge stitch. This creates a new "knit" stitch on the inside, while the seam cannot be seen on the right side.

Single Facings Knit with the Piece

For these facings, you almost always work in ribbing—knit and purl 1 or 2 stitches alternately. Here the selvedge stitch is even more important than for double facings. It should match the knitted piece as closely as possible and also prevent the parts from stretching in length. If you work a seam selvedge, work the selvedge stitches in every row (knit on the right side of the work, purl on the wrong side of the work) and pull the stitches tight. You will get a good edge. A purled garter stitch selvedge is also good, since it can be worked tighter and more evenly than a knit garter stitch selvedge (see also selvedge stitches, pages 26ff.).

For a perfect edge, here's a trick when working 2 x 2 ribbing: Work 4 stitches in stockinette stitch at the outer edge instead of 2 (including the selvedge stitch). The outer stitches roll up by themselves and generally hold this shape.

After frequent wearing and washing, however, the edge can stretch out. It is easy to fix this by sewing it: On the wrong side of the work, sew the outer part of the selvedge stitch to the first part of the knit rib. Work the stitches in every row and from side to side, alternately from right to left and left to right (see also double facing, page 66).

For 1 x 1 ribbing, you achieve the same effect if you work the selvedge stitch and the first stitch of the facing in stockinette stitch on the outer edge. The selvedge stitch then rolls in halfway and does not need to be attached even after you wear and wash the piece many times.

Another problem is if facings that are worked with the piece stretch in length later. This can be from overly loose selvedge stitches, or the individual stitches can become larger, particularly if you worked knit 1, purl 1

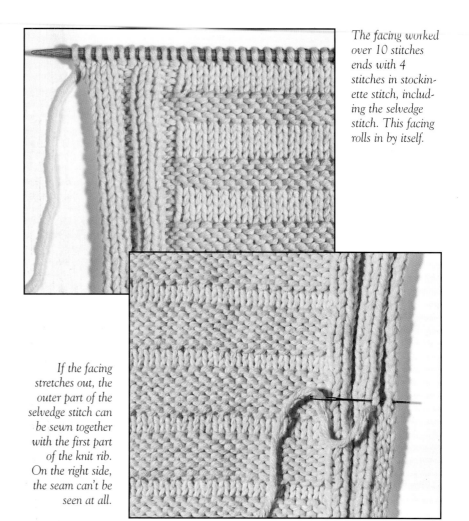

The facing worked over 10 stitches ends with 4 stitches in stockinette stitch, including the selvedge stitch. This facing rolls in by itself.

If the facing stretches out, the outer part of the selvedge stitch can be sewn together with the first part of the knit rib. On the right side, the seam can't be seen at all.

alternately. And if you have buttons on the piece, the buttonholes on one side and the weight of the buttons on the other side will stretch the piece even more. Normally, smaller needles are used for ribbing and facings, specifically for this reason.

You can prevent the facings from stretching in length by working shortened rows. To do this, you can use the buttonhole and button locations as reference points. In textured patterns, you can also select a specific row in the pattern to work the buttonhole and, therefore, the shortened row as shown on the next page for the diamond pattern (see also shortened rows, pages 148ff.).

Always work the facing with an odd number of stitches, such as 9 stitches used for the piece on the next page.

For the left front, start in the first row on the wrong side of the work with the selvedge stitch and 1 purl stitch. For the right front, work to within 9 stitches from the end of the row, then start the facing with 1 knit stitch and end with the next-to-last stitch and the selvedge stitch as purl stitches.

The small buttonhole in the example at the right is worked over 1 stitch. On the left front, work to within 5 stitches from the end of the row, then work 1 yarn over and knit the next 2 stitches together. For the right front, work a single decrease

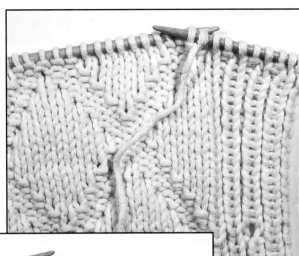

For the shortened rows, work up to the facing and turn with a yarn over.

In the next row on the right side of the work, purl the yarn over together with the first stitch of the facing.

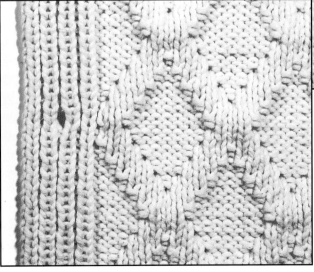

In the next row, on the wrong side of the work, knit the yarn over. The buttonhole will be between 2 knit stitches.

above the fourth and fifth stitch: Slip the fourth stitch, knit the fifth stitch, and pass the slipped stitch over, then work the yarn over. Knit the yarn over on the wrong side of the work. This way, the buttonhole will always lie between 2 knit stitches. It can hardly be seen but is nevertheless good for small to medium-size buttons (see also the section on buttonholes, pages 100ff.).

Buttonholes are worked in the facing on the right front for women's cardigans and on the left front for men's cardigans.

For the buttonhole, in the facing on the left side, work to within 5 stitches from the end of the row, then work a yarn over and knit 2 stitches together.

Sewn-on Facings

Facings sewn on with open stitches are also very attractive. Whether single or double, these facings will almost never flip over, unless you cast on too few or too many stitches.

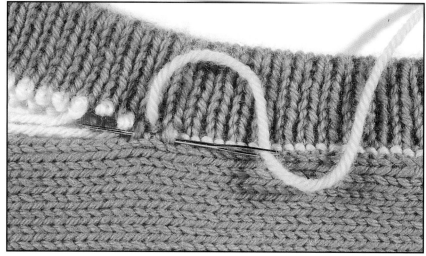

Work ribbing to the desired length, then work 2 more rows in a contrast color.

Then undo the additional rows, 1 stitch at a time, and sew the facing on, using back stitch.

To make sure that the open stitches don't come undone before you sew the facings on, work 2 or 3 additional rows with a contrast yarn on the facing. Always use wool or a rough yarn for the additional rows. If you use cotton or a similar smooth yarn, the stitches will come undone too easily.

Single Facings

For a single facing that is sewn on, cast on the appropriate number of stitches and work to the desired length in the main color, then another 2 rows in ribbing or stockinette stitch with a contrast color.

For open casting on, the number of stitches is based on the number of rows in the piece. Here again, the following general rule applies: You need 3 stitches for 4 rows (see also knit-on facings, pages 60ff). This means: If you worked 120 rows, you need about 90 stitches for the facing. Divide the number of rows by 4 and multiply by 3. A few stitches more generally doesn't hurt, but you should never cast on fewer stitches. If you knit the facings very tightly, you can also choose a

To make this clear, the seam was worked with a contrast color.

different ratio, such as 5 stitches for 6 rows.

Double Facings

Double facings that are sewn on are first knit on. To do this, pick up the stitches on the wrong side of the work and then work a turning edge after the desired length (1 row of purl stitches on the right side of the work or 1 row of knit stitches on the wrong side of the work, or an openwork row for picots, page 58). The second half is worked 1 row

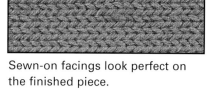

Sewn-on facings look perfect on the finished piece.

longer so that the facing can be sewn down on the outside over the picked-up edge. Then come the rows in the contrast color.

Sewing with Back Stitch

A back stitch is worked from right to left, between the selvedge stitch and the first stitch, using the original yarn and a blunt tapestry needle or yarn needle. As you sew, undo the additional rows 1 stitch at a time.

First insert the tapestry needle through the stitch of the casting-on row and the first stitch of the facing, from bottom to top. As you sew, undo the additional rows 1 stitch at a time. Then go back through the stitch of the casting-on row from top to bottom, and through the knitted piece one horizontal thread farther to the left and through the second facing stitch, from bottom to top. Then continue working as described for the drawing at the bottom right.

However, since you have approximately 25% fewer stitches available on the facing as you have rows on the knitted piece, you need to work around 3 horizontal threads of the knitted piece instead of 2 horizontal threads, approximately after every 3 stitches. Keep precisely to the ratio you calculated previously, otherwise you can end up with too few or even too many stitches. Or pin the facing down carefully along the entire length of the knitted piece, and don't take the pins out too soon.

1 For a double sewn-on facing, pick up the facing stitches on the wrong side of the work, going through the entire selvedge stitch.

2 For this facing, you work 6 rows in stockinette stitch, 1 row of knit stitches on the wrong side of the work, 7 rows in stockinette stitch, and 2 additional rows in a different color.

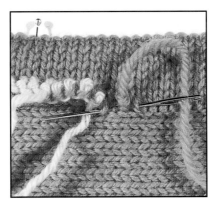

3 Bring the needle out and pin the facing on so that the corresponding stitches are right on top of one another. Now undo the additional rows 1 stitch at a time, and sew the facing on 1 stitch at a time using a back stitch.

4 This is what the facing looks like on the right side of the work.

For back stitch, put the needle through a facing stitch and knitted piece from top to bottom, then through the knitted piece 2 horizontal threads over and facing stitch 2 stitches over, from bottom to top. Then go through the stitch 1 over to the right and knitted piece, from top to bottom, and back through the knitted piece and facing stitch 2 stitches over, etc. As you do this, undo the extra rows 1 stitch at a time.

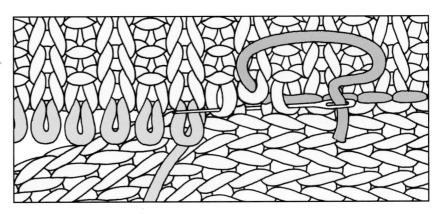

Perfect Details

For **neckbands**, you can also sew on facings with open stitches. This has several advantages: First, the casting-on edge is generally more stretchable than a binding-off edge. Second, you can distribute the stitches evenly around the neckline.

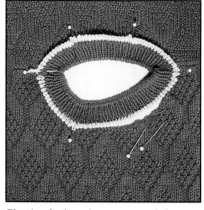

Pin the facing down around the neckline and then sew it on as described on the previous pages.

This way, a neckline edge that didn't come out very neatly can be covered up.

Facings Worked the Long Way

You can also work vertical cardigan facings separately and then sew them on, using invisible stitch. This has the advantage that you can work the facings, just like ribbing, on smaller needles, to prevent them from stretching in length. Also, you can check the exact location for the buttonholes on the finished fronts.

Even as you are working the fronts, make sure that you start the front edges the same on both sides—for example, with selvedge stitch, 2 stitches in stockinette stitch. Then you can match the facing to the pattern. In the example shown here, you end or start the facing with 2 stitches in reverse stockinette stitch, plus 1 selvedge stitch, starting in a row on the wrong side of the work. It looks even better if you work the facing along with the waistband, to the end of the waistband, put the facing stitches on a stitch holder, and first knit the front. At the outside edge of the front and the inside edge of the facing, you then have to cast on an additional selvedge stitch in each instance so that the pattern is complete again after the facing is sewn on.

For a facing worked the long way, you should work the same number of

Add a facing that was knit lengthwise by sewing it to the front, using invisible stitch.

rows as for the front. When you sew the facing on, row to row, the facing has to be stretched a little, but it will never get longer than the other parts. Even for slanted edges, you generally don't have to work any additional rows.

Work both facings to a length that lets them reach the center of the back neckline. However, don't bind

the stitches off. First sew both facings on as far as the shoulder. Then you can check the remaining length and add or undo a few rows, if necessary. Then join the facing stitches in a grafting stitch (see starting on pages 114ff.).

Crocheted Edges

Even though crocheting is not the subject of this book, here are some useful tips for finishing edges by crocheting.

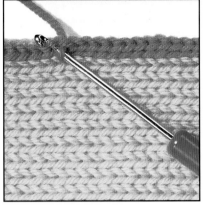

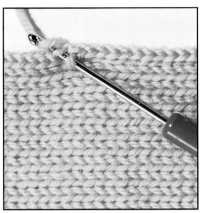

The slip stitches are each worked over 1 knitted row. When the second row of slip stitches is added, the edge turns neatly to the inside.

If you crochet the slip stitches in the same yarn, the double row can hardly be seen.

If you want to do without facings entirely, or if your edges didn't turn out that nice, crocheting is a solution. You can "save" quite a few bad edges this way.

For plain and boat necklines, knit-on neckbands don't always look that good. In this case, reverse crochet or picots make a nice finish. If the binding-off stitches came out unevenly, first straighten out the edge with a row of single crochet.

Working Slip Stitches around the Edge

For all straight edges, such as for side slits or slits in polo sweaters, a neat edge is especially important. Here, 2 rows of crocheted slip stitches work miracles: The edge turns in neatly to the inside.

The slip stitches can be worked between the selvedge stitch and the first stitch, or farther into the piece. Crochet them on the right side of the work, always from right to left. Leave a long enough yarn end at the beginning of the first row of slip stitches, which you will use to crochet the second row. The first row is crocheted through the knitted piece, the second row only through the top part of the first row of slip stitches.

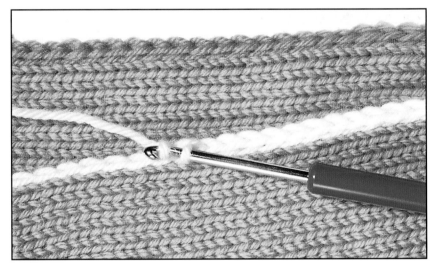

Here the slip stitches are crocheted over 2 knitted rows, i.e., there are always 2 horizontal threads of the knitting between the slip stitches.

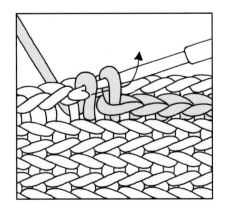

Crocheting slip stitches: Place the yarn underneath the work. Insert the crochet hook between 2 stitches, from top to bottom, and pull the yarn through to the top. At 1 or 2 rows farther along, go through from top to bottom again, pulling another loop through, and pull it through the loop on the needle.

Making an Edge with Reverse Crochet

Reverse crochet is the "classic" stitch for crocheted necklines, because this stitch makes the edge hold together well. Reverse crochet is single crochet worked from left to right, in contrast to every other technique in crocheting.

Reverse crochet can be worked directly onto the edge. However, in most instances, it looks better if you work 1 or 2 rows of single crochet first.

When reverse crochet is worked on the right side of the work, the stitches wrap around the binding-off edge like little ropes (top photo). If they are worked on the wrong side of the work, they form a decorative edge that is somewhat reminiscent of cross stitch (bottom photo). If the crocheted edge of reverse crochet worked on the wrong side of the work is not supposed to be very high, you can do without the first row of single crochet. Work 1 row of single crochet on the wrong side of the work, and then work the row of reverse crochet, without turning.

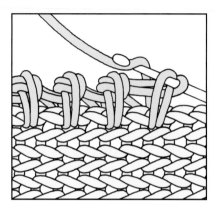

Reverse crochet stitches are single crochet stitches worked from left to right. Bring the yarn through the first stitch from back to front, and bring the working stitch through the loop. *One stitch over to the right, insert the hook and bring a loop through. Put the yarn around the needle and pull it through both loops. Keep repeating from *, going into 1 stitch farther to the right each time.

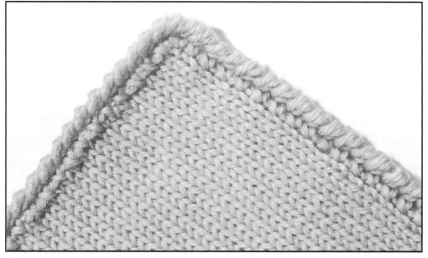

For reverse crochet worked on the right side of the work, work a row of single crochet first. Don't turn the work. Work a row of reverse crochet going into each stitch of the previous row, from left to right.

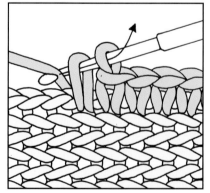

Working single crochet: Insert crochet hook between the selvedge stitch and first stitch, from top to bottom, and pull yarn through to the top. Bring the second loop through to the top 1 or 2 rows farther to the left, put yarn around the hook again, and bring it through both loops.

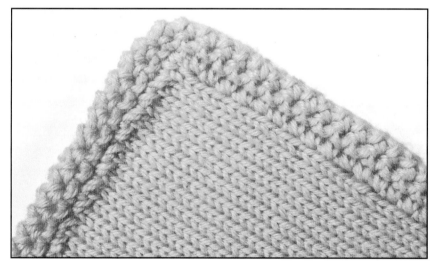

For reverse crochet worked on the wrong side of the work, first crochet a row of single crochet on the right side of the work, then turn the work with a chain stitch and work another row of single crochet. Then work a row of reverse crochet without turning.

Crochet Edge with Picots

Small picots make a nice edge that you can work on the bottom edges of sleeves and sweaters.

Picots are crocheted from right to left. For a picot, you work a single crochet into the knitted piece, then make 3 chain stitches and 1 single crochet into the first chain stitch, and then 1 single crochet into the knitted piece again. For every single crochet that is worked into the knitted piece, skip approximately 2 rows or 1 stitch, depending on the gauge.

Picots with Double Crochet

For the picots of this crocheted edge, a double crochet is worked into the first chain stitch, instead of a single crochet. Since this makes the picot longer, skip approximately 3 rows of the knitted piece each time.

Double crochet: Bring the yarn around the crochet hook from back to front. Bring it through the first single crochet of the picot, put the yarn around the hook again, and pull it through the 2 loops on the hook.

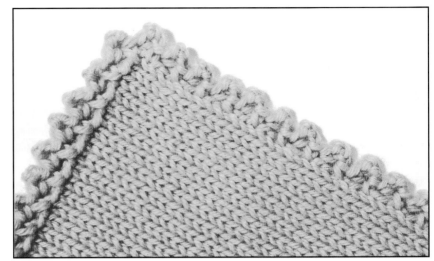

Picots look equally good on lengthwise or crosswise edges.

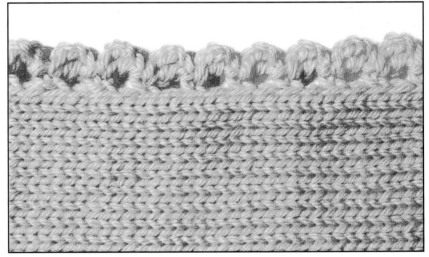

Here the picots were worked with double crochet.

1 For a picot, work 1 single crochet into knitted piece. Make 3 chain stitches, work 1 single crochet into the first of the 3 chain stitches,…

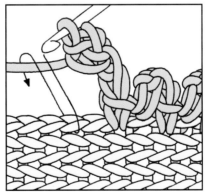

2 …then work 1 single crochet into knitted piece again. For every 1 crochet worked in knitted piece, skip 1 stitch or 2 rows.

Picots with double crochet (instructions above) are slightly longer and also slightly higher than picots with single crochets.

Necklines: Round and Square

Round necklines are probably the ones most frequently used in knitting. You have to work carefully here, because the neckline and the neckband are the first thing people notice about a sweater.

In normal patterns, the neckline width is about one-third of the entire back width. The front neckline is usually 2" to 3" deep, the back neckline is ¾" to 1¼" deep. The wider the neckline, the flatter it should be. A boat neck, which is bound off straight across and not rounded, requires the widest opening.

Start the decreases over the center stitches. To do this, bind off about one-third of the neckline width over the center stitches, or put these stitches onto a stitch holder for knitting the neckband on later. Work the remaining decreases in such a way that the edge becomes rounded. For example, if the neckline is 32 stitches wide, first bind off the center 12 stitches on the front part. Then bind off 3 stitches once, 2 stitches twice, and 1 stitch three times, every other row, on both sides of the center stitches. For the back part, in this case you can bind off the center 20 stitches, or put them on a stitch holder, and then bind off 4 stitches once and 2 stitches once, every other row, on both sides of the center stitches.

Since the decreases are not worked in every row, steps will form. In order to flatten these out, a single decrease is worked first, for the first decrease of 3 stitches to the left of the center; then the other 2 stitches are bound off. If only 1 stitch is going to be decreased, work only the single decrease. To the right of the center,

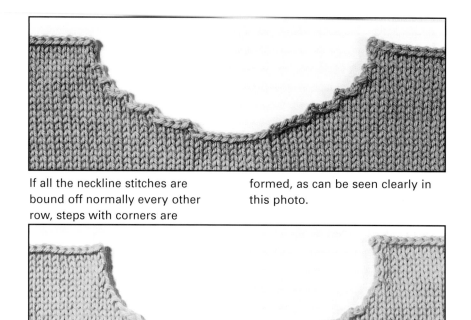

If all the neckline stitches are bound off normally every other row, steps with corners are formed, as can be seen clearly in this photo.

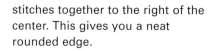

To the left of the center, work a single decrease over the first 2 stitches of the decrease, and purl 2 stitches together to the right of the center. This gives you a neat rounded edge.

With the end of the yarn that is used to continue the right side, even out the step first. To do this, pull the yarn through the first binding-off stitch and then sew it in on the wrong side of the work.

the first 2 stitches are purled together for every decrease, and the other stitches are bound off normally. To decrease only 1 stitch, purl 2 stitches together.

After the shoulder stitches are sewn or knit together, knit the neckband on with a short circular needle. Always start picking up the neckband stitches at a shoulder seam. At the short straight parts just before the rounded part, pick up 4 stitches over 5 rows, between the selvedge stitch and the first stitch. Starting from the larger decreases (2 stitches and more), pick up 1 stitch out of every stitch. As you pick the stitches up, make sure that you pick up the neckband stitches, not from the bound-off stitches, but rather from the whole stitches underneath them. Otherwise the stitches will be off relative to one another, which is not attractive (see detail photos and drawing).

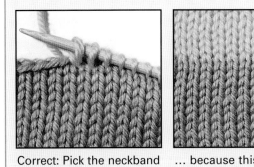

| Correct: Pick the neckband stitches up out of the whole stitches below the binding-off stitches, … | … because this is the only way you can have a neat transition to the neckband. | Incorrect: If the stitches are picked up out of the binding-off row, … | …they look half a stitch off relative to the pattern of the piece itself. |

A drawing of the neckline decreases with "steps." The big steps over 3 stitches at the right edge of the neckline are clearly visible. The stitches shown in a different color show where the neckband stitches should be picked up. Steps of 2 rows are evened out by picking the neckband stitches up, not out of the stitches in the top row, but rather the stitches 1 row farther down, in the case of the stitches before and after the steps.

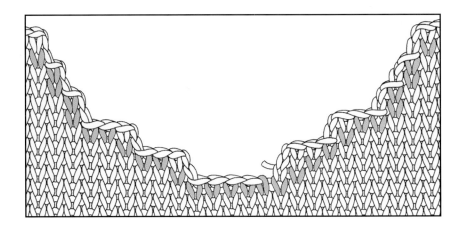

Single and Double Neck Band

A "normal" neckband, with the stitches bound off as they lie, is about 1¼" to 2" high.

If your neckline came out too wide, you can save it by making it a double neckband. First work the outer neckband. Then pick up the stitches for the second neckband on the inside, and work it to be ¼" to ¾" higher than the first one. On the double neckband shown here, the stitches were bound off in kitchener rib (pages 46–49).

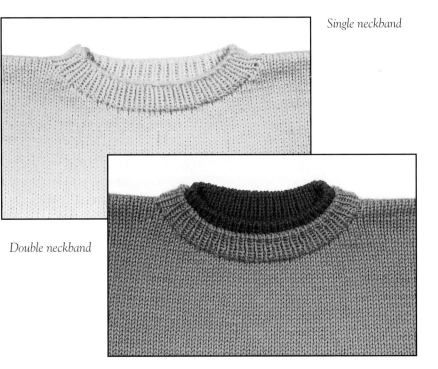

Single neckband

Double neckband

Turned In and Sewn Down

Work a neckband in ribbing to twice the length you want the final neckband to be, then turn it in to the inside halfway and sew it down loosely. A sewn-down neckband is especially good for children's sweaters on which the relatively small neckline has to be very stretchable. It also looks good on heavier sweaters.

Double Neckband Done in Stockinette Stitch

A neckband worked in stockinette stitch blends right in with the sweater. Here, a row of purl stitches was worked as the turning edge; depending on the pattern, you can also use a picot edge.

In order for the neckline to lie flat against the neck rather than standing up, decreases and increases are worked at the shoulder. Every other row before the turning edge, work a double decrease on both sides of the shoulder stitch (page 35). After the turning edge, increase 1 stitch knit twisted out of the horizontal threads on both sides of the shoulder stitch for every other row.

Rolled-edge Neckband

A rolled-edge neckband, which looks very casual, is easy to knit. If you want a wider neckline, you can start with stockinette stitch right after you pick up the neckband stitches. The neckline gets a little tighter if you work ¾" in ribbing first, and then work in stockinette stitch for about 1¼". Bind the stitches off loosely.

Turtleneck Collar

For a turtleneck collar that fits snugly, pick up the stitches as for a single neckband, then work in ribbing for about 8". Bind the stitches off loosely.

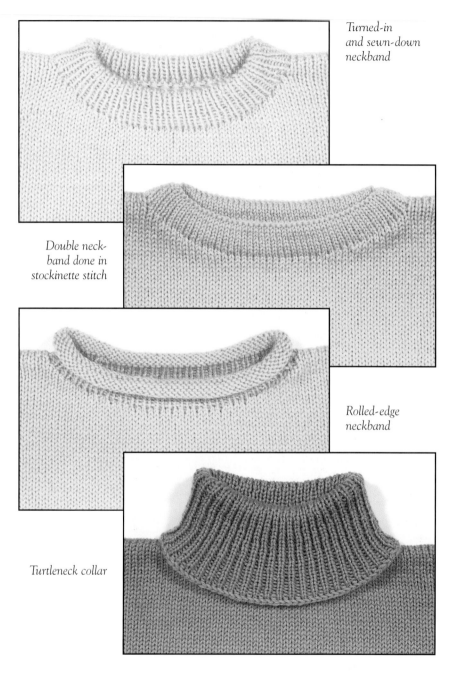

Turned-in and sewn-down neckband

Double neckband done in stockinette stitch

Rolled-edge neckband

Turtleneck collar

If you want the collar to be a little looser, you have to work 10–15 double increases when the collar is about 1¼" to 2" long (page 39). Or continue working the collar in single shaker knitting (page 131).

Open Crew Neck

Start picking up the neckband stitches about 1¾" to the right of the center of the front. After picking up the last stitch, cast on the necessary number of stitches for an additional 3½" for the underneath part of the collar. Then work back and forth with shortened rows (page 144). After the second row, work 1 stitch less at the end of each row twice, then 2 stitches less, until the neckband reaches the desired length. Then work one more row all the way to the edge, bind off all the stitches, and sew the underneath part on.

For the open crewneck collar shown on the right, knit all stitches in the rows on the right side of the work and alternately knit 1, purl 1 on the wrong side of the work.

Open Collar

For this collar, start picking up the neckband stitches ¾" to 1¼" to the right of the center of the front. At the end of the row, cast on the additional number of stitches for an additional 1¾" to 2½". Then work in ribbing pattern for 4" to 4¾", bind the stitches off as they lie, and sew the underneath part on.

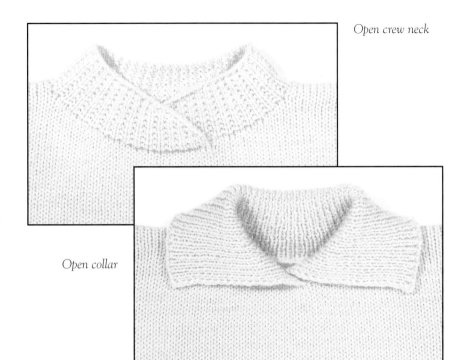

Open crew neck

Open collar

Square Neckline

Preparing for a square neckline is very easy. Here the neckline stitches are put on a stitch holder. Then work straight up both shoulders from there. Bind the shoulder stitches off and sew the seams, or work the seams in grafting stitch.

For the neckband, pick up the stitches with a short circular needle, starting at one shoulder. Pick up about 4 stitches out of 5 rows at the side edges (see facings, pages 60ff.). At the corners, an additional stitch has to be worked each time. In the first round, make sure that these corner stitches are knit. This means that an odd number of stitches have to be worked between the corner stitches along the straight neckline edge.

Now work in the neckband pattern. In every other round, slip the corner stitch knitwise together with the stitch ahead of it, knit the next stitch, and pass the slipped stitches over. If the yarn is very thin, the decreases can also be worked every round. Always work the first round without decreases.

Bind the stitches off normally when the neckband has reached the desired length; work the decreases in the binding-off round too. Or work another 2 rounds to bind off in kitchener rib (see page 46) and then bind off that way, as was done here.

The added knit corner stitch can be clearly seen.

V-necks

Whether you want to show a little more décolleté, or wear an elegant blouse or a casual T-shirt underneath, V-necks offer every possibility.

The finished neckband with the center stitch on top

For all V-necks, the number of stitches is already important right after the ribbing. If you want to work a single center stitch that comes up the front, you need an odd number of stitches, while you need an even number of stitches for 2 center stitches. It is also important to lay the pattern out correctly. Make sure that your basic pattern— whether it is a textured pattern, cable pattern, or openwork pattern—is interrupted as little as possible at the start of the V-neck.

You should fundamentally work selvedge stitches in every row, otherwise it won't be possible to pick the neckband stitches up neatly.

For the slanted edges, even decreases are important. For a neckline that is a little rounder towards the bottom part of the V, you can decrease every other row 4 to 6 times, then every fourth row. If you want to decrease every third row, every other decrease is worked in a row on the wrong side of the work. This means that on the right side of the neckline, you purl 2 stitches together, and on the left side of the neckline you work a single decrease in purl stitch (see decreasing, pages 32ff.).

The decreases of the neckline stitches at the tip of the V are worked every other round or row, for very wide necklines. For narrow necklines, they should be worked in every round. If decreasing in every round is too much, while decreasing every other round is not enough,

alternately work 2 rounds with and 1 round without decreasing. The binding-off round is always worked with decreases.

Neckband with Center Stitch on Top

For this neckband, you need an odd number of stitches for the front. Put the center stitch on a safety pin and continue separately over the 2 sides of the front.

For the slanted edge, on the right side work to within 3 or 4 stitches from the end of the row, then knit 2 stitches together; on the left side, work a single decrease over the sec-

ond and third, or third and fourth, stitches.

When you pick up the neckband stitches, pick up 1 stitch on both sides of the center stitch, from the stitches next to it, and simply slip the center stitch onto the needle. Now work 1 round in the neckband pattern without decreases. Make sure that the center stitch is knit, not purled. Then work a double decrease over the 3 stitches at the tip of the V, every round or every other round (drawing on page 81). Work the decreases in the binding-off round too.

1 Put the center stitch on a safety pin. Catch a stitch on either side of the center stitch with the safety pin so that the pin does not stretch out the stitch.

2 Pick up 1 stitch on both sides of the center stitch, out of the stitches next to it, but just slip the center stitch onto the needle.

Decreases Offset to the Outside with Slipped Stitches

Slipped stitches are normally slipped in the rows on the right side of the work, purled in the rows on the wrong side of the work. However, if you want to work the decreases over the slipped stitches in such a pattern, you must slip these stitches as if to purl in the rows on the wrong side of the work, and knit them in the rows on the right side of the work. The appearance of the slipped stitches remains unchanged.

Between the slipped stitches, always work 1 or 3 stitches in reverse stockinette stitch. In the center of the front, there are 3 slipped stitches. For the neckband, put the center one of these slipped stitches on a safety pin. Here the slant is worked every other row. On the right side of the V-neck, knit the single slipped stitch together with the stitch in front of it; just slip it in the row on the wrong side of the work. On the left side of

Here, the neckband was worked with a double decrease, as described below.

the V-neck, work a single decrease: Slip the slipped stitch as if to knit, knit the next stitch, and pass the slipped stitch over the knit stitch.

For a double decrease with the center stitch on top, slip 2 stitches knitwise, knit the next stitch, and pass the slipped stitches over.

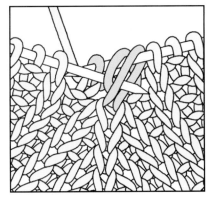

Neckband with 2 Knit Stitches Running Up the Center

The pattern of the sweater with this neckband is worked as follows: *4 stitches in stockinette stitch, 1 stitch reverse stockinette, 1 stitch knit garter stitch, 1 stitch stockinette, 1 stitch knit garter stitch, 1 stitch reverse stockinette, repeat from*. In the center of the front, there are 4 stockinette stitches.

For the neckline, put the center 2 stitches on a safety pin. Move the decreases 6 stitches in from the edge—i.e., purl the outer stitches, in reverse stockinette, of the pattern ribs next to the edge together with the stitch before or after them, depending on the side you are on.

Here the decreases were worked every other row 5 times, then every fourth row. This makes the V a little rounder towards the tip.

For the neckband, pick up the stitches with a circular needle beginning at a shoulder; pick up the 2 center stitches along with the rest. For this neckband, the number of stitches must be divisible by 4. Arrange the pattern in such a way that the 2 center stitches are knit stitches; work 2 purl stitches and 2 knit stitches alternately on both sides of them. Now, in every round, knit the first of the 2 center stitches together with the stitch in front of it, then work a single decrease over the next 2 stitches. Work these decreases in the binding-off row too.

Matching the pattern: the textured ribs on both sides of the neckband

Overlapping V-neck Band

For this shape of V-neck, bind the center 6 to 8 stitches off after the piece has reached the desired length. Here, a single decrease was worked over the second and third stitches, every fourth row. On the right side, the last 2 stitches before the selvedge stitch are knit together for the slanted edge.

For the neckband, first cast on a new selvedge stitch and then begin picking up the neckband stitches on the left-slanted side. Cast on an additional selvedge stitch at the end of the row too. Make sure that at the end of the neckband, which will be on top, there is a line of knit stitches next to the selvedge stitches. As is the case for cardigans, the right neckband is on top of the left neckband for women's sweaters, while the left is on top of the right for men's sweaters.

When you pick up the neckband stitches, cast on additional selvedge stitches at the beginning and end of the row.

The finished neckline.

Sew the narrow edge of the top part of the neckband on using invisible stitch and the edge of the part that is underneath with slip stitches.

The same neckline with 1 x 1 ribbing.

Neckband Sewn on Top of Itself

For this neckline, the decreases are moved 2 stitches into the knitted piece. To do this, on the right side knit to within 3 stitches from the center of the front, knit the next 2 stitches together, and knit the last stitch; cast on a new selvedge stitch next to that. Then finish the right side of the front first.

For the slanted edge, every fourth row always work to within 4 stitches from the end of the row, then knit 2 stitches together. On the left side of the front, cast on a new selvedge stitch, then work a single decrease over the next 2 stitches. After the first row, work a single decrease over the third and fourth stitches for every fourth row.

The neckband is worked without a point in rows on the right and wrong side of the work. First cast on a new selvedge stitch and then start picking up the neckband stitches on the left side of the V point, and at the end cast on another selvedge stitch.

Make sure that 2 stitches next to the selvedge stitch are worked in stockinette stitch, at least at that end of the facing that will be on top.

The side edges of the top part of the facing are sewn on using invisible stitch; the part underneath is sewn on with slip stitches.

Knit-on Neckband Using Seed Stitch

Seed stitch, whether large or small, is great as a finishing touch, since the edges do not roll up. For this sweater, 8 stitches are alternately worked in stockinette stitch and large seed stitch. The seed stitch pattern is arranged in the center of the front.

Here, first work the slanted edge of the neckline over the left side. To do this, work to the end of the seed stitch pattern stitches in a row on the wrong side of the work, turn, and work the first stitch as a selvedge stitch (seam selvedge worked in stockinette stitch). Now work the last seed stitch pattern stitch together with the next stitch, matching the pattern, every fourth row. It looks best if the last seed stitch pattern stitch is a purl stitch; then you can purl the 2 stitches together. If the last stitch in the large seed stitch pattern has to be worked as a knit stitch, it is better to work another 2 rows before starting with the decreases.

Work the right side of the front in reverse. To do this, cast on 8 new

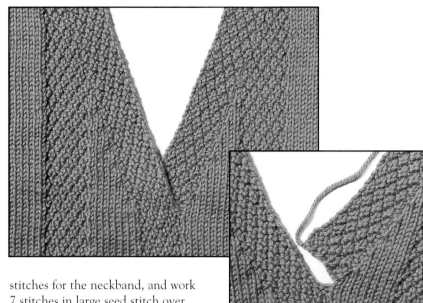

stitches for the neckband, and work 7 stitches in large seed stitch over these stitches. Then join these stitches to the piece and complete the work in reverse. Sew the underneath part of the neckband to the inside with slip stitches.

You can also continue this neckband for the back neckline. To do this, cast on an additional selvedge stitch on the inside edge, before or after the seed stitch pattern stitches, depending on which side you are

working, at shoulder seam level, and work over these 9 stitches to the center of the back neckline. Sew the neckband stitches together using grafting stitch, and sew the neckband onto the back neckline.

Without a Neckband

This neckline was worked without any neckband. To do this, it is important to work the selvedge stitches very evenly and tightly. Here, the selvedge stitches are purled in every row and pulled tight.

For this neckline, the center stitch has to be a purl stitch, so the number of stitches must be divisible by 4 plus 1 stitch plus 2 selvedge stitches. After the selvedge stitch, start with 1 purl stitch in the rows on the right side of the work, and with 1 knit stitch in the rows on the wrong side of the work.

Double the center stitch in the last row on the wrong side of the work before you divide the front into the two halves. Then continue working

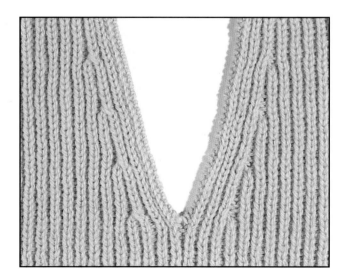

over the right half and work the first of these 2 stitches as a selvedge stitch. The double decreases (see shaker

knitting, page 130) are worked every sixteenth row here, 5 stitches in from the neckline edges in each instance.

Polo Collars

Polo sweaters, named after the game, are a tradition in hand knitting. Here are some examples for beautiful collars.

For polo sweaters, the front placket can be knit later or with the piece. In most cases, it is knit on later. The collar stitches are then picked up from half the placket parts and the neckline. You will find some tips about how to pick up the placket stitches starting on page 60. And there is a detailed explanation about how to pick up the stitches for the collar in the section on round necklines (starting on page 76). For women's cardigans and polo sweaters, the right placket, with the buttonholes, is on top; for men's sweaters, the left placket is on top.

Knit-on Plackets

For the slit of the collar shown above, bind off the center stitches on the front over a width of about 1¼". Depending on the yarn thickness, this will come to approximately 6 to 10 stitches; in the case of the placket shown above, 6 stitches were bound off.

The placket and collar are worked with needles one size smaller than

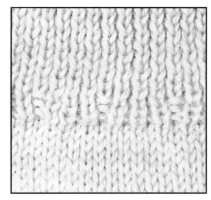

For the necessary collar width, the increases have to be worked at regular intervals.

the rest of the sweater. Pick up the stitches from the edges of the slit and cast on an additional selvedge stitch at the bottom edge. When working 1 x 1 ribbing, make sure that you have an odd number of stitches and work a line of stockinette stitch next to both of the selvedge stitches.

For the collar, pick up an odd number of stitches from half the plackets and the neckline, arranging a purl stitch next to the selvedge stitches in the first row, on the wrong side of the work. After 4 rows, work a double increase (page 39) every sixth stitch (= purl stitches) at the back neckline to create the necessary fullness. Work the collar to a length of about 4 to 4¾". Don't bind the collar stitches off too tightly.

Sew the bottom edge of the top part of the placket on, using invisible stitch, alternately catching 2 horizontal threads of the placket and a whole or a half stitch of the sweater.

Knit-in Plackets

For the polo collar shown on the right, the placket is knit with the rest of the sweater. The top placket is worked over the knit stitches of the front, the bottom placket is worked out of the wrong side of the work.

First mark the center 6 stitches of the front. If the left placket is supposed to be on top of the right placket, work to just before these 6 stitches. Now alternately work 1 stitch purl twisted out of the horizontal thread, and knit 1 stitch 5 times, working the last stitch as a chain selvedge stitch or as a seam selvedge stitch in stockinette stitch. At the beginning of the row, especially after the selvedge stitch, the stitches have to be worked very tightly.

If the right placket is supposed to be on top of the left one, work up to these 6 stitches. The first of these stitches is the new selvedge stitch. Now alternately knit 1 stitch and increase 1 stitch purl twisted out of the horizontal thread, then continue in the basic pattern. Work the buttonholes (see pages 100ff.) in the top placket.

Work the 11 placket stitches for the underneath placket out of the wrong side of the front placket stitches. Work the ribbing pattern in reverse. Start with selvedge stitch, 1 knit stitch.

At the top edge of the neckline, put the 11 placket stitches on a stitch holder and then work the rounded part of the neckline. Then sew the shoulder seams.

Now, for the collar, first bind off the first 5 stitches of both placket parts without knitting them, then work the remaining placket stitches and pick up the other stitches for the collar from the neckline. Make sure that a purl stitch is worked next to the selvedge stitch so that a knit stitch will be on the outside edge when the collar is turned. After 4 rows, work double increases (page

By increasing at the front edges, the collar reaches farther down.

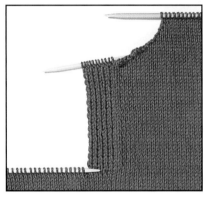

For the front placket, work the purl stitches twisted out of the horizontal threads. At the top edge, put placket edges on a stitch holder, then work the rounded part of the neckline.

Work the stitches for the underneath placket out of the stitches of the front placket, on the wrong side of the work.

39) every sixth stitch (= purl stitches) at the back neckline to create the necessary fullness. Work the collar to a length of about 4 to 4¾" in total.

In order for the collar to close well at the front, as in the example shown, stitches are increased every third row, 4 stitches in from the edge. Here, this comes to a total of 6

stitches. These increases can also be worked every second or fourth row. Keep to the pattern and alternately increase 1 stitch knit twisted and 1 stitch purl twisted from the horizontal thread.

With Double Pickup

A double pickup at the neckline is also good for polo sweaters and cardigans, since it holds its shape and looks good from both sides.

Work the double pickup with flex or circular knitting needles. Since normal knitting needles are stiff, it would be difficult to pick up the stitches for the second pickup with them.

For 2 x 2 ribbing, the number of stitches picked up, including the selvedge stitches, must be divisible by 4. The stitches are worked in such a way that on the outside of the work 2 stitches in stockinette stitch always lie next to the selvedge stitches. Of course you can also work the collar with 1 x 1 ribbing, but then the number of stitches must be odd and 1 stitch in stockinette stitch has to be worked next to the selvedge stitches.

Pick up the stitches from the slit edges as for a single facing. To do this, use a knitting needle 3 sizes larger than the needles being used for the placket. Then work 3 rows in stockinette stitch with the placket needles, casting on an additional selvedge stitch in the first row at the bottom edge.

On the inside, pick up the stitches from the horizontal threads of the stitches picked up as knit stitches previously (= 1 stitch less). Since these stitches were picked up with a larger needle before, the horizontal threads are easy to knit with the placket needle. Here again, work 3 rows in stockinette stitch.

Now continue in the ribbing pattern. In the next row on the right side of the work, always work 1 stitch from the front needle together with 1 stitch from the back needle: If they are knit stitches, insert the needle first into the front stitch; if they are purl stitches, insert the needle first into the back stitch (see photos of the method below). So that the number of stitches is evened out, work 1 stitch of the front pickup by itself in the center of the work.

Pick up stitches with a larger needle also from the neckline and half of the plackets. When picking up the stitches from the plackets, catch the entire selvedge stitch each time. This way both sides of the pickup are covered here too. Work the 2 sides of the double pickup as described above.

1 For the double pickup, pick up the stitches from the outside with a larger needle, and pick up the stitches on the inside from the horizontal threads of the outside pickup, using the placket needle.

2 Knit or purl the stitches of the pickups together, as appropriate.

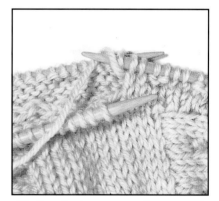

3 For the increases, always work the second stitch of a rib only from the front needle, the first purl stitch only from the back needle.

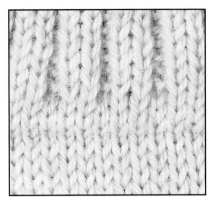

Enlarged view of the increases.

This collar looks good...

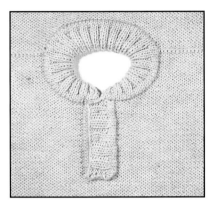

...from both sides.

In order for the collar to be full enough, you have to work increases. These are worked when the stitches are knit together in the first row of the ribbing pattern. Here, double the stitches every third or fifth stitch, depending on the gauge. In the first row on the wrong side of the work,

first purl 2 stitches after the selvedge stitch together with the back stitches, then knit 1 stitch together with the back stitch. Work the next knit stitch only from the front needle, the next purl stitch only from the back needle. Then purl 1 stitch together from both needles and knit

1 stitch together from both needles, followed by 2 individual stitches. In order for the number of stitches to be correct at the end of the row (you have to end with 2 purl stitches and 1 selvedge stitch), you can leave out a few increases at the shoulders.

With Double Pickup and Nehru Collar

For the pattern of this Nehru collar (photograph below), you need an odd number of stitches. In the rows on the right side of the work, knit all the stitches. In the rows on the wrong side

of the work, alternately knit 1, purl 1. This means that you alternately work 1 stitch in stockinette stitch and 1 stitch in garter stitch.

The double pick-ups are worked as for the example on page 86. The stitches of the pick-ups are always knit together in a row on the right

side of the work. The row on the wrong side of the work then begins with selvedge stitch, 1 purl stitch.

In order for the collar to lie closely against the neck, the stitches have to be bound off very tightly.

You can also work the collar in 1 × 1 or 2 × 2 ribbing.

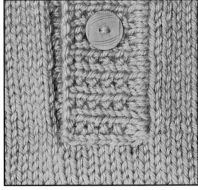

Sew down the narrow edge of the placket on top with invisible stitch, the underneath placket with slip stitch.

Shawl Collars

There are 2 ways of making attractive shawl collars: knitting them on later or working them right with the piece.

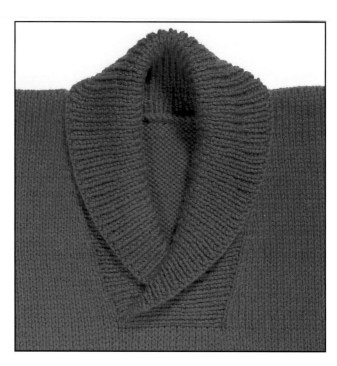

The necessary collar fullness is obtained by increasing at the back neckline.

Whether a shawl collar is worked on a cardigan or a pullover, it always looks best when it lies close against the neck. For this reason, the neckline should not be too large. A total width of 6¼" to 7" is enough. On a pullover, the neckline should begin at chest height, in other words about 10" below the shoulders. On a cardigan, the slanted edge can start even lower down.

Increases on shawl collars

In order for a shawl collar not to pull up, like a turtleneck, stitches always have to be increased at the back neckline to get the necessary fullness. For a collar knit on in 1 × 1 ribbing, work double increases. To do this, increase 1 stitch purl twisted out of the horizontal thread after a knit stitch, knit the next purl stitch, and then increase 1 stitch purl twisted out of the next horizontal thread again. The pattern repeat of the ribbing pattern continues without interruption.

When a shawl collar is worked with the piece itself, shortened rows have to be worked instead of increases at the back of the collar.

Shawl Collar Knit onto a Pullover

On the pullover shown above, the center 14 stitches are bound off straight across for the inset piece.

After that, make the slanted edges for the neckline by knitting 2 stitches together, next to the selvedge stitch, on the right side of the sweater, and working a single decrease over these stitches on the left side. For the back neckline, bind off the center 20 stitches, then 3 stitches once and 2 stitches once, on both sides of the center, every other row.

After you sew the shoulder seams, pick up an odd number of stitches from the back neckline with a circular needle or flex needles, starting and ending at a shoulder. Turn the work, slip the first stitch knitwise, and then work in ribbing pattern. At the end of the row, pick up several stitches from the slanted edge of the front. Always pick up the stitches on the front to the next decrease made on the slanted edge. Here, the decreases were made every sixth row so that at the end of each row, you should pick up an additional 6 stitches. Turn the work, slip the first stitch, then work in ribbing pattern. Continue working the same way, picking up 6 stitches at the end of each row until you have reached the

bottom end of the neckline edge. Cast on an additional selvedge stitch here so that you can sew the collar on later. Also make sure that there is a knit stitch on the right side of the work next to the selvedge stitch.

At the same time, when the collar is about ¾" long at the back neckline, work double increases evenly distributed over the back neckline. This is the only way the collar can be turned over loosely to the outside later! Work the increases about 2–3 stitches after the shoulder, before and after a purl stitch, then work 5 stitches and make another double increase. Keep repeating these increases up to the other shoulder. The frequency of increases is the same for almost all thicknesses of yarn.

Once all the stitches have been picked up, continue working until the selvedge is as long as the bottom neckline edge is wide, then bind the stitches off. Sew the top part of the shawl collar onto the bottom edge of the neckline with invisible stitch. Since the ribbing pattern requires more rows for the same length, as compared with stockinette stitch, always sew around 2 crosswise threads of the ribbing and alternately a whole stitch twice, and a half stitch once on the sweater, or alternately a whole stitch and a half stitch, depending on the gauge. Sew the underneath part of the collar on with slip stitches.

Shawl Collar Knit onto a Cardigan

For the slanted edge of this cardigan (bottom photo), the decreases were worked every fifth row, over the third and fourth stitch in each instance. On the right side of the cardigan, knit the 2 stitches together in a row on the right side of the work, purl them together in a row on the wrong side of the work. On the left side of the neckline, work a single decrease in a row on the right side of the work; work a single purl decrease in a row on the wrong side of the work (page 34). If the gauge calls for decreases every fourth or sixth row, they are worked only in the rows on the right side of the work.

For the collar, first pick up the stitches from the back neckline, as described for the pullover sweater, then start picking up from the slanted edges at the end of every row (here, you pick up 5 stitches each time). At the same time, when the collar is about ¾" long at the back neckline, work the increases for the necessary fullness of the collar.

At the end of the slanted edge on the front, along the straight edge, pick up 3 stitches over 4 rows, or, depending on the gauge and how you knit, 4 stitches over 5 rows (see knit-on facings, pages 60ff.), and work over all the stitches until you reach the desired facing length.

On the left side of the pullover sweater, pull the stitches through with a crochet hook and lift them onto the knitting needle.

In order for the collar to turn well, the stitches have to be bound off loosely.

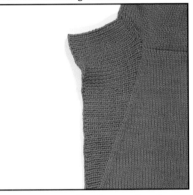

From the side: The front edge forms a straight line. The collar stitches should not be bound off too tightly.

At the back neckline, work several double increases for the necessary collar fullness.

The finished shawl collar fits perfectly.

Shawl Collar Knit with a Cardigan

For this collar, the front facing is worked along with the body of the cardigan, starting from the waistband. To do this, work 11 stitches in 1 x 1 ribbing, starting with a chain selvedge stitch and 1 knit stitch.

Start widening the ribbing for the shawl collar 10" to 12" below the shoulder. To do this, work the facing stitches, knit the next stitch, and increase 1 stitch purl twisted from the horizontal thread next to that stitch = 13 stitches in the ribbing pattern. Continue to work these increases every sixth row, widening the ribbing by 2 stitches each time, until the collar is about 31 stitches wide. Then continue without increasing up to the shoulder.

After the shoulder stitches have been bound off or put on a stitch holder, continue knitting just the collar stitches, adding 1 selvedge stitch at the shoulder edge in the first row. This edge will be sewn into the back neckline later.

In order for the shawl collar to have the necessary fullness, shortened rows must be worked over about three-quarters of the stitches (24 stitches in this instance) 5 to 6 times on every side, after 4 rows each

The finished cardigan with a shawl collar.

time. These shortened rows can be worked with yarn overs or with stitches passed over (pages 144–147). The shawl collar shown here, and the slanted shoulders, were worked with stitches passed over.

Work the collar to the center of the back neckline, then put the stitches on a stitch holder. Work the other half of the front in reverse.

At the end, put the knit and purl stitches of the two halves of the collar onto 2 needles for each half,

and sew the seam using grafting stitch (page 116). Then sew the side edge of the collar to the back neckline.

1 For the slanted edge, work 2 more stitches in ribbing after every sixth row, increasing the second stitch from the horizontal thread.

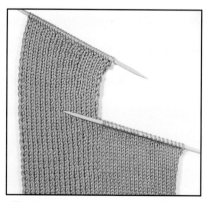

2 For the necessary collar fullness, work shortened rows every fourth row. Slanted shoulders assure a better fit of the cardigan.

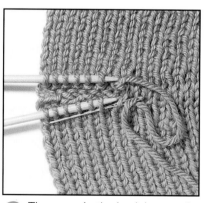

3 The seam in the back is sewn in grafting stitch (see page 116).

Shawl Collar Knit with a Pullover

The sweater shown on the right was worked with a very wide shawl collar; the center 12 stitches were doubled. If you want to, and depending on the gauge, you can also start the collar over 6 or 8 stitches, or over 14 or more.

First mark the center 12 stitches of the front. If the left end of the collar is supposed to lie on top of the right end, work to just before these 12 stitches. Now alternately work 1 stitch purl twisted out of the horizontal thread and knit 1 stitch 11 times. Work the last stitch as a seam selvedge stitch or a chain selvedge stitch = 23 stitches in ribbing. Then continue working over these stitches.

If the right end of the collar is supposed to lie on top of the left end, you also work to just before these 12 stitches. The first of these stitches is the new selvedge stitch. Then alternately knit 1 stitch and increase 1 stitch purl twisted out of the horizontal thread. Then continue in the basic pattern.

Now widen the ribbing pattern by 2 stitches every sixth row, as for the cardigan: Knit the stitch next to the selvedge stitches and then increase 1

The collar turns easily because of the shortened rows.

stitch purl twisted from the horizontal thread next to it. These increases to widen the ribbing were worked 8 times for the sweater shown here = 18 additional stitches—i.e., 41 collar stitches in total.

Now continue over these 41 stitches, and the knit stitch next to them, to the center of the back neckline, casting on an additional selvedge stitch (for sewing the collar on) = 43 stitches. For sufficient fullness, starting from the shoulder,

work shortened rows over the outer 30 stitches every fourth row, 6 times.

For the second half of the collar, pick up 23 stitches from the inside edge of the top part of the collar, and finish the piece in reverse.

Put the knit and purl stitches of the collar parts onto a needle each, and sew the seam using grafting stitch (page 116). Then sew the collar onto the back neckline.

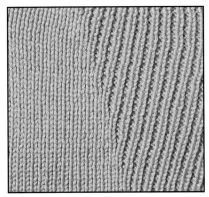

1 For the collar, work 2 more stitches in ribbing after every sixth row, increasing the second stitch purl twisted from the horizontal thread.

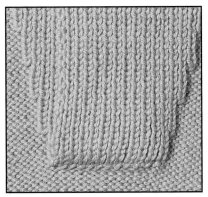

2 For the inside of the collar, pick up stitches from the front part of the collar on the wrong side, or cast them on and sew collar on later.

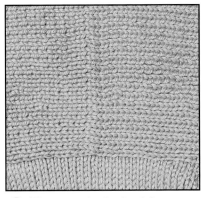

3 The seam in the back is sewn in grafting stitch from both sides.

Pockets

A cardigan usually has pockets. The bigger the pockets, the more comfortable the cardigan. Pockets can be inconspicuously worked into the piece, or they can be used as a decorative element. Whether the pockets are worked horizontally, vertically, or diagonally, there is a perfect solution for every cardigan.

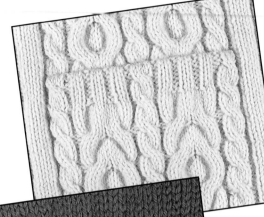

N eat facings are especially important for pockets. They can be worked with the pocket or knitted on later with the side edges being sewn on.

When you knit the pocket facing along with the rest of the sweater, you work with the same size needle as for the other parts. For this reason, you must be sure to bind the stitches off tightly.

If you knit the facing on later, you can work with a needle one or two sizes smaller. This makes the facing tighter, but you should still make sure to bind off tightly, because a loose edge always looks unattractive.

Ribbing, seed stitch, or even garter stitch prevents the facing from rolling up. The edge of a double facing is particularly attractive. Here, the outside part is worked in ribbing or seed stitch, the inside part in stockinette stitch on slightly smaller needles. That prevents this facing from riding up.

When you are working patterns that tighten, such as cable patterns, make sure that you decrease a few stitches at the start of the facing, in accordance with the gauge, so that the pocket facing does not become too wide.

Pocket facings should always be worked symmetrically. Always start and end with 1 or 2 knit stitches next to the selvedge stitches. In the case of 1 x 1 ribbing, this means you need an odd number of stitches, and in the case of 2 x 2 ribbing, you need a number divisible by 4 (including selvedge stitches). Pay attention to this when you pick up the stitches. One stitch more or less is hardly noticeable, but an asymmetrical facing is very noticeable.

Another way is to work entirely without a facing. Here you need a turning edge, such as a row of purl stitches or decorative picots. The inside pockets should not ride up, if possible. If you are working a simple textured pattern, they can be worked with this pattern, but if you are working wide cables, for example, this would cause the cardigan to bulge here. For this reason, the inside pockets are generally worked in stockinette stitch or reverse stockinette stitch. But always work the last 1¼" to 2" in the basic pattern so that the plain part of the inside pocket does not show. Also pay attention to the number of stitches: For patterns that tighten, like cable patterns, you need fewer stitches for the inside pockets. Before you continue working in the basic pattern, you must adjust the number of stitches, which means you need to increase (work increases purl twisted from the horizontal thread). For patterns that stretch, such as shaker knitting patterns, the inside pocket is worked with more stitches. Before you continue in the basic pattern, you need to decrease stitches. To do this, knit 2 stitches together as needed, uniformly divided over the pocket stitches.

Always cast on 2 additional selvedge stitches for the seam. These stitches are bound off before the inside pocket is inserted into the piece.

On the following pages, you will see all the possibilities in detail.

Horizontal Pocket with Facing Knit On

Work about 8 to 10 rows in ribbing or in seed stitch, over the desired width, when the piece has reached the length where the pocket is supposed to go. In ribbing, make sure that the facing is symmetrical—for example, it starts and ends with a knit stitch. If the pattern requires an even number of stitches, you can decrease a stitch within the pocket facing. Then bind the facing stitches off. For a tighter edge, you can also pass the stitches over without knitting them (see page 102) or bind them off by knitting them together.

For the inside pocket, cast on the required number of stitches plus 2 selvedge stitches, and work either in the basic pattern or in stockinette stitch or reverse stockinette stitch. Then work the last 1¼" to 2" in the basic pattern. Before inserting the inside pocket into the body of the piece, bind off the 2 selvedge stitches. Then continue working over all the stitches.

1 Bind off tightly the stitches of the pocket facing. Insert stitches of the inside pocket here later.

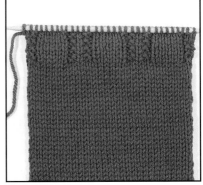

2 Work the inside pocket in stockinette stitch, then work the last 1¼" to 2" in the basic pattern.

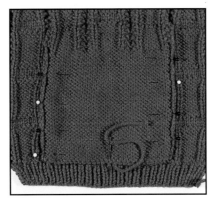

3 Pin the inside pocket down on the wrong side of the work and sew down first the bottom edge, then the side edges.

4 The finished pocket with a tight binding-off edge.

If the pattern does not allow a wide pocket opening...

...you can simply widen the pocket itself by several stitches below the facing. Just cast on about 5 or 6 stitches on both sides. Then work the pocket until it reaches the facing, and bind the additional stitches off straight across. Or you can work a slanted edge on the top part of the pocket for which you knit 2 stitches together every second row on both sides. Then insert the stitches into the piece.

Pocket Worked In Later

Pockets worked in afterwards have a great advantage: They can be worked precisely to your measurements—farther up if your arms are short, farther down if they are long. You can also determine the precise width. For patterned cardigans, you should pay attention that you don't interrupt the pattern at an inappropriate point. For example, undoing a row with crossed stitches would make your work unnecessarily difficult.

A fast solution: a rolled edge

Instead of making a pocket facing in ribbing, you can also knit on a rolled edge that is about 1¼" long. If the edge is worked in stockinette stitch, it will roll to the outside (top photo). If it is worked in reverse stockinette stitch, it will roll to the inside (bottom photo).

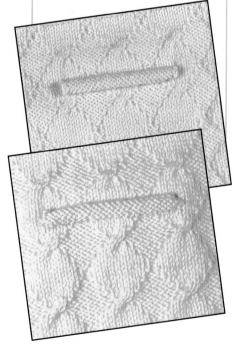

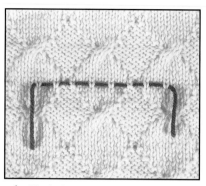

1 Mark the position and the width of the pocket. Include the length of the pocket facing in your calculation. Then cut a stitch in the middle of the marked section.

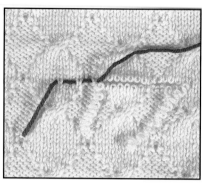

2 Now undo this row on both sides until you reach the end of the marker. The yarn ends will be sewn in on the wrong side of the work.

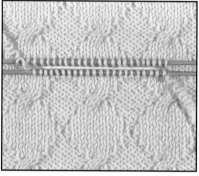

3 With a thin knitting needle, pick up the top and bottom stitches. Also pick up on the top edge the "half" stitches on both sides. You will have 1 stitch more on the top needle.

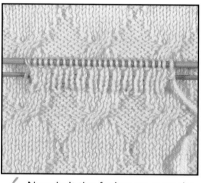

4 Now knit the facing on over the stitches on the bottom needle. In the first row, cast on a selvedge stitch on both sides. Make sure that the number of stitches is uneven, and work a knit stitch next to the selvedge stitches on both sides.

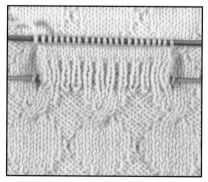

5 At the desired length, work inside facing in stockinette stitch on needles 1 size smaller and 1 row less than the facing worked in ribbing. In the first stockinette stitch row, bind the selvedge stitches off on both sides.

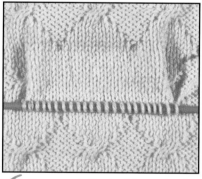

6 Now work the inside pocket in stockinette stitch over the stitches on the top needle.

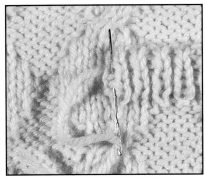

7 Sew inside facing down. Then sew the narrow edges on, using invisible stitch. Alternately catch 2 horizontal threads of the front and…

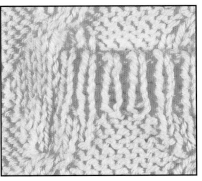

8 …of the pocket facing. The seam runs between the selvedge stitch and the first knit stitch of the facing.

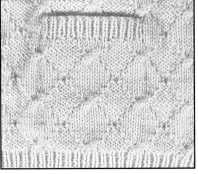

9 The pocket does not ride up even with a double facing, and it looks perfect.

Pocket Knit On in Cable Pattern

For this pocket, the stitches for the facing are put on a stitch holder at the desired length, and the stitches of the inside pocket are inserted into the work. The pocket facing is worked last.

For cable patterns that tighten, stitches have to be decreased—i.e., knit together—for the pocket facing. For narrow cables, 1 decrease is generally enough; for wide cables, you generally need to decrease 2 to 3 stitches per cable.

In the example on the right, the narrow cables continue in the facing, while 2 stitches are purled together twice over the wide cables. This means that the purl ribs next to the cables don't have to be offset.

For the double facing, cast on a selvedge stitch on both sides in the first row. When the facing has reached the desired length, continue in stockinette stitch on needles one size smaller, binding off the selvedge stitches in the first row of stockinette stitch and knitting 2 stitches together once over each of the narrow cables.

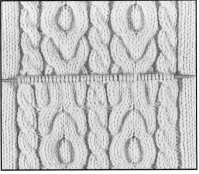

1 Put the stitches for the pocket facing on a stitch holder or a piece of heavy yarn in accordance with the pattern.

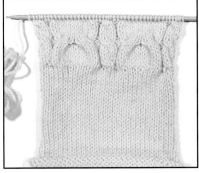

2 Work the inside part of the pocket and insert the stitches into the work in place of the stitches on the stitch holder. Continue working over all the stitches.

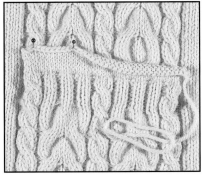

3 Match the outside facing to the pattern as closely as possible. Work the inside facing in stockinette stitch on smaller needles.

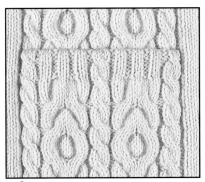

4 The pocket facing matches the pattern of the cardigan even better when it includes small cables.

Pocket Worked Diagonally

Diagonal pockets are the right touch for some cardigans. For example, long cardigans worked in plain stockinette stitch need something extra. Here, diagonal pockets will make the hipline look slimmer.

Work the waistband and the front to the bottom edge of the pocket. Now put the outer third of the stitches on a stitch holder and first work the front, with the slanted edge for the pocket. To do this, decrease 1 stitch every second row: On the left front, work a single decrease (slip 1 stitch, then knit 1 stitch, and pass the slipped stitch over). On the right front, knit 2 stitches together. You can work these decreases over the selvedge stitch and the first stitch, or, as shown, over the second and third stitches. When you decrease over the second and third stitches, you don't need a facing; the selvedge stitch will turn in by itself.

For the inside pocket, cast on the stitches or pick them up from the horizontal threads of the purl stitches of the first row above the ribbing, on the wrong side of the work. The pocket has to be at least as wide as the number of stitches decreased for the slant. However, it is better to make the inside pocket 10 to 15 stitches wider (depending on the gauge). When the pocket has reached the desired length, bind off the additional stitches of the inside pocket, or knit them together with the outside stitches. Then continue working over the entire front.

For the pocket facing, pick up stitches from every row of the edge (odd number of stitches!), and in the first row, cast on a selvedge stitch on both sides. Sew the side edges of the pocket facing on, using invisible stitch.

1 For the inside pocket, pick up the stitches from the first row of the basic pattern, or cast them on.

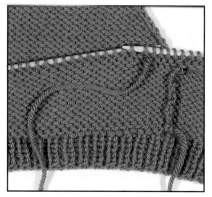

2 Work to the bottom edge of the pocket, then join the stitches with those of the third to the side.

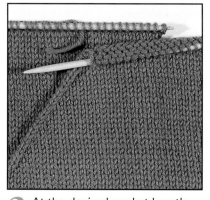

3 At the desired pocket length, knit the additional stitches of the inside pocket together with those on the outside.

4 The pocket edge looks good even without a facing.

5 For the facing, pick up stitches from every row of the side edge. Work to the desired facing length and bind off tightly.

6 The finished pocket on the right side of the cardigan.

Perpendicular Pocket with Inside Pocket Knit On

For this pocket, put about one-third of the stitches at the side edge on a stitch holder, either right after the ribbing or at the desired point. Then continue working over the other stitches until the pocket has reached the desired length. Then continue working over the side one-third, casting on as many stitches as necessary for the inside pocket, and work to the same length as the other part.

Now continue working over all the stitches, knitting or purling the stitches additionally cast on for the inside pocket together with the stitches of the outside pocket, as appropriate. The additional stitches can also be bound off and sewn on later.

From the lengthwise edge of the outside pocket, pick up stitches and work about 1¼" in ribbing pattern. Work a stockinette stitch on either side of the selvedge stitch.

To finish, sew the inside pocket and the narrow edges of the facings down.

Tip

If the pocket is worked not directly above the ribbing, but higher up, the inside pocket can be made larger towards the bottom, as in the diagonal pocket. To do this, cast the stitches for the inside pocket on separately, work about 2" to 3¼" in the pattern, and then join these stitches with the stitches of the side part.

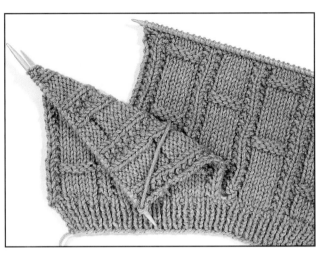

The inside pocket is worked in the basic pattern, or it can also be worked in stockinette stitch.

Bind off the stitches of the inside pocket, or knit them together with the stitches of the outside pocket.

To finish, knit on the pocket facing.

Sewn-on Pockets

Sewn-on pockets offer a variety of decorative possibilities. On the right is an example with stripes. The knitted piece was worked with horizontal stripes, and the pocket with vertical stripes. Here you can also work with diagonal stripes, with openwork or textured patterns, or with embroidery. In addition, you can sew the pockets on wherever you want, such as a large one at the hip, a small one on the chest, etc.

Since the edges of stockinette stitch roll up, you always need a facing for the pocket opening. To make this facing on a piece knit crosswise, pick up 3 stitches over 4 rows along a side edge (see also facings starting on page 60).

Of course you can also work the entire pocket in seed stitch. Then you don't need a facing.

Pin the pocket onto the knitted piece precisely where you want it to go. Pinning the pocket down is very important for pockets knit crosswise or diagonally, since stitches and rows don't have the same length. When you sew the pocket on using invisible stitch, you must work very carefully to make sure that everything lies flat and you don't create any bulges.

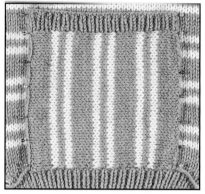

1 Pin the pocket, worked crosswise, onto the knitted piece.

2 Always catch one stitch of the pocket…

3 …and 1 to 2 horizontal threads of the knitted piece.

4 For the facing, alternately catch 2 horizontal threads of the knitted piece and of the facing.

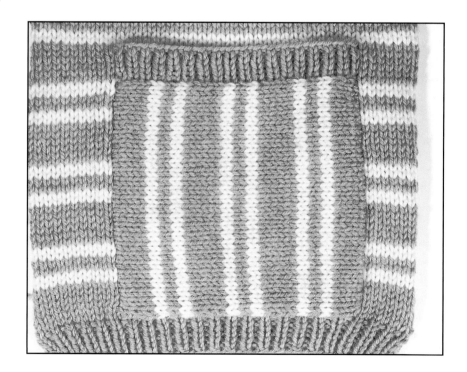

Ribbing Pocket

If you have a very long waistband worked in ribbing, you can make inconspicuous pockets. Work the ribbing to the desired length and then bind off the stitches for the pocket very tightly. Instead of knitting the stitches as you bind them off, you can simply pass them over (see horizontal buttonholes, page 102). This will make the binding off edge even tighter.

Ribbing pockets are even more inconspicuous if you bind the stitches off in kitchener rib (starting on page 45).

Pick up the stitches for the inside pocket from the casting-on edge, on the wrong side of the work. On the purl stitches, pick them up from the crosswise thread. On the knit stitches, pick them up from one part of the stitch each time.

Then work to the length of the ribbing, insert the stitches into the work, and continue in stockinette stitch or the basic pattern. The side edges of the inside pocket are sewn on later.

1 Pick up the stitches for the inside pocket on the wrong side from the casting-on row…

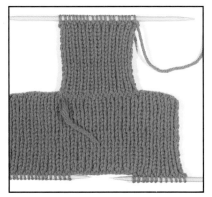

2 …and work in ribbing pattern. Turn the ribbing up and continue working over all the stitches.

The finished pocket with the edge bound off "normally"…

…and with the edge bound off in kitchener rib.

Double Knit-in Pocket

While double knit-in pockets ride up a little more, they don't have the problem of sewing the inside pocket on.

Work the front to the desired length at the top edge of the pocket. Then put the stitches on both sides of the pocket on stitch holders and first work a row of knit stitches, on the right side of the work, over the pocket stitches. In the next row, on the wrong side of the work, make a picot edge by alternately purling 2 stitches together and working a yarn over. In the next row, on the right side of the work, knit all the stitches and yarn overs.

Then continue in stockinette stitch until the piece reaches twice the pocket length, but work the last 1¾"

1 Work the inside pocket to twice the pocket length.

2 On this pocket, picots make a nice turning edge.

to 2" in the basic pattern again (pay attention to the number of stitches). Now put the two halves of the pocket together, right side on right side, and continue working the front

over all the stitches. To finish, sew the side seams of the pocket and attach the outside stitches to the top pocket edges with a few sewing stitches.

Buttonholes

Whether they are round, horizontal, or vertical, whether they are knit in, crocheted on, or sewn on— here's a suitable buttonhole for anything you want to knit.

Before you make buttonholes, you should know how large the buttons are as well as how many buttonholes you need to make. If possible, knit a facing on and determine the number and size of the buttons on the facing. When you knit the facing with the piece, you need to know the location of the buttonholes right from the start.

To determine the size of the buttonholes, put the button on the facing, stretch the knitting slightly, and count out the stitches. It is better to make buttonholes a little smaller rather than too large, since knitting stretches over time anyway, and the buttons would come open easily.

Round Buttonholes

On facings in 1 x 1 ribbing, work a small buttonhole like an openwork pattern with a yarn over. It can hardly be seen in the finished facing, since it lies between 2 knit stitches.

This buttonhole is usually the right size for shoulder facings on children's sweaters or for button plackets on polo sweaters.

On facings knit up and down, there should be a purl stitch in the middle so that you can work the buttonhole over it. Work a yarn over before this

purl stitch (i.e., after a knit stitch) and then knit the purl stitch together with the next knit stitch. In the next row, work the yarn over in keeping with the pattern, knitting it not twisted.

On facings in 2 x 2 ribbing, a round buttonhole is always worked over the purl stitches. In a row on the right side of the work, work a single decrease over the second knit stitch and the first purl stitch (slip the knit stitch knitwise, knit the purl stitch, and pass the slipped stitch over). Now make 2 yarn overs and knit the next 2 stitches (the second purl stitch and the first knit stitch of

the next rib) together. In the next row on the wrong side of the work, knit the first yarn over and knit the second yarn over twisted.

If this buttonhole is too large, you can also work just 1 single decrease, and in the next row on the wrong side of the work knit 1 stitch and knit 1 stitch twisted over it.

In a row on the right side of the work, work a yarn over after a knit stitch, and knit the next 2 stitches together.

On facings worked in 2 x 2 ribbing, work a single decrease and 1 or 2 yarn overs, then knit 2 stitches together.

The buttonhole with 1 yarn over (top) is slightly smaller than the buttonhole with 2 yarn overs (bottom). Both lie neatly in the purl rib of the facing.

Vertical Buttonholes

On a 1 x 1 ribbing, the buttonhole is worked over a purl stitch. In order to maintain the knit stitches on both sides of it, this stitch has to be doubled in the last row on the wrong side of the work before the buttonhole. To do this, knit 1 stitch and knit 1 stitch twisted out of the stitch above which the buttonhole is going to lie.

In the following rows, work ½ of the facing with the first purl stitch as a selvedge stitch, and put the stitches on a stitch holder when the buttonhole has reached the desired length. Work the selvedge stitches in every row and pull them especially tight.

Now work the second half of the facing, using the second stitch as a selvedge stitch.

When this side has reached the desired length, work over the entire width again, and in the first row knit or purl the 2 "selvedge stitches" together, as applicable.

On a 2 x 2 ribbing, the work for the buttonhole is divided up between 2 purl stitches. One purl stitch, in each instance, forms the selvedge stitch on each side here.

1 For a vertical buttonhole in 1 x 1 ribbing, double 1 knit stitch in a row on the wrong side of the work, and work the first purl stitch of the row on the right side of the work as the selvedge stitch.

2 Work the second half of the facing to the desired length with the second stitch forming the selvedge stitch. Continue working on all the stitches, knitting or purling them together in the first row, as applicable.

The purl stitches of 2 x 2 ribbing form the selvedge stitches of the buttonhole edges.

On garter stitch facings, vertical buttonholes are hardly noticeable if the selvedge stitches are worked as a garter stitch selvedge. Knit them in every row and pull tight.

Knitted Buttons

If you can't find matching buttons, you can knit them with the same yarn in a contrast color. Cast on 6 to 10 stitches, depending on the yarn thickness, with a different-colored yarn. Work 4 to 6 rows in stockinette stitch with the actual yarn. Cut the yarn to about 4" long and draw it through the stitches with a tapestry needle. Undo the yarn in the different color and draw the yarn end through those stitches too. Now tighten the yarn ends slightly and fill the button with a small scrap of wool. Sew the narrow edges closed with 2 stitches, then pull the yarn ends tight and knot them. Pull the yarn ends through the knitted piece and sew them in.

Horizontal Buttonholes

You can work horizontal buttonholes several different ways. The usual way is to bind the stitches off in a row on the right side of the work and cast them back on in the next row on the wrong side of the work. The disadvantage of this is that the buttonhole usually gets very wide, because of the stitches being passed over.

On a facing in 1 x 1 ribbing, work this buttonhole over an odd number of stitches, starting and ending with a knit stitch.

On a facing in 2 x 2 ribbing, the buttonhole should be worked over an even number of stitches. If it is 2 stitches wide, it is worked over 2 knit stitches; if it is 4 stitches wide, it is worked over 1 purl stitch, 2 knit stitches, and 1 purl stitch.

This means that the last binding-off stitch is always passed over a purl stitch, and the buttonhole fits perfectly into the ribbing pattern. However, if the buttonhole is supposed to be 2 stitches wide, you should try to work a round buttonhole over 2 purl stitches, since this type of buttonhole is even less conspicuous.

A horizontal buttonhole comes out tighter…

…if you don't knit the stitches before binding them off, but rather simply pass them over: Put 2 stitches from the left needle onto the right needle, slipping the purl stitches purlwise and the knit stitches knitwise. Now pass the first stitch over the second stitch. Then slip 1 stitch onto the right needle again, etc., until the buttonhole is 1 stitch less wide than you want it. Put the last stitch back onto the left needle.

1 For a "normal" buttonhole in 1 x 1 ribbing, bind off tightly 3 (or 5) stitches in a row on the right side of the work,…

2 …and cast them on again very tightly in the next row on the wrong side of the work.

The finished buttonhole worked over 3 stitches.

The finished buttonhole worked over 2 stitches (top) and over 4 stitches (bottom) in 2 x 2 ribbing.

1 In 1 x 1 ribbing, for a buttonhole over 5 stitches, first bind off 4 stitches without knitting them. Just pass the stitches over. Put the last stitch back onto the left needle.

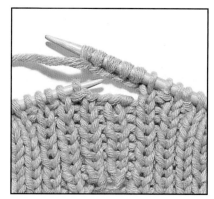

2 Now cast on 5 new stitches as tightly as possible. Then knit the last buttonhole stitch together with the next knit stitch.

Cast on as many new stitches on the right needle as the entire buttonhole is wide. Pull these stitches as tight as possible. Then knit or purl the last buttonhole stitch together with the next stitch the same way as the second stitch on the left needle lies. In the example shown on page 102, bottom photo 2, the stitches are knit together.

You should always work these buttonholes over an odd number of stitches in 1 × 1 ribbing, and start and end over a purl stitch. There will be a knit stitch on both sides of the buttonhole to give the ribbing a neat appearance.

In 2 × 2 ribbing, the buttonhole has to be worked over an even number of stitches. If it is only supposed to be 2 stitches wide and worked over 2 purl stitches, a round buttonhole will look more attractive. If the buttonhole is 4 stitches wide, work it over 1 purl stitch, 2 knit stitches, and 1 purl stitch. If it is 6 stitches wide, work it over 2 purl stitches, 2 knit stitches, and 2 purl stitches.

In 2 × 2 ribbing, the buttonhole over 4 stitches begins with a purl stitch (top). A buttonhole over 6 stitches begins with 2 purl stitches (bottom).

Working with Contrast Yarn

Another way for getting really tight buttonholes is working an additional row in a contrast yarn. The buttonhole stitches are crocheted together later.

Without Contrast Yarn

…is another way you can work this buttonhole. To do this, cut a stitch in the middle of the buttonhole, carefully pull the yarn out on both sides, and put the stitches on thin cable needles. Crochet the buttonhole and sew in the yarn ends. The buttonhole will spread apart a little more than one worked with contrast yarn.

1 Work with a different-colored yarn over the desired number of stitches. There are 5 here. Then slip the stitches back onto the left needle and work them once again with the original yarn. This means that you are knitting the buttonholes twice!

3 Crochet the open stitches of the bottom part, then top part, in 1 direction without using extra yarn. Draw the last stitch of the bottom part through the first stitch of the top part. Draw the last loop through to the wrong side and sew it in.

2 Pull the contrast yarn out and pick up the bottom 5 and top 6 stitches with cable needles (catch the half stitches of the stitches next to the ends on both sides).

4 Crocheting the stitches gives you a tight, durable buttonhole.

Crocheted Button Loops

Crocheted button loops are quick and easy. They can be used on polo sweater plackets and shoulder facings.

On polo sweaters, work the slit in the center of the middle. In the row in which the sides are divided, increase 1 selvedge stitch for the button loop edge, and 2 to 3 stitches for the underneath part. Since the loops are crocheted between the selvedge stitch and the first stitch, you should work a seam selvedge in stockinette stitch (page 26).

In order to be able to distribute the loops evenly, first count the rows of the slit edge. For example: If you want to distribute 3 loops over 30 stitches and assume 5 rows per loop, this leaves 2 rows for the top edge, 5 rows between loops, and 3 rows for the bottom edge. Viewed from the bottom edge, this is 3 rows without a loop; then, 2 times: 5 rows with a loop, 5 without, then another 5 with, and 2 without.

Now work 1 row of slip stitches between the selvedge stitch and the first stitch, using a crochet hook approximately the same size as the knitting needles used (or a little smaller; see drawing on page 105). Above that, work another row, from right to left again, with slip stitches and chain stitches. Leave a long enough yarn end at the beginning of the first row. This way you can use it to work the second row and don't have to sew the end in.

The slip stitches of the second row are now crocheted only in the top part of the first row of slip stitches. The number of slip stitches and chain stitches is determined by the arrangement and the size of the buttons.

1 Insert the crochet hook between the selvedge stitch and the first stitch, and crochet a row of slip stitches from right to left. Then start from right to left again, and work alternately 4 slip stitches and 5 chain stitches.

2 To reinforce the button loops, you can crochet around them with half a piece of yarn and single crochets; just work slip stitches over the slip stitches.

3 The finished facing worked in the same color. If necessary, reinforce the edge of the underneath part with a row of single crochets.

Sewn Button Loops

Preparing the knitted piece for sewn button loops is the same as for crocheted button loops. Here again, where the knitted piece divides for the slit, increase 1 selvedge stitch for the part on top, and 2 to 3 stitches for the part underneath. The loop placement is calculated the same way as for the crocheted loops.

If the selvedge stitches are very neat, you can sew the loops on between the selvedge stitches and the first stitch. If the selvedge stitches came out a little uneven, first crochet a row of slip stitches between the selvedge stitch and the first stitch, and then sew the loops on.

These loops are always made with half the yarn.

The finished facing worked in the same color. If needed, work a row of single crochets along the edge of the underneath part.

Tip

If you don't have matching thread to sew the buttons, then use the knitting yarn! For most types of yarn, this isn't a problem. Depending on the yarn thickness, you have to divide the yarn in halves or into thirds.

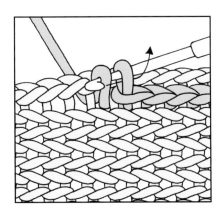

Crocheting slip stitches: Put yarn under the work. Insert crochet hook between 2 stitches, from top to bottom, and bring the yarn through to the top. Insert hook from top to bottom again, 1 or 2 rows farther along, bring another loop through, and draw it through the loop on the needle.

1 Start at the bottom edge of the slit, and sew a double loop between selvedge stitch and first stitch, or into the middle of the row of slip stitches, whichever is applicable.

2 Sew around the loops with buttonhole stitch. At the end, insert needle into the stitch and come out again a few rows farther along. Then sew the next loop.

Since the yarn is thick and the selvedge stitches are uniform, you can do without the row of slip stitches.

Zippers

Sewing in zippers is a very special topic in knitting. To keep the knitted piece and the edge next to the zipper from becoming wavy, you have to work very accurately. The zippered closure should look good from both sides.

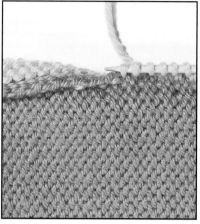

For the inside facing, pick up 1 stitch from each of the loops of the front facing stitches, and work the facing like the outside facing.

The zipper neatly sewn in, as seen from the wrong side.

Zipper with Double Facing

On the cardigan shown to the right, the zipper was sewn in between a double facing.

After you have worked the neck band, pick up 3 stitches over 4 rows from the edges. Use a knitting needle that is 2 to 3 sizes larger than the needles used for the neck band. Don't let the size of the stitches bother you. Half of this will be pulled to the inside for picking up the stitches for the inside facing.

Now work 3 rows of stockinette stitch (= 1 row of purl stitches on the wrong side, 1 row of knit stitches on the right side, 1 row of purl stitches on the wrong side) with the facing needles. Then bind off the stitches in a row on the right side of the work with purl stitches.

If you are using heavy yarn, 2 rows of stockinette stitch may be enough. But if you are using very thin yarn, you might have to work 4 rows of stockinette stitch. The facing must be approximately as wide as the fabric edge of the zipper.

On the inside, pick up 1 stitch from the loops of every stitch previously picked up on the right side, and work the facing the same way as on the

The zipper neatly sewn in as seen from the right side.

outside. The inside facing will be 1 stitch narrower than the outside facing.

Pin the zipper to the edges of the facings so that the zipper teeth are exposed, and sew it down between the purl stitch and the binding-off stitch with strong sewing thread in a matching color. Then sew the inside facing down.

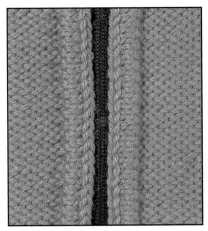

The same zipper with a binding-off edge worked with knit stitches. Here the seam is sewn through the middle of the binding-off stitches.

The same zipper with the edge bound off with knit stitches, as seen from the wrong side.

Sewn-in Zipper in Cable or Ribbing Pattern

In the example shown, 2 stitches in reverse stockinette are worked between each of the cables. The zipper is sewn into this rib of reverse stockinette. You can work zipper closures in any vertical ribbing pattern this way.

At the point where the 2 halves of the piece divide, cast on 2 additional stitches on both sides, between the purl stitches, for the underneath parts. The zipper is then sewn on using invisible stitch, between the last stitch of the cable and the purl stitch. To do this, alternately catch a crosswise thread and sew a short stitch through the fabric of the zipper. On the wrong side of the work, sew the zipper tapes to the underneath part of the knitting.

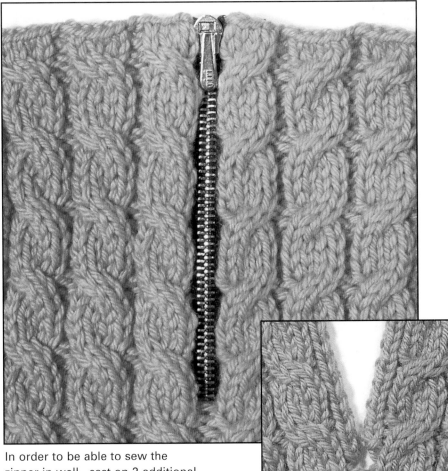

In order to be able to sew the zipper in well , cast on 2 additional stitches for the underneath part on both sides (right photo inset). The zipper fits perfectly between 2 cables.

Straightening Out Zipper Edges with Slip Stitches

This technique is good for the front closures of polo sweaters and turtle-neck sweaters as well as for zippered back closures, such as in children's sweaters.

For the slit, just bind off the 2 center stitches. Then continue the 2 sides separately, working evenly over the same number of stitches.

Before you sew in the zipper, first straighten out the edges with slip stitches (see drawing on page 73). To do this, put the yarn under the work. Insert the hook between the 2 bound-off stitches at the bottom of the slit, and bring the yarn through to the top. Leave enough yarn to work the row of slip stitches on the other side.

Now crochet the slip stitches on 1 side first. Insert the crochet hook into the middle of the first binding-off stitch, from top to bottom. Bring the yarn through to the top and pull it through the loop on the hook. Keep working the following slip stitches through the selvedge stitches, 1 or 2 rows higher. Work slip stitches over the second edge the same way.

Then work a second row of slip stitches over the first. To do this, start again at the bottom of the slit, as described above, and now work the slip stitches through the half of the previous slip stitches that faces the slit.

For the inside facing, cast on 10 stitches and work in stockinette stitch for about ¾". Then bind off the 2 center stitches and continue the 2 halves separately. Pin the facing on and sew it down.

1 First crochet a row of slip stitches onto the selvedge stitch.

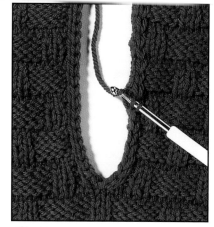

2 Above that, crochet a second row of slip stitches through the part of the first slip stitches that faces the slit.

Sew in the zipper with sewing thread, going through the outer row of slip stitches.

Pin the inside facing down on the wrong side of the work and sew it down with slip stitches.

Zipper in a Turtleneck Sweater

This turtleneck sweater is worked in single shaker knitting with the rough side on the outside. The collar, worked in 1 x 1 ribbing, is sewn down on the inside. The front zipper reaches to the top edge of the turned collar. Since the neck can be worn open, the zipper should be covered by a facing on the inside.

At the division into the 2 sides, work the center purl stitch as a selvedge stitch on 1 side. For the other side, cast on a new selvedge stitch.

Sew the zipper in so that it ends about ⅛" below half of the collar. Turn the collar to the inside and loosely sew it on with slip stitches.

For the inside facing, cast on 9 stitches and work in stockinette stitch for about ¾". Then bind off the center stitch and finish the 2 halves separately. Pin the facing on and sew it down.

On this turtleneck sweater, the zipper reaches up into the collar.

Sew the inside facing onto the wrong side of the work.

Shortening a Zipper

If you can't find a zipper of the correct length, buy one that is a little longer and shorten it to the desired length. Sew a new stop at the appropriate location, using a double buttonhole thread. Then cut off the rest of the zipper below it.

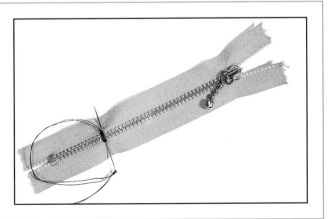

Finishing

A nice-fitting sweater comes from how you sew the individual pieces together. Here are the best tricks for perfect seams.

Invisible Seams to Join Selvedges

The best way to sew side and sleeve seams is with invisible stitches.

You can use this stitch to sew pieces worked in stockinette stitch, reverse stockinette, or even shaker knitting—almost invisibly together. Of course, you must first have perfect edges (see also selvedge stitches, pages 26–27).

Before you sew the pieces together, block them and let them dry under damp cloths (see page 121).

To sew the seams, you need a tapestry or wool needle. If possible, you should sew the pieces together with the same yarn you used for knitting. That works well for all smooth or only slightly fuzzy yarns. When using long mohair yarn or specialty yarns with nubs or fringes, it is better to use a smooth yarn that matches in color. But do not use sewing thread, because it does not stretch enough.

Put the knitted pieces onto a sufficiently large work area with the right side of the work on top. Always start at the bottom edge and work from right to left.

Stockinette Stitch Pieces

First sew the selvedge stitches of the casting-on rows together. To do this, insert the needle next to the selvedge stitches, going from bottom to top of one piece to the other. Then catch the first horizontal thread between the selvedge stitch and the knitted piece of the top piece. On the bottom piece, now catch the first and the second horizontal threads, then the second and third horizontal threads on the

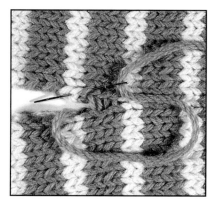

1 On pieces worked in stockinette stitch, begin sewing with 1 horizontal thread,...

2 ...then catch 2 horizontal threads of the top and bottom pieces each time.

3 Because of the offset, even stripes and textured patterns match up perfectly.

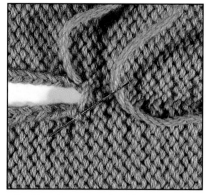

1 On pieces worked in reverse stockinette, only catch 1 stitch of the bottom piece...

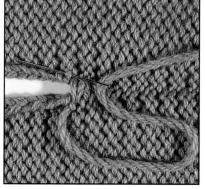

2 ...and 1 stitch of the top piece.

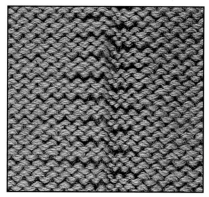

3 After tightly pulling the yarn, the seam can hardly be seen.

first piece, etc. You always catch 2 horizontal threads with the needle, offset relative to one another. Don't pull the yarn too tight so that the seams remain stretchable.

Because of the offset of the stitches, even patterns such as stripes or textured patterns match up perfectly.

Reverse Stockinette Pieces

A seam worked in invisible stitch is almost impossible to see in reverse stockinette too. Here, however, from the beginning you only catch 1 horizontal thread per side. The yarn has to be pulled a little tighter. It

forms a back-and-forth line in the knitting.

Shaker Knitting Pieces

For a seam using invisible stitch, you have to work a purl stitch on the right side of the work, next to the selvedge stitch (odd number of stitches). It is also important that your selvedge is worked very tightly. This seam is slightly thicker, but almost invisible.

After you have sewn the casting-on rows together, always catch the center of the purl stitches next to the selvedge stitches (it is made up of 2 threads), going from side to side. The

2 half stitches from each side produce a whole stitch.

Garter Stitch Selvedges

If the pattern allows, such as in the case of faux shaker knitting, garter stitch selvedges are the best edges for an especially attractive seam. Since the little knots always form at the beginning of a row, they fit into each other like the teeth of a zipper when they are sewn together. The finished stitch then looks like an additional purl stitch.

1 For shaker knitting, alternately catch the middle of the purl stitch next to the selvedge stitch…

2 …on the top and bottom pieces.

3 This seam is a little thicker, but it is still almost invisible.

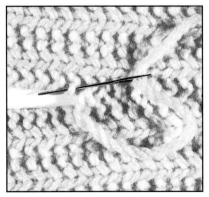
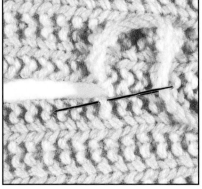
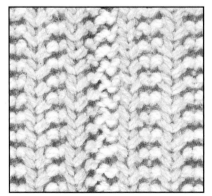

1 Alternately insert the needle through a knotted selvedge stitch on the top…

2 …and bottom pieces. Don't pull the yarn too tight.

3 The seam is very flat and looks like an additional purl stitch.

113

Invisible Seams with Grafting Stitch

The great advantage to sewing seams using grafting stitch is that no visible seam is formed. This looks better, particularly when using heavier yarn or when sewing a top shoulder/sleeve seam of a sweater worked in 2 parts, such as a sweater with dolman sleeves.

To sew grafting stitches, you need a tapestry or blunt wool needle. The yarn for sewing has to be about three times as long as the width of the pieces when lying flat. If you use the end of the yarn you knit with, this is one less yarn end to sew in. It is better to leave the yarn a little longer rather than too short, because you can't add more yarn if you run out.

You can sew the stitches right as they come off the needle. You need a little practice to do this, because sometimes they slip off the needle too quickly, especially if you knit loosely.

Or you can work another 2 rows in stockinette stitch in a different-colored yarn on both pieces. These additional rows will be undone little by little as you sew the pieces together. Use wool or a wool blend for these additional rows, because cotton comes undone too easily.

When you sew parts together using grafting stitch, you create a new row. Therefore, you should work the knitted piece 1 row shorter. For example, if you are working stripes of 4 rows each, work 2 rows on one side; the finished row and the stitches on the knitting needle will be visible. On the other side, knit just 1 row; here the stitches on the needle will form the row of grafting stitches.

1 To sew off of knitting needles, insert tapestry needle in the selvedge stitches of bottom and top pieces, from bottom to top. Then insert needle into bottom piece from top…

2 Now insert the tapestry needle into the previous stitch, alternately in the top and the bottom pieces, and out through the next stitch on the needle.

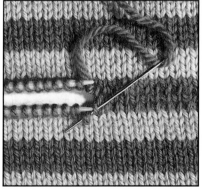

3 The stitches on the needle and the seam itself form a row in the knitting. For a pattern repeat…

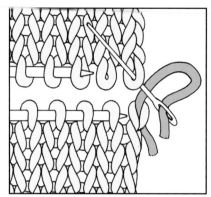

…to bottom, and come out of the next stitch from bottom to top. Then allow the second stitch to slip off the needle.

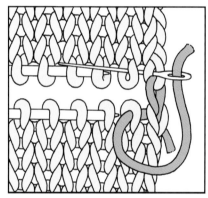

Don't pull the yarn too tight. With every working step, you catch 2 half stitches.

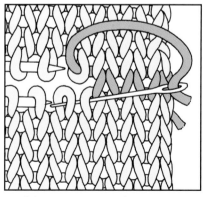

…of 4 rows, you need 1 row on one needle and 2 on the other.

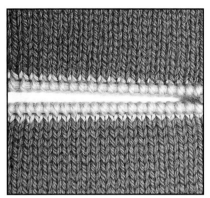

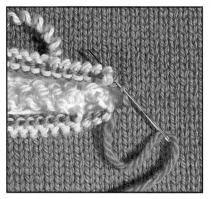

1 For sewing with open stitches, first work 2 rows in stockinette stitch in a different-colored yarn. Place the parts next to each other and pull the knitting needles out.

2 Work as when sewing from the knitting needles, alternately joining 2 stitches of the bottom and top pieces after the selvedge stitches. Undo the additional rows as you work.

3 The result is the same as when sewing from the knitting needles. The finished seam is invisible.

Put the pieces next to one another in the way they are going to be joined, with the right side of the work on top. The working yarn is attached to the bottom piece. The way you work in stockinette stitch is explained in detail on these pages.

For pieces worked in reverse stockinette, the stitches are similarly sewn together. You only have to insert the needle from bottom to top instead of from top to bottom, and bring it out the opposite way.

This means that you insert the needle into the selvedge stitch from top to bottom. Then insert the needle in the other selvedge stitch from bottom to top, and out of the next stitch from top to bottom, etc. If the piece was worked entirely in reverse stockinette, you can also turn the work and sew it together using grafting stitch for stockinette stitch.

When you have a patterned design, such as textured or ribbing patterns, it is not as practical to use grafting

stitch to join the pieces, because the stitches move over by half a stitch each time. In this case, it looks better if you knit the stitches together or sew them together after they are bound off.

Sewing Bind-off Stitches Together

On some patterns, such as openwork patterns, it is difficult to sew open stitches together using grafting stitches. In this case, it is easier to bind off the stitches and then sew them together with grafting stitches. A slightly raised area will form on the inside with this seam, but it can hardly be seen on the outside.

Similar to sewing open stitches together, to sew the bind-off stitches together with grafting stitches, you need a tapestry or wool needle, and a working yarn

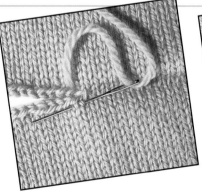

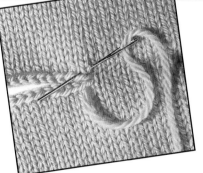

that is about three times as long as the width of the piece.

Put both pieces down, right side of the work on top, next to one another. Start with the selvedge stitches, just as you do for open stitches. Then again,

catch 2 stitches from the bottom and top pieces. Don't pull the working yarn too tightly, otherwise the seam will be hard and rigid, and the line on the inside will become thicker.

Sewing Together Pieces Worked Crosswise

For some patterns, you have to knit sweaters crosswise, such as if you want to work lengthwise stripes and don't want to work with a lot of different skeins of yarn.

It's true that you can start the sweater at the sleeve and work it in 1 piece over the shoulders. But if you use thick, country-type yarn, the sweater gets very heavy; and if you use soft yarn, it can easily stretch out of shape.

Here, you can work all the parts separately and then sew the sleeves onto the casting-on or binding-off edge of the front and back in open stitches. In order to finish at the same length on both sides, start in the middle of the sleeve—i.e., at the shoulder. Leave half the working yarn hanging on the right side of the work, and first sew 1 side to the corner of the sleeve. Then begin at the same point in the middle again, and sew the other side.

At the end, sew the side edges of the front and the back together using grafting stitch, and sew the sleeve seam using invisible stitch (pages 112–113).

1 When you sew sleeves onto pieces knit crosswise, put half the sleeve stitches on 1 needle, the other half on another.

2 Start working the grafting stitch in the center of the sleeve, i.e., at the shoulder, and first work towards the left edge of the sleeve.

3 Then turn the piece and finish the other side. At the casting-on edge, catch the whole stitch. At the open edge, catch 2 half stitches each time.

Sewing Ribbing Together

Cardigan or vest facings that were knit with the piece, or wide shawl collars, are generally worked in simple ribbing: knit 1, purl 1. For the section from the shoulder to the center of the back neckline, you work only these facing stitches, then they are joined in the center of the back.

Since the stitches of a seam sewn with grafting stitch shift over half a stitch, you can't sew this seam invisibly nor can the stitches be knit together. Since ribbed stitches also contract a lot, try this technique:

First put all the knit stitches on 1 needle and the purl stitches on another so that only the knit stitches are on the needle on both sides. Then put the pieces next to one another and first sew the knit stitches from the 2 needles on top together with grafting stitch. Then turn the work and sew the stitches from the needles on the bottom together in the same way.

Sewing In Sleeves

You have to set the sleeves in with special care. This seam should always be sewn before you sew the side and sleeve seams.

Sewing sleeves on using invisible stitch: Always alternately catch 1 whole stitch of the sleeve, and 1 or 2 horizontal threads of the front or back.

Straight and Slightly Rounded Sleeves

These sleeves should always be sewn in from the outside, using invisible stitch or back stitch. This is the only way to keep the seams straight with the stitches.

Lay the pieces, opened out, onto a counter or tabletop. Pin the sleeves exactly into place so that nothing can pull out of shape while you are sewing. Start pinning at the shoulder, in the center of the sleeve, and at the corners of the sleeves. Then pin the rest of the top sleeve edge at intervals of 2".

While you are sewing, pay attention to the gauge. For parts worked in stockinette stitch, you have to go around 1 horizontal thread instead of 2 every 3 stitches when sewing invisible stitch, and around 3 instead of 2 horizontal threads when sewing back stitch. If you have pinned the parts together carefully, it should be easy to check the seam.

If you have bound off the sleeve stitches, you can now work in invisible stitch. Always go alternately around 1 sleeve stitch and 1 or 2 horizontal threads of the front or back.

The seam will be even flatter if you sew the open sleeve stitches on using back stitch. To do this, first bind the

When sewing a sleeve on in back stitch, undo the binding-off row 1 stitch at a time.

The back stitches form a seam that looks similar to a row of purl stitches.

stitches off loosely, so that they won't come undone when you block the piece. Now pin the sleeve to the front and back, as described, and undo the binding-off row, little by little, as you sew the seam. Work the seam from right to left as follows:

First draw the yarn through the front or back, from bottom to top, next to the selvedge stitch, then through the first sleeve stitch. Now insert the needle directly to the right, from top to bottom, and come out again from bottom to top, 2 horizontal threads farther along,

catching the second sleeve stitch. Then go back down through the first sleeve stitch and the front or back, and 2 horizontal threads farther along through the front or back, and out through the third sleeve stitch. Go back down through the second sleeve stitch and back out again 2 horizontal threads farther along, and through the fourth sleeve stitch, etc. (see also sewing on facings, pages 70–72).

Full and Puffy Sleeves

When you join in very full sleeves, you can work either from the outside or inside. With full sleeve seams, it is easier to sew them before you sew the side seams and sleeve seams.

On the Wrong Side of the Work

The more popular method of joining uses back stitch on the wrong side of the work. Pin the pieces together, right side to right side. Put the pins in place close together so that the pieces can't slip out of place. Distribute the additional width at the top of full, rounded sleeves over the shoulder region.

Put the parts down so that the front and back are at the top and the sleeve is at the bottom. To make sure that the seam is in line with the stitches, always insert the needle directly next to the selvedge stitch of the top or bottom.

On the Right Side of the Work

When you work this way, it is easier to make sure you are staying in line with the stitches than when you sew on the wrong side. First pin the pieces together, wrong side to wrong side, distributing the additional width over the shoulder region. Then sew the seam using invisible stitch, as described on the previous pages. Work from 1 pin to the next and don't remove the pins too quickly. At the shoulder, depending on the fullness, catch 2 or more stitches at the same time, then a horizontal thread of the front or back.

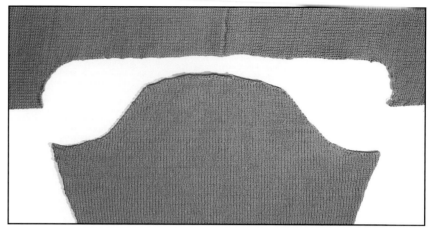

Put the body of the sweater and the sleeve next to one another. Spread them out and mark the center of the sleeve. Pin the sleeve in place and then sew the 2 pieces together using invisible stitch.

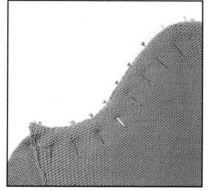

Either pin the pieces together, right side to right side, and then sew the seam using back stitch, or...

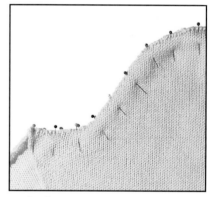

...pin the pieces together, wrong side to wrong side, and sew the seam using invisible stitch.

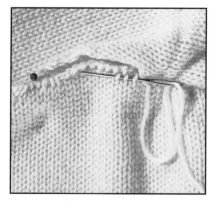

At the gathered parts, always put several stitches onto the sewing needle at the same time, and join them with 1 horizontal thread from the front or back.

Both seams look perfect when seen from the outside.

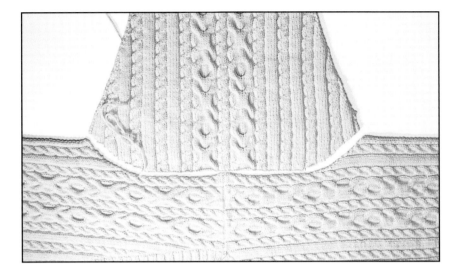

The best way to do it: Put the pieces, right side up, onto a large counter or table. Pin the outside edges of the sleeve in place, and then pin the center of the sleeve to the shoulder seam. Now sew the sleeve on, using invisible stitch with the original yarn, if possible. Don't take the pins out too quickly so that the seam won't pull out of shape.

The instructions for the cardigan with cable patterns are on page 200; those for the pullover sweater with jacquard and textured patterns are on pages 198–199.

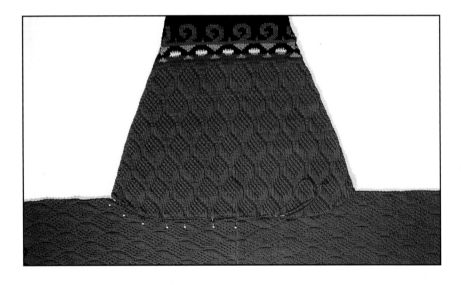

A contrast yarn makes it easier to count rows and increases. In every row where you work an increase, put the yarn to the back ahead of the center stitch (or the stitch next to it), and after you work the center stitch, put it to the front again. This makes it easy to check the number of increases and the number of rows between increases.

Leave the yarn in the knitted piece until you have finished the sleeve. Since it also marks the center of the sleeve, the sleeve can be pinned to the shoulder seam at this point.

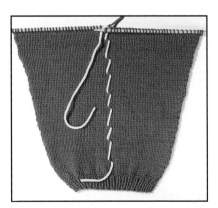

TIP

Here is a simple trick for rounding the top of the sleeve evenly without having any "steps": After the first big decreases, in all the following rows knit the first 2 stitches together twisted on the right side of the work and purl them together on the wrong side of the work. Bind off the following stitches normally. If only 1 stitch is supposed to be bound off, just knit the stitches together appropriately.

Starting and Finishing Yarn Ends

When your yarn comes to an end, making a knot is a taboo in knitting.

Starting a New Skein

If possible, don't start a new skein within the knitted piece. Even if the remaining piece of yarn looks pretty long, it often won't be long enough for the whole row. Leave it hanging at the side; you can use it later for sewing the parts together. If the yarn end bothers you as you are knitting, cut it off to about 4" long.

In order for the stitches not to become loose easily when you start a new skein, work the selvedge stitch at the end of the row with the old yarn and the new yarn. Turn the piece and work the selvedge stitch and several stitches with the new yarn. Then pull on both yarns so that the stitches will not get any looser again.

Sewing In Yarn Ends

Since knitted pieces are more stretchable in width than in length, yarn ends are always sewn individually and vertically into the selvedge stitches. If they were sewn in horizontally, the ends could easily come through to the front.

It doesn't matter whether you sew the yarn ends in before or after you sew the pieces together. When you are working with thin yarn, it is better to sew the yarn ends in after you have sewn the pieces together. Since the selvedge stitches and frequently also the stitches next to them become thicker when you sew the yarn ends in, it might not be possible to distinguish the individual stitches clearly any more. That makes it more difficult to sew the pieces together. Also, you can use the yarn ends for sewing.

1 In order that the first stitches with the new yarn don't come loose, work the last selvedge stitch with both yarns and turn the piece.

2 Work the selvedge stitch and several stitches of the row with the new yarn, and then pull the yarn ends tight.

1 If you must sew yarn ends in within a knitted piece, put the needle through the stitch next to the yarn end so that the stitch is completed.

2 Then sew the yarn end in vertically. Never catch whole stitches, just parts of them, and don't pull the yarn too tight.

When you are using heavy yarn with small lengths of yarn on a skein, it could easily happen that a skein ends in the middle of a piece. Whatever you do, don't make a knot! Not only are knots unattractive, they can unravel while the piece is being worn or washed, and then the piece is almost impossible to save.

Cut the yarn ends to about 4" long and sew them in as described on middle photos 1 and 2 above.

You can sew in yarn ends at the edges before or after you sew the pieces together. Always sew them individually and vertically into the selvedge stitches or seam.

Blocking Your Work

Before you sew the pieces together, you should block them. This makes the edges lie flat and the overall look of the stitches becomes more even.

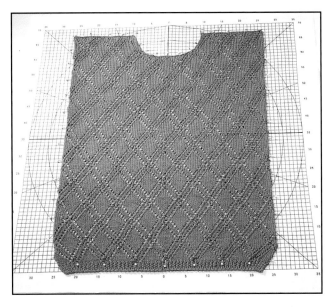

Block all the pieces according to the measurements of the pattern, and allow them to dry under damp cloths.

This blocking and steaming pad is available in most needlework stores.

Before you block your work, you should sew in any yarn ends that are within the piece. Yarn ends at the sides can be sewn in the seams after you sew the pieces together.

All of the pieces are pinned to a smooth surface, according to the measurements of the pattern. You can use a large ironing table, a piece of carpet, a Styrofoam sheet covered with a kitchen towel, or a blocking and steaming pad with foam (available in needlework stores). You can use normal pins to pin the pieces in place, but somewhat longer blocking pins are more practical.

Put the pins through the selvedge stitches as flat as possible and not too far apart. Check your measurements frequently as you pin, so that the front, back, and sleeves are the same size later. Don't stretch the ribbing. Now put damp cloths on top of the piece, press down lightly with your hands, and allow everything to dry for several hours or overnight. Remove the cloths. Before removing the needles, allow the parts to rest for about an hour more.

Do not put weights, such as books or other heavy items, on the pieces. This would flatten the patterns, and even pieces worked in stockinette stitch would lose their texture.

Steam Ironing

Before you steam iron your knitted pieces, carefully check the label. If there is a picture of a crossed-out iron, you can't iron or steam iron this yarn. You can carefully apply steam only to pure wool and cotton. Any other yarn mixtures—which means most yarns—don't take steam very well; the pieces become limp.

For applying steam, place a damp cloth on the knitted piece. Put the iron down just briefly and lift it to move it to the next spot. In other words, don't move it back and forth as in normal ironing. This would cause the stitches to pull out of shape. It is better to use a steam iron that you don't put down on the piece, but rather move above the piece, not touching it.

Special Techniques

This chapter contains some beautiful knitting techniques. From openwork to cables and shaker knitting, to jacquards, contrast piping, and intarsia—everything is explained in detail. This even makes knitting short-ened rows a pleasure…

Shaker Knitting

Shaker knitting patterns have a lot of "depth." And once you get the hang of it, they're very easy to knit.

Yarn labels always have recommended needle sizes, such as size 3 to 6. Since shaker knitting stretches a lot—double shaker knitting in width, single shaker knitting in length—you should knit these patterns relatively tightly and, therefore, you shouldn't use the biggest needle size indicated. If you tend to knit loosely, size 3 will be big enough; if you tend to knit tightly, use size 4.

For the same reason, the sample for gauge (pages 50–51) has to be stretched slightly before you measure it so that your sweater doesn't turn out too big. Don't worry if the knitted pieces look small. They won't have the correct size until after they are blocked or washed.

In shaker knitting, the selvedge stitches have to be knit very tightly. A purled garter stitch selvedge is best. Purl the selvedge stitches in every row and pull them tightly. Very nice examples of this are the V-necks on page 83. A purled garter stitch selvedge is so even that no additional facing is required. For edges that won't disappear in a seam, such as scarves or the front edges of a cardigan, a selvedge worked in shaker knitting looks the most attractive (see selvedge stitches, pages 26–27).

Also make sure that there is always a purl stitch next to the selvedge stitches on the right side of the work. You will need this purl stitch to make an invisible seam later. This means that in double and single shaker knitting, you must cast on an odd number of stitches, and already make sure in the ribbing that in the first row on the wrong side of the work, you knit a stitch next to the selvedge stitch.

Bind off shaker knitting as the stitches lie—i.e., in double and single shaker knitting, you alternately bind off a knit and purl stitch. Work tightly, especially at the shoulder seams, so that they don't stretch too much later. Instead of binding off these stitches by passing them over, you can also bind them off with a crochet hook or by knitting them together. Instead of using yarn over, double and single shaker knitting can be worked by inserting the needle in the stitch of the previous row. To many knitters, this seems a simpler way of doing it, but the knitting becomes much looser because an entire stitch is opened up. In most instances, the finished piece looks as if it was knit unevenly—and it doesn't go any faster either! Also, when you use some yarns, such as nubby or bouclé yarn, the stitches don't necessarily unravel by themselves.

TIP

For shaker knitting, as compared with stockinette stitch, you need about 30%–50% more yarn. Make sure you choose "light" yarn that isn't twisted too tightly. Wool and wool blends are lighter than cotton yarns. Even a sweater knit in stockinette stitch comes out fairly heavy when it is made of cotton. The heavier the sweater, the more it will "grow" later!

Double Shaker Knitting

For knitting with yarn over:
Odd number of stitches.
Row 1 (WS): selv st, * k1, slip 1 purlwise with yo *, k1, selv st.
Row 2 (RS): selv st, * slip 1 purlwise with yo, k next st tog with yo *, slip 1 purlwise with yo, selv st.
Row 3: selv st, * k st tog with yo, slip 1 purlwise with yo *, k st tog with yo, selv st.
Repeat **Rows 2 and 3.**

For knitting by inserting the needle in the stitch of the row below:
Row 1 (WS): Between the selv st, k all the st.
Row 2 (RS): selv st, * k1, knit next stitch in the row below (the st above it will come undone) *, k1, selv st.
Row 3: selv st, * knit next stitch in the row below, k 1 *, knit next stitch in the row below, selv st.
Repeat **Rows 2 and 3.**

Two-color Double Shaker Knitting

This pattern has to be worked on circular knitting needles in open

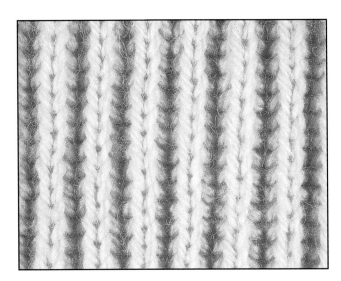

Pieces worked in double shaker knitting look the same from both sides.

rows, since 2 rows on the right side of the work and 2 rows on the wrong side of the work always have to be worked consecutively. After working the first row on the right side of the work, push the needles from the left tip of the needle back to the right tip, and work the second row on the right side of the work. Then work the first row on the wrong side of the work, etc.

In order for the selvedge stitches to be tight in this pattern, they are always purled in the odd rows and knit in the even rows. In the example shown below, all the white selvedge stitches are purled, all the ochre selvedge stitches are knit.

In this pattern, the ochre side is the right side of the work. You need an odd number of stitches.
Row 1 (RS) in white: selv st, * p1, slip 1 purlwise with yo *, p1, selv st. Now push the stitches to the right tip of the needle.
Row 2 (RS) in ochre: selv st, * slip 1 purlwise with yo, k next st tog with yo *, slip 1 purlwise with yo, selv st. Turn the work.
Row 3 (WS) in white: selv st, * k st tog with yo, slip 1 purlwise with yo *, k st tog with yo, selv st. Push the stitches to the right tip of the needle.
Row 4 (RS) in ochre: selv st, * slip 1 purlwise with yo, p next st tog with yo *, slip 1 purlwise with yo, selv st. Turn the work.
Row 5 (RS) in white: selv st, * p st tog with yo, slip 1 purlwise with yo *, p st tog with yo, selv st. Push the stitches to the right tip of the needle.
Repeat **Rows 2 to 5.**

Two-color double shaker knitting: The pattern described is seen on the right side of the work…

…and with the opposite colors on the wrong side.

Single Shaker Knitting

As the name says, single shaker knitting is worked with the yarn over on only one side. This pattern looks smooth on one side, almost exactly like double shaker knitting. On the other side, the pattern looks "rough"; that is the side that is worked with the yarn over. You must decide right from the start which side is going to be the right side of your work.

Again, make sure that you work a purl stitch next to the selvedge stitches. The number of stitches has to be odd.

If you follow the instructions given below, the smooth, single shaker knitting side is the right side of the work.

Row 1 (WS): selv st, * k1, slip 1 purlwise with yo *, k1, selv st.
Row 2 (RS): selv st, * p1, k next st tog with yo *, p1, selv st.
Repeat **Rows 1 and 2**.

For a "rough" look on the right side of the work:

Row 1 (WS): selv st, * slip 1 purlwise with yo, k1 *, slip 1 purlwise with yo, selv st.
Row 2 (RS): selv st, * k next st tog with yo, p1 *, k next st tog with yo, selv st.
Repeat **Rows 1 and 2**.

Of course you can also work this pattern by inserting the needle in the stitch of the previous row. In this case, you knit all the stitches on the rough side of the work and alternately purl 1 stitch and knit 1 stitch in the stitch of the previous row.

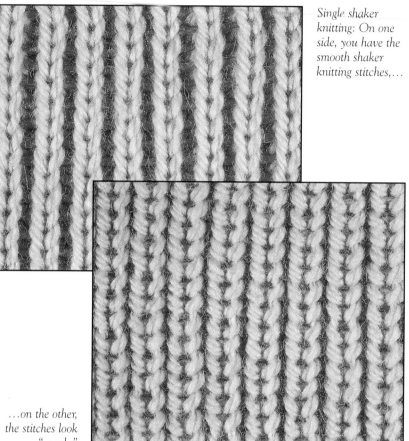

Single shaker knitting: On one side, you have the smooth shaker knitting stitches,…

…on the other, the stitches look "rough."

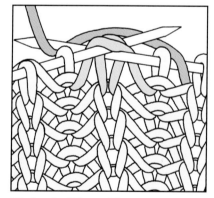

Shaker knitting with yarn over:
If you slip a stitch with a yarn over, the yarn will be at the front of the work, at first. You then insert the right needle into the next stitch as if to purl, slip it, and bring the yarn to the back of the work. If you are working in double shaker knitting, you knit the next knit stitch together with the yarn over of the previous row. If you are working in single shaker knitting, you knit the stitch.

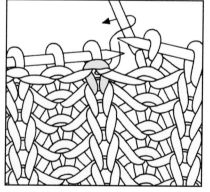

Needle inserted in stitch of row below:
Instead of bringing the yarn over the purl stitch, you can also simply knit a stitch. In the next row, you then have to insert the needle into the stitch of the row below. The stitch, which looks like a purl stitch on this side, will come undone.

Single Shaker Knitting Worked Twisted

Shaker knitting stitches worked twisted have a completely different look. To work this, you need an even number of stitches.

Row 1 (WS): selv st, * slip 1 purlwise with yo, k1 *, selv st.
Row 2 (RS): selv st, * p1, k next st tog with yo twisted (insert needle into the back part of the stitch and the back loop of the yarn over, and k), p1 *, k next st tog with yo twisted, selv st.
Repeat **Rows 1 and 2**.

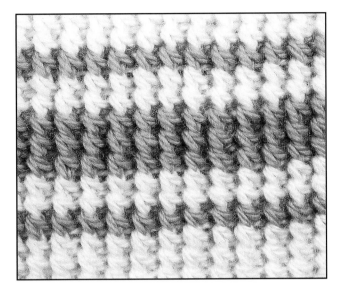

Shaker knitting stitches worked twisted look completely different.

Double-ribbed Shaker Knitting

This pattern, in which the yarn over is always knit together with 2 stitches, is also very striking. The drawing below shows how the yarn overs and stitches are worked.

The number of stitches must be divisible by 4 + 2 + 2 selvedge stitches.

Row 1 (WS): selv st, * k2, slip 2 purlwise with yo *, k2, selv st.
Row 2 (RS): selv st, * slip 2 purlwise with yo, k next st tog with the yo, leaving the yo on the left needle and putting only the st on the right needle, then k the second st tog with the yo *, slip 2 purlwise with yo, selv st.
Row 3: selv st, * k the first st tog with the yo, leaving the yo on the left needle and putting only the st on the right needle, then k the second st tog with the yo, slip 2 purlwise with yo *, k next st tog with the yo, leaving the yo on the left needle and putting only the st on the right needle, then k the second st tog with the yo, selv st.
Repeat **Rows 2 and 3**.

In double-ribbed shaker knitting, the yarn overs are worked over 2 stitches.

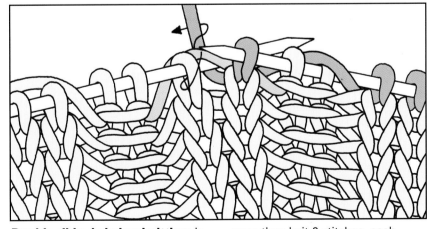

Double-ribbed shaker knitting: In double-ribbed shaker knitting, slip 2 stitches purlwise with a yarn over, then knit 2 stitches, each individually, together with the yarn over of the previous row.

Triple-ribbed Shaker Knitting

Here, 3 knit shaker stitches and 1 purl shaker stitch are worked alternately. The first and third knit shaker stitches in the rows on the right side of the work are knit together with the yarn over. For the second knit stitch, the yarn over is worked in the rows on the right side of the work, and the stitch is purled together with the yarn over on the wrong side of the work. You can expand this to 5, 7, or more knit stitches so that the ribs on the wrong side of the work are farther apart.

For triple-ribbed shaker knitting, the number of stitches has to be divisible by 4 + 1 + 2 selvedge stitches.

Row 1 (WS): selv st, * k1, slip 1 purlwise with yo, k1, slip 1 purlwise with yo *, k1, selv st.

Row 2 (RS): selv st, * slip 1 purlwise with yo, k next st tog with the yo *, slip 1 purlwise with yo, selv st.

Row 3: selv st, * k next st tog with yo, slip 1 purlwise with yo, k next st tog with yo *, k next st tog with the yo, selv st.

Repeat **Rows 2 and 3.**

Triple-ribbed shaker knitting: On one side with 3 shaker knitting stitches next to one another,...

...on the other side a completely new textured pattern with ribs of shaker knitting stitches.

Faux Shaker Knitting

This pattern is actually a textured pattern, not a real shaker knitting pattern, since it is not worked with yarn overs or with the needle inserted in a stitch of the previous row. It is good for country-look sweaters and cardigans as well as scarves, since it looks the same on both sides like shaker knitting.

The number of stitches is divisible by 4 + 3 + 2 selvedge stitches.

Row 1 (RS): selv st, * k3, p1 *, k3, selv st.

Row 2 (WS): selv st, k1, p1, * k3, p1 *, k1, selv st.

Repeat **Rows 1 and 2.**

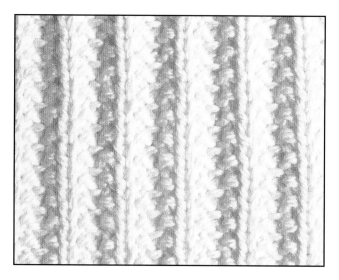

Faux shaker knitting: Actually, a simple textured pattern.

Brioche Stitch

Brioche stitch is worked almost
entirely with knit stitches. The pattern is shifted over every 2 rows, so
you always repeat 4 rows. The yarn
overs are worked in the rows on the
wrong side of the work, and knit
together with the corresponding
stitch in the next row on the wrong
side of the work.

This pattern is worked with an
even number of stitches.

Row 1 (WS): selv st, *slip 1
purlwise with yo, k1*, selv st.

Row 2 (RS): selv st, *k2, slip the yo
of the previous row purlwise*, selv st.

Row 3: selv st, * k1 tog with the yo,
slip the next st purlwise with the yo
*, selv st.

Row 4: selv st, * k1, slip the yo of
the previous row purlwise, k1 *, selv
st.

Row 5: selv st, * slip 1 purlwise with
yo, k next st tog with yo *, selv st.

Repeat **Rows 2 to 5.**

Two-color brioche stitch is worked
the same way as single-color brioche
stitch, but always alternately knit 2
rows in the same color. Start the new
color in a row on the wrong side of
the work.

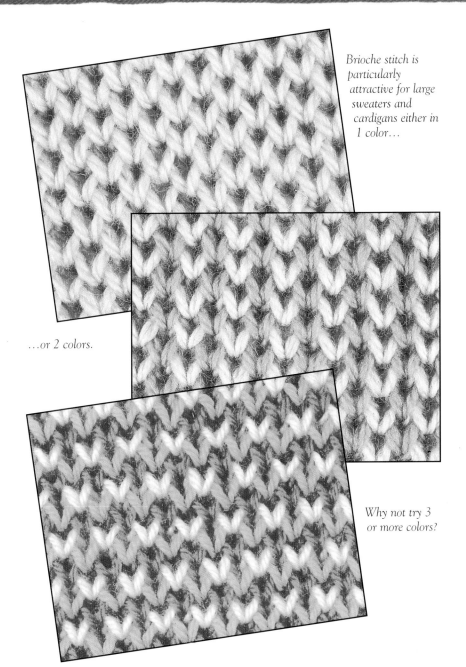

Brioche stitch is particularly attractive for large sweaters and cardigans either in 1 color…

…or 2 colors.

Why not try 3 or more colors?

Brioche stitch: In the first row on the wrong side of the work, slip every second stitch with a yarn over, purlwise. In the rows on the right side of the work, you knit the stitch that is sort of hiding under the yarn over, and slip the yarn over purlwise. Then knit the next stitch.

In all the following rows on the wrong side of the work, you knit the stitch together with the yarn over, and slip the stitches in between with a yarn over, purlwise.

Decreases in Shaker Knitting

Whether they're for a V-neck or raglan sleeves, decreases in shaker knitting are always worked on the right side of the work.

In shaker knitting, don't work decreases right next to the selvedge stitch, since it will make the edges uneven. Decreases moved over 3 or 5 stitches towards the inside of the piece come out much more even.

The decreases are especially attractive if they are worked as double decreases. This holds true for both raglan edges and V-necks.

For V-necks **with a facing knit on later**, put the knit center stitch on a stitch holder. In order for you to have a knit stitch in the middle, the number of stitches must be divisible by 4 + 3 stitches + 2 selvedge stitches. You must be able to count an odd number of knit stitches on the right side of the work.

For V-necks **without a facing** (see also V-necks, page 83), the number of stitches must be divisible by 4 + 1 stitch + 2 selvedge stitches. The number of knit stitches must be an even number. Work the center purl stitch as a selvedge stitch on one side. For the other side, pick up an additional selvedge stitch.

If you work **single decreases**, you will have a knit stitch next to the decreased shaker knitting stitch after every other decrease. Until the next decrease, don't work this stitch in the shaker knitting pattern. Instead, purl it in the rows on the wrong side of the work or slip it purlwise in the rows on the right side of the work with the yarn at the back of the work.

A finished V-neck with the center stitch on a stitch holder and the facing knit on.

For a double decrease to the left, work 2 more stitches in the pattern after the selvedge stitch, slip the next knit stitch knitwise together with the yarn over, then knit 2 stitches (= 3 loops) together...

...and pass the slipped stitch over together with the yarn over. Then continue in the shaker knitting pattern.

For a double decrease to the right, work to within 6 stitches from the end of the row. Knit the next 3 stitches together. Including the yarn overs, this comes to 5 loops.

Then work the last 3 stitches in the shaker knitting pattern.

Increases

Just like decreases, increases in shaker knitting should be worked as double increases. Here again, it looks nicer if they aren't worked right next to the selvedge stitches. For this slanted edge of a sleeve, the increases are worked after 3 stitches.

Work 3 stitches at the right edge, then purl 1 stitch twisted and knit 1 stitch twisted from the horizontal thread (the yarn over of the previous row).

At the left edge, work to within 3 stitches from the end of the row, then knit 1 stitch twisted and purl 1 stitch twisted from the horizontal thread.

After the seam has been sewn with invisible stitch, 2 ribs of shaker knitting will run up the sleeve next to one another.

In order for the pattern after the ribbing not to look mismatched, you should always work double increases here as well.

After a knit stitch, increase a purl stitch twisted, knit the next stitch, which was previously a purl stitch, then increase another purl stitch twisted from the next horizontal thread. This allows the ribs to continue in the same pattern.

Working in the Round

I don't recommend working an entire sweater in shaker knitting in the round, if only because it will get too large and heavy. But if you want to knit a really luxurious turtleneck and don't want to have a seam, **single shaker ribbing** is a good solution.

You should work the first ¾" to 1¼" in simple ribbing (alternating knit 1, purl 1) to keep the neckline from getting too wide.

If you want to wear the single shaker knitting pattern with the smooth side on the outside, turn the work—that is, work in rounds on the wrong side of the work—as follows:

Round 1: Slip the k st with yo, p the p st.
Round 2: k the st tog with the yo, p the p st. Repeat **Rounds 1 and 2**.

If you don't turn the work, the rough side will be on the outside once the turtleneck collar has been turned over.

You can also work **double shaker knitting** in rounds. To do that, every other round, slip the purl stitches with a yarn over and knit the knit stitches together with the yarn over. In the other rounds, slip the knit stitches with a yarn over and purl the purl stitches together with the yarn over.

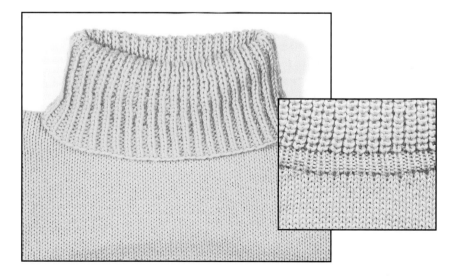

Cable Patterns

This simple technique of crossing stitches is the basis for textured patterns with a lot of depth. The cables formed this way can be worked in individually or distributed over the sweater or cardigan in different combinations, such as in Aran Isle knitting.

Cable patterns look best if they are worked with smooth yarn or wool. Note that designs with cable patterns require more yarn, since cables contract in width.

You also have to take that into account when you bind off. To keep from having too much width at the shoulders and sleeves, knit 2 stitches together several times as you bind off, or bind off by knitting stitches together (see also pages 43–44).

If you want to make a sweater with different kinds of cable, you have to make a sample gauge for each of these cables using the original yarn. If you are a little short of the desired sweater width, you can add small or large seed stitch (see page 30) or narrow cables.

Some of the stitches that form the cable are placed on a cable needle in front of or behind the work. You then work the indicated number of stitches before continuing with the stitches from the cable needle.

The examples on page 133 show you how to work the cable stitches. Each cable is made up of 6 stitches. These stitches are knit on the right side of the work, purled on the wrong side of the work—in other words, worked in stockinette stitch. The cables stand out even more if you work a few stitches of reverse stockinette stitch on both sides of them. The number of rows between cable crossings can be varied however you want; the cables shown on page 133 were crossed every sixth row.

Simple cables (top): crossed just to the right, alternately to the right and the left, or just to the left. **Plait cables** (bottom) are a combination of stitches crossed to the right and left.

Horseshoe or chain cables (top) are made up of 2 cables next to one another and worked in reverse. **Fancy cables** (bottom) are a combination of different cable widths and lengths.

Left Cross Cables

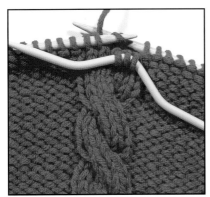

1 Slip the first 3 stitches of the cable onto a cable needle and place them in front of the work. Knit the next...

2 ...3 stitches on the left needle. Knit the 3 stitches from the cable needle.

3 Then work another 5 rows without crossing the cable.

Right Cross Cables

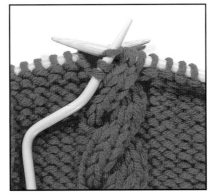

1 Slip the first 3 stitches of the cable onto a cable needle and place them behind the work. Knit the next...

2 ...3 stitches on the left needle. Knit the 3 stitches from the cable needle.

3 Then work another 5 rows without crossing the cable.

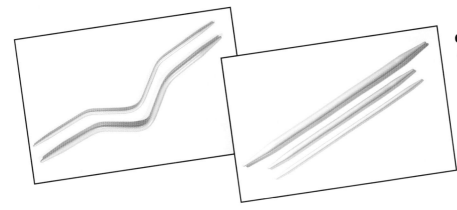

Cable needles are available in different sizes in angled shape or straight. You can also use a short double-pointed needle as well. The angled needles have the advantage that the stitches won't slip off the needle as easily.

Making Cables Without a Cable Needle

Crossing stitches with a cable needle takes a lot of time, especially when you are working an interwoven pattern. Since the little "cables" in these patterns are generally worked over only 2 or 4 stitches, with a little practice you can work without a cable needle.

In comparison to stockinette stitch or even normal cables, interwoven patterns tighten a lot, so you should knit them a little looser. Use at least the largest needle size indicated. If you have a little "play" in the yarn, it is also easier to cross the stitches.

You can work the interwoven pattern explained in the photos on the right as perpendicular strips or all the way around. However, entire sweaters in the interwoven pattern are relatively stiff and heavy, so this pattern is not good for all sweaters. A country-look cardigan, on the other hand, will be especially warm. You need an even number of stitches for this interwoven pattern.

Left Cross Mini-cables

For mini-cables crossed to the left, there's a trick you can use to make crossing the stitches easier. The difficult stitch in the row on the right side of the work is always the second stitch of the cable, which is the first stitch on the wrong side of the work. So if you purl this stitch "the wrong way" in the previous row on the wrong side of the work, it will be on the needle twisted in the next row on the right side of the work—in other words, the front part of the stitch will be behind the needle. You can then knit the stitch "twisted." Insert the needle into the back part of the stitch and get a normal knit stitch.

1 In the right side rows, insert the needle into the front of the second stitch, going behind the first stitch, and pull the yarn through.

2 Then knit the first stitch and let both stitches drop from the left needle.

3 In the wrong side rows, purl 1 stitch at both edges, and in between work as follows every 2 stitches. Insert the needle into the second stitch, going in front of the first stitch, and purl it.

4 Then purl the first stitch and let both stitches drop from the left needle.

1 In the previous row on the wrong side, pull the loop for the purl stitch through from the top to the bottom. This puts the stitch on the needle "twisted." In the row on the right side, knit the second stitch of the cable twisted: Insert the needle from right to left, behind the first stitch into the back loop of the second stitch, and pull the yarn through.

2 Then insert the needle into the front of the first stitch, from right to left, and knit the stitch. Then allow both stitches to drop from the left needle. The twisted stitch of the previous row will now lie "correctly" under the crossing.

Left Cross Wider Cables without a Cable Needle

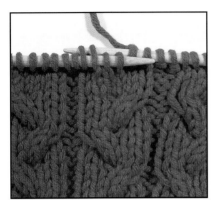  

1 For stitches crossed to the left, skip the appropriate number of stitches (in this case, 2 stitches) and insert the right needle into the next 2 stitches behind the left needle.

2 Allow the 4 stitches to slip from the left needle, and then quickly catch the first 2 stitches with the left needle.

3 Slip the 2 cable stitches on the right needle back onto the left needle, and knit all 4 stitches.

Right Cross Wider Cables Without a Cable Needle

1 For stitches crossed to the right, skip the appropriate number of stitches (in this case, 2 stitches) and insert the right needle into the next 2 stitches in front of the left needle.

2 Allow the 4 stitches to slip from the left needle and then quickly catch the first 2 stitches with the left needle.

3 Slip the 2 cable stitches on the right needle back onto the left needle, and knit all 4 stitches.

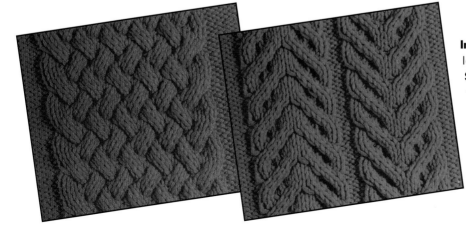

Interwoven cables (left) look like basket lattice. **Staghorn cables** (right) are very attractive as a single pattern element of a sweater. The pattern charts for these cables and for the patterns on page 132 are on pages 216–217.

Openwork Patterns

Openwork patterns, also called filigree patterns, are the laciest patterns you can make.

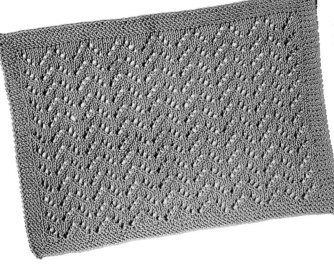

Smooth cotton yarns are especially good for patterns like this arrowhead lace.

There are no limits on the patterns you can come up with. The larger the pattern designs, the lighter and airier the piece will look.

The holes are made with simple yarn overs, which can be arranged horizontally, vertically, or diagonally. The working yarn is placed over the needle from front to back. In most patterns, these yarn overs are purled in the row on the wrong side of the work. Every yarn over forms a new stitch, so the number of stitches has to be corrected with corresponding decreases.

Openwork patterns are frequently worked over the entire piece. However, they can also be very effective as a single separate design, horizontal borders, or vertically arranged pattern strips. Leaf and diamond patterns are especially attractive. Lace patterns with a lot of openwork, which are practically an art in themselves, are always fashionable.

Make sure that the openwork patterns start 1 to 2 stitches in from the edges, so that you don't have any problems when you sew the pieces together.

By the way, the most inconspicuous buttonholes are worked like a mini-openwork pattern (see buttonholes, starting on page 100).

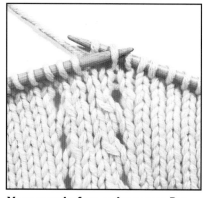

Yarn over before a decrease: Put the yarn over the needle from front to back, slip 1 stitch, knit the next stitch, and pass the slipped stitch over.

Yarn over after a decrease: Slip 1 stitch, knit the following stitch, and pass the slipped stitch over, then put the yarn over the needle from front to back and continue knitting normally.

Yarn over before 2 stitches knitted together: Put the yarn over the needle from front to back, then knit the next 2 stitches together.

Yarn over after 2 stitches knitted together: Knit two stitches together, then put the yarn over the needle from front to back.

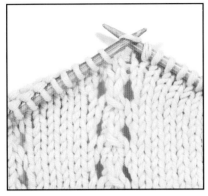

Left double decrease with 2 yarn overs: Put the yarn over the needle, then slip 1 stitch knitwise,…

…knit the next 2 stitches together and pass the slipped stitch over, then put the yarn over the needle again.

Double decrease with center stitch on top and 2 yarn overs: Put the yarn over the needle, then slip 2 stitches knitwise,…

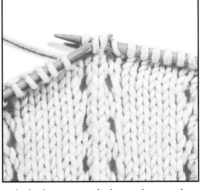

…knit the next stitch, and pass the slipped stitches over together. Then put the yarn over the needle again.

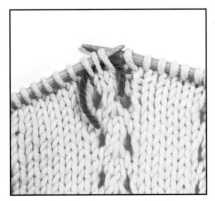

Right double decrease with 2 yarn overs: Put the yarn over the needle, knit 3 stitches together,…

…then put the yarn over the needle again.

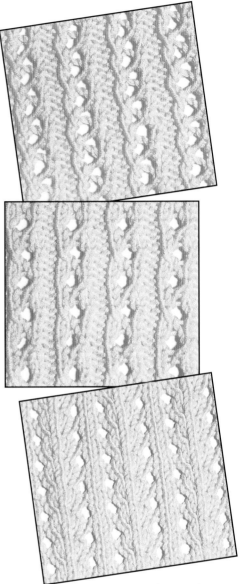

For vertical strips of openwork, the arrangement of the yarn overs before and after stitches knit together is important. The pattern charts for all these patterns are on pages 219 and 221.

Twisted Stitch Patterns

Patterns with twisted stitches have a lot of texture. In ribbed patterns, the knit ribs are even more prominent. The stitch in the previous row is always the one that is twisted.

For ribbing, knit all the knit stitches twisted on the right side of the work and purl all the purl stitches normally.

On the wrong side of the work, knit all the knit stitches normally and purl all the purl stitches twisted.

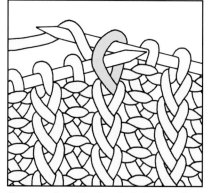

For a **twisted knit stitch**, insert the needle into the back of the stitch on the left needle, from right to left, and knit it.

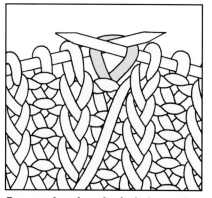

For a **twisted purl stitch**, insert the needle into the back of the stitch on the left needle from behind the work, from left to right, and purl it.

Ribbing with twisted stitches also looks very nice. Only work every other stitch twisted, namely the stitch that appears as a knit stitch on the front of the work. The stitch in between is purled normally in the rows on the right side of the work and knit normally in the rows on the wrong side of the work. Knitting both stitches twisted is not good for ribbing; the ribbing loses its elasticity.

Check patterns, ribbing cables, and slipped stitches have even more texture when they are worked with twisted stitches. Some examples are shown on page 139.

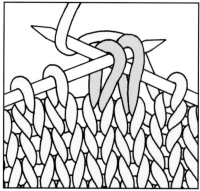

To **knit 2 stitches together twisted**, insert the needle into the back of the next 2 stitches at the same time, from right to left, and knit them together.

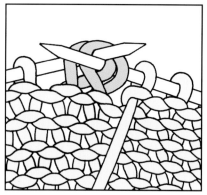

To **purl 2 stitches together twisted**, insert the needle into the back of the next 2 stitches at the same time, from behind the work, from left to right, and purl them together.

Check pattern

Ribbing and hourglass cable

Diamonds and zigzag lines

Oval designs

Check Pattern

In a check pattern, all the stitches that appear as knit stitches on the right side of the work are twisted in every row—i.e., knit twisted on the right side of the work, purled twisted on the wrong side of the work. All of the stitches that appear as purl stitches on the right side of the work are purled on the right side of the work, knit on the wrong side of the work.

Ribbing and Hourglass Cable

In the ribbing and hourglass cable, all the stitches that appear as knit stitches on the right side of the work are twisted in every row. For the hourglass shape, the stitches are crossed (see cable patterns, page 138).

Diamonds and Zigzag Lines

For the diamonds and zigzag lines, only the stitches that appear as knit stitches on the right side of the work are twisted.

Oval Design with Slipped Stitches

In this oval design, the knit stitches are knit twisted in every row on the right side of the work and only slipped, not purled, in the rows on the wrong side of the work. This results in a knit twisted slipped stitch.

The pattern charts for the patterns described here are on page 224–225.

Slip Stitch Patterns

Whether they are worked in the same or different colors, you can create impressive patterns with slipped stitches. And they're really simple to do!

Slipped Stitches in Single-color Patterns

Slipped stitches give reverse stockinette stitch and even stockinette stitch a lot of texture. They are particularly attractive when worked in smooth yarn, since the stitches on top stand out more.

The stitches are generally slipped in a row on the right side of the work, and purled on the wrong side. To slip them, insert the right needle into the stitch from right to left and slip it off. In other words, the stitches are slipped purlwise; the yarn is at the back of the work. Purl the stitch on the wrong side of the work.

The stitches can also be slipped in the rows on the wrong side of the work and knit on the right side of the work; the effect is the same. In this case, you also insert the needle into the stitch as if to purl; the yarn is at the front of the work. Knit the stitches in the rows on the right side of the work.

You can also achieve an attractive effect if you cross slipped stitches (see cables, pages 132–135). The background can be worked in stockinette or reverse stockinette stitch. In the example shown at the right, you can see that crossed slipped stitches really stand out well against a stockinette stitch background.

Slipped Stitches in Multicolor Patterns

Although you only work with 1 yarn at a time, these patterns often look

For a slipped stitch on the right side of the work, insert the right needle into the stitch as if to purl and slip it off. Then work the next stitch, bringing the yarn along loosely at the back of the work.

In this pattern, 1 or 3 stitches are worked in reverse stockinette stitch between the slipped stitches.

Crossed slip stitches: The interior of the diamonds is alternately worked in stockinette stitch and reverse stockinette stitch. The pattern chart for this pattern is on page 230.

as if they were done using intarsia or jacquard technique.

In the pattern with **vertical slip stitches** (figure below), the yarn color is changed after every row—i.e., 2 rows on the right side of the work and 2 rows on the wrong side of the work are worked one after the other. To do this, you have to work on a circular knitting needle. After the first knit row on the right side of the work in white, push the stitches back and knit the second row on the right side of the work in turquoise. Then turn the work and purl the first row on the wrong side of the work in white; push the stitches back and purl the second row on the wrong side of the work in turquoise. For this reason, the slipped stitches sometimes have to be worked in a row on the right side of the work, sometimes in a row on the wrong side of the work.

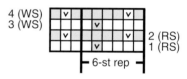

Every row is shown in the pattern chart. Read the 2 RS rows from right to left, the WS rows from left to right. Repeat these 4 rows.

Perpendicular Slip Stitches: This pattern (chart above) has to be worked on a circular needle, since 2 RS rows and 2 WS rows must be knit consecutively each time.

The **diamond pattern** looks like a jacquard pattern. Alternately work 2 rows of turquoise, 2 rows of white. The slipped stitches are shifted over, which is shown on the pattern chart.

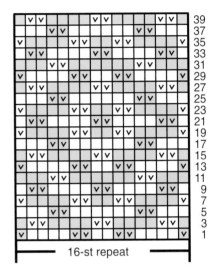

16-st repeat

The pattern chart for the diamond pattern shows only the RS rows. Purl the stitches on the wrong side and slip the slipped stitches again. Repeat these 40 rows.

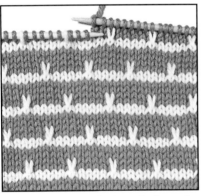

Slip the **individual slip-stitches** of this pattern over 2 rows each.

Individual slip-stitches (left) loosen up a pattern with wide turquoise stripes. Two rows of white alternate with 4 rows of turquoise. The slip stitches are worked every sixth stitch, shifted from 1 row of white to the next, and over 2 rows.

Three slip stitches (below), which are always worked over 2 rows in different colors and shifted over, interrupt the horizontal stripes. This pattern, too, is worked with only 1 color yarn at a time. For the vertical breaks, 3 stitches are always slipped when the stripes in the second color are being worked.

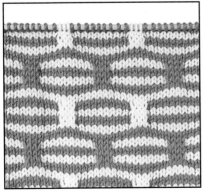

Three slip-stitches are slipped twice over the stitches in the other color. After 10 rows, the pattern is shifted over by 6 stitches.

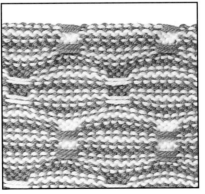

The yarn carried behind the work can be seen behind the 3 slip stitches.

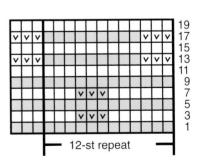

12-st repeat

The pattern chart for 3 slip stitches shows only the RS rows. Purl the stitches on the wrong side and slip the slipped stitches again. Repeat these 20 rows.

Jacquard Patterns

Patterns with at least 2 colors in a row are called jacquard patterns. They are also called Fair Isle patterns.

Jacquard patterns are almost always worked in stockinette stitch: On the right side of the work, knit the stitches; both yarn colors are at the back of the work. On the wrong side of the work, purl the stitches; both yarn colors are at the front of the work. If you work jacquard patterns in the round, knit all the stitches and keep the yarn at the back of the work. The selvedge stitches are always worked with both yarn colors.

You'll find a sweater with this jacquard border on page 198.

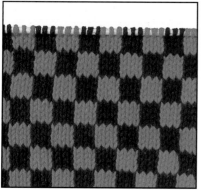

When you work small checks like these, use the jacquard technique. If you make larger checks, interlock the different colors (see intarsia).

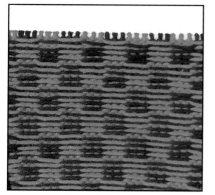

A view of the mini-checks from the back.

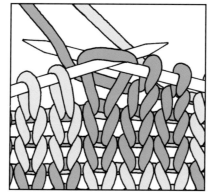

1 On the right side, hold both yarn colors behind the work and alternately knit with the front yarn...

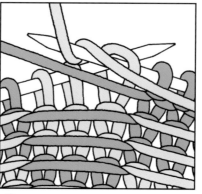

3 On the wrong side, hold both colors in front of the work and alternately purl with the front yarn...

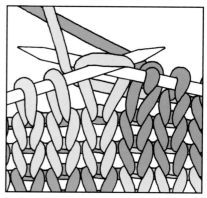

2 ...and the back one.

4 ...and the back one.

142

Holding the Yarn

You can get special yarn guides for 2-color or multicolor knitting. You hook or thread the yarn into the eyes.

Another way is keeping both yarn colors on your left hand at the same time. First put 1 color yarn around the pinkie finger of your left hand and then around your forefinger from back to front. Put the other color yarn around your pinkie finger the same way, but then put it around your forefinger from front to back. The 2 colors cross in front of your forefinger.

Now alternately work with the front and the back yarn as the pattern requires. In the case of irregular patterns, if you are knitting

The diamonds are staggered in such a way that the greatest distance the yarn has to be carried on the back is over 7 stitches.

with more of 1 color, you have to tighten the yarn on your pinkie finger from time to time so that the stitches you knit with it don't become too loose.

Yarn Tension

The yarn that is not used is carried along at the back of the work. It should not be pulled too tight, since this would make the knitted piece tighten, but it should also not be too loose. This is particularly important over several stitches in the same color.

Here is a little trick for maintaining proper yarn tension: Every time you change colors, work only 1 stitch in the new color. Then spread the stitches on the right needle out to the correct width and correct the length of the yarn being carried along.

Sample for Gauge

In jacquard patterns, the stitches are longer than in single-color patterns, so you need fewer rows for the same length. The density of the pattern determines how big the difference is as compared with single-color knitting. If you work 2 colors in every row, and if the patterns are very small, the stitch length can actually be the same as the stitch width. For example, a 4" square can have 22 stitches and 24 rows.

If you want to make a sweater in which different patterns, such as single-color textured patterns and jacquard patterns, are to be worked next to one another to produce the same length, you have to work shortened rows on the single-color side to make up for the difference (pages 146–150). Or you can make 2 different pieces and sew them together later, using invisible stitch (don't forget to include the additional selvedge stitches). When you change patterns over the length, all that matters is the stitch width, and that is the same for stockinette stitch, textured patterns, and jacquard patterns.

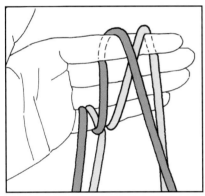

Holding both yarn colors on your left hand at the same time.

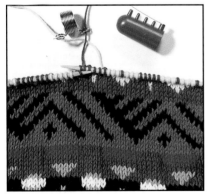

The guide with 2 eyes (left) is for 2-color knitting. The one with 4 notches (right) is for up to 4 colors.

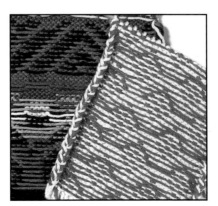

The yarn not in use is carried evenly at the back of the work.

Reading Patterns

You usually work from a multicolor pattern chart for jacquard patterns. Sometimes the different colors are also identified with symbols. Every box represents 1 stitch. Pattern charts in colors are easier to follow. If you are working from a complicated pattern shown with symbols, it might be a good idea to transfer it to graph paper and color it in.

In almost all cases, the pattern chart shows every row. Pay attention to the row numbers. The numbers for the rows on the right side of the work are on the right side, the ones for the rows on the wrong side of the work are on the left.

You can keep your place with a ruler or place marker.

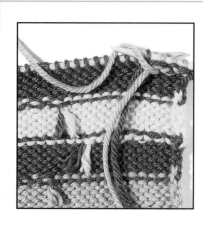

On the right are the pattern charts for these knitted pieces. Some have all the rows in colors, some use symbols. The pattern charts show the rows on both sides of the work.

You read a pattern chart the same way as you knit, from bottom to top. The rows on the right side of the work read from right to left, those on the wrong side of the work from left to right.

If only the rows on the right side of the work are shown, the stitches are worked in the same colors on the wrong side of the work.

In order to keep your place, put a marker above the row you are working on. This way you can check the pattern again for the rows you have already worked. If you put the marker underneath the row you will be working "blind" and won't be able to compare the stitches on the needle with the pattern.

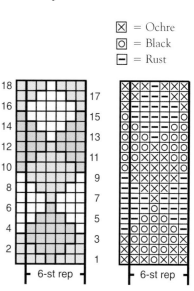

⊠ = Ochre
Ⓞ = Black
⊟ = Rust

6-st rep   6-st rep   6-st rep

Weaving in Yarn Ends

If you change colors at the beginning of a row, such as for sweaters with narrow stripes, you can weave the yarn ends in. Just make sure that the tension of the knitting yarn remains constant. Otherwise, the stitches could easily pull out of shape.

First work the selvedge stitches with the old and the new yarn, and then 1 stitch just with the new yarn. Then pull up both yarn ends and cut them to a length of about 4". Now work 8 to 10 stitches, placing the yarn ends alternately over and under the working yarn. Don't cut the yarn ends too short.

Weaving In Yarn Carried Across the Back of the Work

If you are working large jacquard patterns, where the individual parts of the design are more than 7 stitches apart, you should occasionally weave in the yarn you are not using, or even weave it in continuously.

If you use the weaving technique—in other words, if you weave in the yarn not being used continuously—the appearance of the stitches can easily become irregular on the front of the work and the colors of the yarn being carried on the back can show through on the front. For this reason, the yarn being woven in always has to be pulled up rather tight. Also, the knitting usually becomes tighter than normal in jacquard patterns because of the yarn being woven in.

For a better overview, the drawings show the yarn woven in at only 1 point (photo at bottom). Make sure that as you are knitting, you always have the same yarn color at the front of your forefinger, otherwise you won't be able to reproduce the steps shown in the drawings. Here the yellow yarn is at the front, the rust-colored yarn at the back.

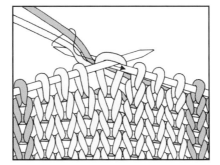

1 On the right side rows, alternately knit the front yarn normally. Then insert right needle into the stitch, bring the tip of the needle over both yarns to the back, catch the front yarn from top to bottom, and bring it forward and through the stitch, passing over the back yarn.

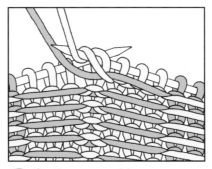

3 On the wrong side rows, alternately work the front yarn normally. Then catch it going over the back yarn.

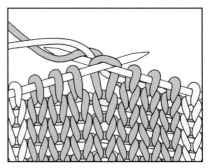

2 Alternately knit the back yarn normally, then catch the yarn going under the front yarn.

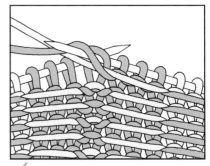

4 Alternately work the back yarn normally. Then insert the right needle into the stitch, bring the tip of the needle over the front yarn from the front, catch the back yarn from top to bottom, and bring it forward and through the stitch, passing over the front yarn.

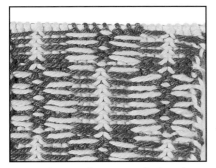

Long pieces of yarn carried at the back of the work are woven in at 1 or more points.

If you use the weaving technique for every stitch, the piece gets very stiff. If the yarn is heavy, the woven yarn can show through on the right side of the work.

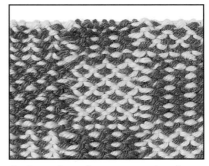

A view of continuous weaving from the back. Here, alternately work 1 stitch "normally," using the jacquard technique (page 142), and 1 stitch using the weaving technique.

Intarsia Patterns

Whether you are working a complicated sweater with a picture design, or diagonal areas of color, patterns in which areas of color are worked with several skeins of yarn are called intarsia patterns.

For intarsia work, the yarn must be crossed within the knitted piece at every color change (see photos and drawings). Crossing the yarn prevents holes from forming in the knitted piece.

In order not to get your yarn all tangled if you are working with a lot of different colors, put the skeins of yarn next to one another in the order in which they are going to be worked. The yarns will cross in the first row. Now turn the piece to the front, turning the tip of the needle towards your body and to the right. When you work the row on the wrong side of the work, the yarns will uncross. At the end of this row, turn the work to the back—in other words, turn the tip of the needle away from your body and to the right. Now the yarns will cross again. For all the subsequent rows, always turn the work alternately towards your body and away from your body. The skeins only have to be resorted if new yarn, such as a new color, is added or a color is eliminated. It is best that when you stop knitting, you always interrupt your work after a row on the wrong side of the work, so that when you start working again you can put the skeins next to one another in the proper order.

1 On the right side rows, put the "old" color yarn over the "new" color yarn at the back of the work and continue working with the "new" color.

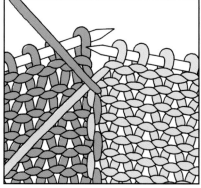

On the back of the work, a 2-color "chain" forms where the yarns cross.

If areas of color are shifted over by several stitches, prepare to cross the yarns ahead of time: Cross the "new" yarn 1 stitch before or after the stitch to be knit in this color...

2 On the wrong side rows, put the "new" color yarn over the "old" color yarn at the front of the work and continue with the "new" color.

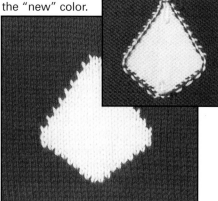

If areas of color are shifted over by only 1 stitch, cross the yarns the same way as for straight areas of color. Small photo: A view from the back. The yarn ends are sewn in on the area of color that they match.

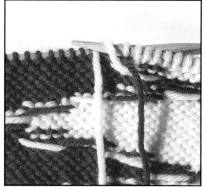

...so that the yarn will come from the "correct" side and the first new stitch will not be pulled in the wrong direction.

For Attractive Color Changes

Just as at the beginning of each row, when you change colors the first few stitches in a new color have to be worked tight (see also page 29). In spite of this, the stitches of the 2 areas of color will generally have 2 to 3 very loose stitches in 1 row, and 2 to 3 very tight small stitches in the rows above and below that row.

You can correct this uneven appearance of the stitches, although it requires some time and effort: Use

If you are working a lot of small areas of different colors, yarn bobbins are very helpful. You can make them out of cardboard, but they are also available in needlework stores.

a knitting needle to pull each part of the large stitches, individually and one after the other, from the outside to the inside—i.e., towards the color change. At the point where the yarns cross, put the knitting needle into the small stitch underneath, and pull the excess yarn through to the bottom. Hold the stitches you have just corrected in place with your thumb. Now distribute the excess yarn over the first 2 stitches.

Ribbing with Areas of Color

If the areas of color already start at the ribbing, the stitches have to be cast on appropriately. Since the first row in the ribbing pattern is supposed to be a row on the wrong side of the work, the stitches have to be cast on exactly as the areas of color are supposed to appear later. In this example, you start with the red yarn.

If the second piece is worked in reverse—that is, if the red area is on

the left—start casting on with the natural-color yarn.

Sewing in the Yarn Ends

In order for the starting stitches of every area of color to have the correct shape, the yarn ends must first be sewn in the direction in which you normally would have continued knitting with this yarn:

If the area of color started in a row on the right side of the work, or ended in a row on the wrong side of the work, the yarn ends on the back are first pulled through the horizontal thread of the next stitch to the left, or through the perpendicular yarn crossing, and then sewn into the same area of color to the right.

If an area of color started in a row on the wrong side of the work, or ended in a row on the right side of the work, the yarn ends on the back are first pulled through the yarn carried on the back of the work to the right, and then sewn into the same area of color to the left.

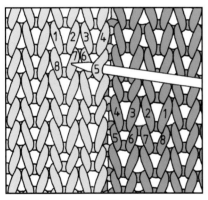

Pull the stitches in the top row up in the direction of the color change in the sequence indicated, and then distribute the excess yarn over the small stitches on the previous row.

The stitches before (top) and after (bottom) the correction.

If the areas of color already start at the ribbing, cast the stitches on in the same color sequence as that in which they are worked.

Here, the area of color started in a right side row and ended in a wrong side row. First pull all the yarn ends through the yarn of the other color to the left, and then sew them in.

Shortened Rows for Slanted Patterns

Hardly anyone who knits likes to work shortened rows. But it's not really difficult once you get the hang of it.

Working shortened rows means working fewer rows over some stitches. These rows are needed if you want to make a shawl collar or a dart, or if you are combining patterns that require a different number of rows for the same length, such as garter stitch and stockinette stitch.

Shortened Rows with Yarn Over

There are 2 ways of preventing a hole from forming when you work shortened rows. The first is shown on these pages using the example of a garter-stitch facing that is knit on. Here, you turn with a yarn over, and in the next row knit the yarn over together with the first of the stitches that was not worked before.

If you knit a facing on in ribbing pattern, you should add shortened rows from time to time, because when you knit 1, purl 1 alternately, the knit and purl stitches pull into each other slightly, which makes the stitches larger, and the facing will stretch out more easily. Also, facings are normally worked with smaller-size needles, and that is not possible when they are worked together with the main piece. In this case, however, in contrast to what is shown here, you don't work more rows over the stitches of the facing, but rather over the other stitches (see knit-in facings, pages 66–67).

Shortened Rows at the Right Edge of a Facing

1 In a row on the right side of the work, knit to the end of the facing. Turn the work and make a tight yarn over ahead of the first stitch.

2 Then knit back along the row. In the next row on the right side of the work, …

3 … knit the facing stitches up to the yarn over. Then knit the yarn over together with the first stitch of the pattern.

4 After the next row, the shortened row can hardly be seen. Here, the shortened rows are worked every 6 rows.

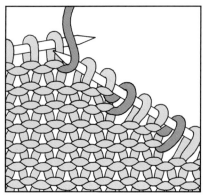

1 For darts on the left side, the shortened rows are worked within the piece. Turn with a yarn over, as described,…

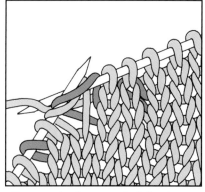

2 …and when you knit back along the row, knit the stitch after the yarn over together with the yarn over.

148

Shortened Rows at the Left Edge of a Facing

1 Work a row on the wrong side of the work to the end of the facing. Turn, make a tight yarn over ahead of the first stitch, and work back along the row of facing.

2 In the next row on the wrong side of the work, knit the facing stitches up to the yarn over. Slip the yarn over onto the right needle knitwise.

3 Also slip the next purl stitch onto the right needle.

4 Insert the left needle, from right to left, into the stitch and the yarn over at the same time...

5 ...and put both loops back onto the left needle. Now the yarn over is ahead of the stitch— i.e., on the back of the work.

6 Now the yarn over and the stitch can be purled together.

7 After the next row, the short-ened row can hardly be seen even on the right side of the work.

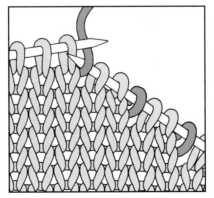

1 For darts on the right side, turn the work with a yarn over,...

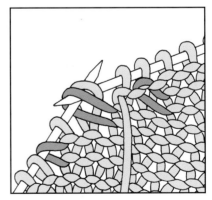

2 ...and when you knit back along the row, first reverse the yarn over and the next stitch, as described above, then purl them together.

Shortened Rows with Stitches Passed Over

A completely different way of working shortened rows is passing stitches over. Here again, you turn at the point where the shortened row is supposed to end.

But now you don't work with a yarn over, but rather place the working yarn at the front of the work. Then insert the needle into the stitch from right to left, and slip the stitch onto the right needle without knitting it. Now pull the working yarn from front to back over the right needle and continue knitting normally. Two parts of the stitch of the previous row will now be on the needle. Of course these 2 parts of the stitch count as only 1 stitch, as they are worked together in the next row. On the right side of the work, you will only see 1 stitch here; in all other rows, there are 2 stitches in height.

Shortened Rows on the Left Side

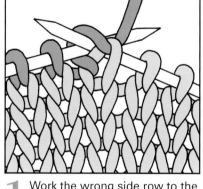

1 Work the wrong side row to the desired length, then turn the work. Put the yarn to the front of the work. Insert the needle into the first stitch from right to left and…

…slip the stitch onto the right needle. Put the yarn over the right needle from front to back, and don't pull it too tight. Knit back along the row.

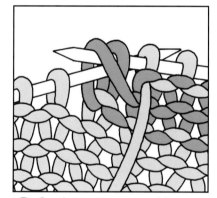

2 On the next wrong side row, work to the stitch that was passed over (at this turning stitch, there are 2 threads on the needle), insert…

…the needle from right to left into both threads—i.e., parts of the stitch—and purl them together.

You can see the shortened rows very clearly in the different colors. There is always only 1 stitch in white or purple at the left end of these rows.

The single-color sample was worked the exact same way as the multicolor one. No transition is evident between the shortened rows and the "normal" ones.

3 On the right side of the work, only 1 stitch can be seen at the end of the shortened rows.

Shortened Rows on the Right Side

1 Turn the work at the desired point. Put the yarn to the front of the work. Insert needle into the first stitch from right to left and slip it onto the right needle. Put the yarn over the right needle from front to back,…

2 In the next right side row, work to the stitch that was passed over. At this turning stitch, there are 2 threads on the needle. Now…

…and don't pull it too tight. You can see the 2 parts of the stitch of the previous row. Put the yarn to the front, ahead of the slipped stitch, and work back along the row.

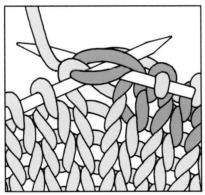

…insert the needle from left to right into both threads and knit them together.

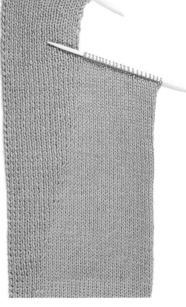

When you make a cardigan with a shawl collar (see also page 90), the collar has to be worked with shortened rows in order to have the necessary width. Slanted shoulders worked with shortened rows assure a better fit.

3 On the right side of the work, only 1 stitch can be seen at the end of the shortened rows.

A contrast yarn …

… makes it easier to count rows. Since the shortened rows are almost invisible, this little aid will help you to consistently work the shortened rows after the same number of rows.

Simply put a piece of yarn in a contrast color around a stitch in the knitting in every row in which you are working the shortened rows. This way, you only have to count the rows from 1 marker to another.

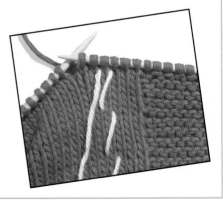

Pattern Variations with Shortened Rows

Knitting such patterns and still keeping them "straight" is not magic. You simply have to make sure that you work the shortened rows to the same point from both sides. The single stitch at the end of the shortened row is a perfect reference point. To make sure you don't work 1 row shorter than the other, work the passed-over stitch precisely on top of this single stitch. That is what was done in all 4 of these pattern variations, although it does not look that way at first glance. For every stripe, I worked more or less 6 stitches. The 3 rows in purple are slanted because of the shortened rows.

You should not work this type of pattern over too many rows, because the rows worked over all the stitches would stretch too much. But 5 times 2 rows, as in these examples, is no problem.

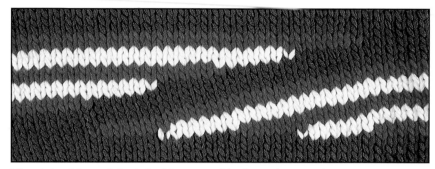

The right side and the left side start with short shortened rows.

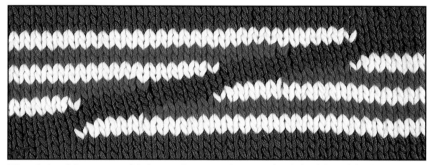

The right side starts with long shortened rows, the left side with short shortened rows.

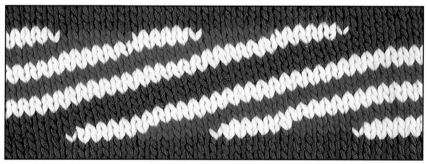

The right side starts with short shortened rows, the left side with long shortened rows.

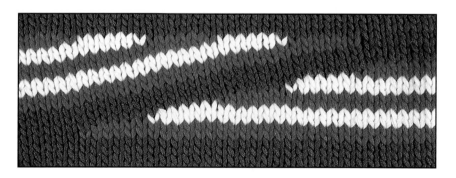

The right side and the left side start with long shortened rows.

Embossing

In addition to bobbles, sections of embossing are a nice way of creating interesting effects.

Embossing can be worked over a few stitches or over an entire row. You can create a very attractive design of different lengths distributed at irregular intervals over an entire sweater. And you can use all kinds of colorful bits of yarn.

If the sections of embossed knitting are close together, the yarn for the embossed knitting can be carried along at the back of the work, just as in intarsia work. If the sections of embossed knitting are farther apart, you should work with individual pieces of yarn or small skeins.

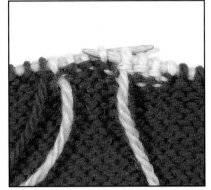

1 Leave the yarn of the main color hanging on the back, and use the embossing yarn …

2 … to work the desired width and length—in this case, 6 rows of stockinette stitch.

3 Use a thin cable needle to pick up the stitches of the last row below the embossing. Make sure you have the same number of stitches.

4 Turn the work and put the needles one behind the other. Then knit 1 stitch from the front needle and from the cable needle together each time. Insert the needle into the front stitch knitwise and into the back stitch knitwise twisted.

If sewing in the yarn ends of the embossing yarn is too much trouble …

… try a tailor's knot. Make an overhand knot with the 2 yarn ends held together. Then push the knot towards the knitted piece with a needle, pulling the ends tight. You should check the knots from time to time to make sure that they haven't come undone.

5 Finally, work the row to the end.

Narrow or Wide

Embossing can be worked over only a few stitches or over the entire width of the piece.

Embossing in Stockinette Stitch

This embossing was worked in stockinette stitch over 4, 6, and 8 rows. Two examples of each are shown. Embossing with different stripes is even livelier.

Embossing in Reverse Stockinette Stitch

Embossing worked in reverse stockinette stitch looks like little rolls of knitting. The first row of the embossing, worked in reverse stockinette stitch on the right side of the work, always has to be knitted rather than purled. Otherwise, the horizontal threads of the last row of the background color will show.

Embossing with Picots

Whether you work it in 1 or 2 colors, embossing with picots is very striking. For the examples of narrow embossing over 6 rows, the third row is an openwork row. For the examples of wide embossing over 10 rows, it is the fifth row. For this row of openwork, you need an odd number of stitches. After the selvedge stitch, first knit 1 stitch, then alternately make a yarn over and knit 2 stitches together. In the next row, on the wrong side of the work, purl all stitches and yarn overs. For the 2-color embossing, work 5 rows in the first color (i.e., including the openwork row) and 5 rows in the second color. On the right side of the work, the picot edge will still show in the first color.

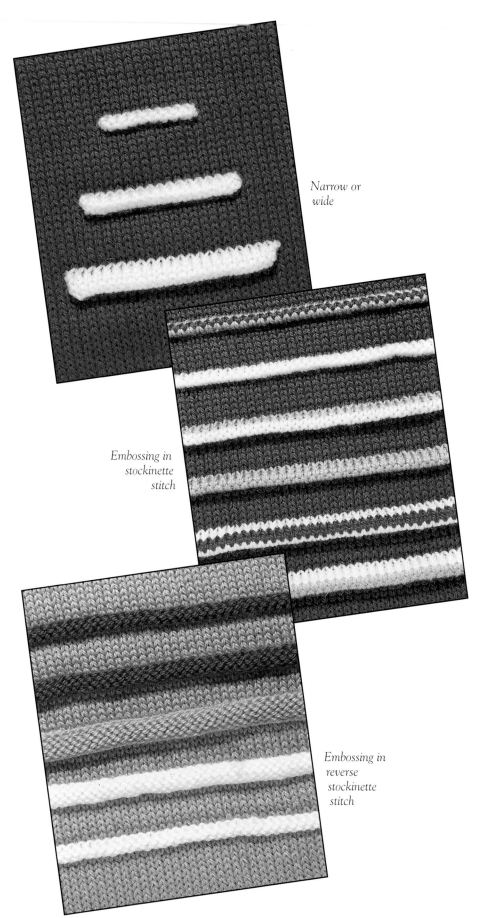

Narrow or wide

Embossing in stockinette stitch

Embossing in reverse stockinette stitch

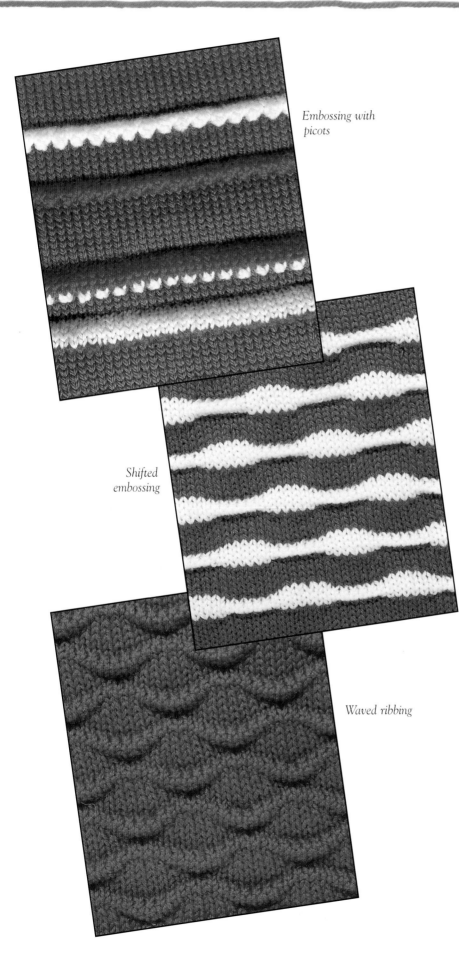

Embossing with picots

Shifted embossing

Waved ribbing

Shifted Embossing

Shifted embossing patterns are particularly attractive. However, you should only work patterns like this over the entire width of the sweater. Alternately work 6 rows in the main color and 4 rows in the piping color. In the first row of the main color, alternately work 6 stitches as embossing and 6 stitches not as embossing. When you work the next stripe, do the opposite.

If you start and end a row with 3 embossed stitches or 3 normal stitches, as needed, the pattern will also match at the side seams after you have sewn the pieces together.

Waved Ribbing

Waved ribbing patterns are very striking, but require quite some effort. To work this way, first slip the horizontal thread of the first previous row (= on the wrong side of the work, the second horizontal thread below the stitch you want to work) in front of the knit stitch and knit both together. Then, in order, do that for the horizontal threads of the second, third, fourth, fifth, fourth, third, second, and first previous row. Then knit a normal knit stitch.

In the next row, Row 8, work the pattern shifted over: Where you worked the normal knit stitch, slip the horizontal thread of the fifth previous row (= on the wrong side of the work, the sixth horizontal thread below the stitch you want to work) and work a simple knit stitch where you previously inserted the needle the farthest down. For this pattern, the number of stitches has to be divisible by 10 + 1 stitch + 2 selvedge stitches.

Entrelac Patterns

The traditional Entrelac pattern may look complicated at first glance, but once you get the hang of it, it's easy to knit.

If you want to work a sweater in Entrelac pattern, you should choose either a V-neck, boat neck, or square neck. You can't make individual decreases for a rounded neckline. Also, the sleeves have to be knit from the top down. A decrease of half a pattern piece every other row of the pattern is the simplest answer for the slanted edges of the sleeves.

The various schematic drawings show you how the triangles and squares can be divided up. Always work a sufficiently large sample for gauge. It should be at least 3 squares wide and high. Then you can calculate the size of the sweater. As in the examples shown, draw the entire sweater (or at least the front or back) and 1 sleeve on graph paper.

In this pattern, there are no limits on how you vary the colors. You can use 2, 3, or more colors. Or you can work each rectangle or triangle in a different color. It might be worthwhile checking your scrap basket.

The size of the pattern pieces can also vary. On pages 158–159, the pattern is explained step by step, using the example of pattern pieces worked over 10 stitches. The pattern pieces can be made smaller or larger, following the same principle.

Sweater

In this 3-color sweater, the pattern pieces are worked over 10 stitches. The layout of the triangles and squares is shown in the full diagram and photo. Four triangles were left out for the front neckline. The wristband and waistband ribbing and the neckband were knit on later.

This child's sweater can be worked in any size. The diagram shows the different areas of color of the sweater.

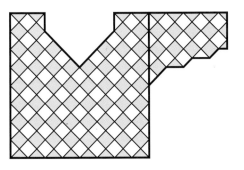

Block the finished pieces of the child's sweater only slightly so that it doesn't get too flat. Sew all the seams from the outside using invisible stitch.

This example shows a rounded, straight neckline. If the colors are laid out vertically, the front and the back should be worked crosswise— i.e., from side seam to side seam. Otherwise, the yarn ends have to be sewn in for every color change. The sleeves are worked from top to bottom, as in the other examples.

Two ways of making V-neck sweaters: For a very wide neckline, continue the V all the way to the shoulder.

For a slightly narrower neckline, knit another small triangle at the top edge of the neckline on both sides.

Instructions for Entrelac pattern:
The individual areas of color are worked in stockinette stitch over 10 stitches, and the selvedge stitches are also worked in every row. The stitches for the individual pattern pieces are always picked up from the outer part of the selvedge stitches of every second row.

Row 1 is worked from right to left. Then alternately repeat Row 2 from left to right, and Row 3 from right to left.

Finish the work with triangles. If you end the work after a second row, the last row of triangles will be worked from right to left; see Row 4. If the desired length requires you to finish the work after a third row, the last row is worked from left to right, and an additional small triangle has to be worked at the beginning and end of the row; see Row 5. The pattern can be worked on normal knitting needles, but circular needles are better.

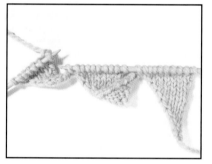

Row 1 with triangles
For the first triangle, cast on 2 st, p 1 row, k 1 row, p 1 row. In Row 4 (RS), and then in every second row, at the left edge, before the selv st, always inc 1 st k twisted from the horizontal thread, until there are 10 st on the needle. Now don't turn the work. Stop working on the first triangle and cast on 2 st for the second triangle by knitting them on. Then continue working as described. Work all the other triangles the same way.

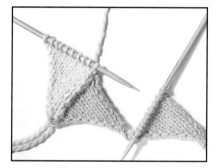

Row 2, first edge triangle
The second row of pattern pieces starts in a row on the wrong side of the work with a triangle: p the last 2 st of the last triangle, turn (= t) - k1, increase 1 st (k twisted out of the horizontal thread), selv st, t - p1, p the third stitch tog with the next st of the triangle (= p tog), t - k2, inc 1, selv st, t - p2, p the fourth stitch tog with a st of the triangle, etc., until all the triangle stitches have been used. By working the increases, you have 10 stitches on the needle again.

Row 2, square
Now don't turn, rather work 10 st out of the side edge of the next triangle, going through the selv st from back to front and bringing the st through to the back. Or turn the work and pull the st through to the front with a crochet hook and put them onto the knitting needle. * t - k10, t - p9, p the last st tog with the 1st st of the triangle, rep from * until all st of the triangle have been used. Work all the other rectangles the same way.

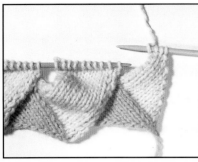

Row 2, last edge triangle

At the end of the row, work another triangle: p10 st out of the side edge of the last triangle, t - k10, t - p8, p2 tog, t - k9, t - p7, p2 tog, etc. Pull the working yarn through the last st and cut it off.

Row 3, squares

Here, you work squares over the entire row: Knit 10 st out of the side edge of the triangle, t - * p10, t - k9, single dec (= slip the last st knitwise, k the first st of the square of the second row and pass the slipped st over), t - rep from * until all the stitches of the square are used. Then don't turn and k another 10 st out of the side edge of the next part. Work the following squares the same way and, at the end, cut the yarn off.

Row 4, end triangles from right to left

Work the last st of the previous triangle with the new yarn, then pick up 10 st knitwise out of the side edge (= 11 st), t - p9, p2 tog, t - k9, 1 single dec, t - p8, p2 tog, t - k8, 1 single dec, t. Continue according to the same principle until only 1 st is left on the needle. Then pick up another 10 st out of the side edge. Work all the following triangles the same way.

Row 5, end row from left to right, first small triangle

For the first small triangle, p the first 2 st of the last square you worked, t - k1, inc 1, selv st, t - p2, p the third st tog with the first st of the square (= p2 tog), t - k2, inc 1, selv st, t - p3, p2 tog, t - k3, inc 1, selv st, t - p4, p2 tog, t - k4, inc 1, selv st, t - p5, p2 tog, t - k6, t - p2 tog, p3, p2 tog, t - k5, t - p2 tog, p2, p2 tog, t - k4, t - p2 tog, p1, p2 tog, t - k3, t - p2 tog 2ˇ, then pass the first st over the second = 1 st left.

Row 5, triangle

Pick up 10 st purlwise out of the side edge of the square, t - k11, t - p2 tog, p8, p1 st of the triangle tog with the first st of the previous square (= p2 tog), t - k10, t = p2 tog, p7, p2 tog, t - k9, t - p2 tog, p6, p2 tog, t. Continue working according to the same principle. P the last 2 st of the end triangle tog, put the st back onto the left needle, and then p tog with the last st of the square.

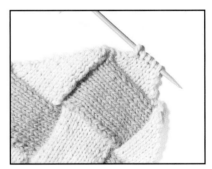

Row 5, last small triangle

P 10 st out of the side edge of the last square, t - k11, t - p2 tog, p7, p2 tog, t - k9, t - p2 tog, p5, p2 tog, t - k7, t. Continue working according to the same principle. At the end, p2 tog, put the st back onto the left needle, and p the last 2 st tog. Cut off the yarn and pull the end through.

Reversible Patterns

Reversible patterns, also called double-face or double knitting, look good on both sides. They are good for scarves, warm blankets, and heavy cardigans. With this type of knitting, you have stockinette stitch on both sides. The color pattern on the "wrong" side of the work is the reverse of the front.

Opened up: If the knit and purl stitches are placed on separate needles, you can hardly see any transition in casting on with kitchener rib.

Casting On with Kitchener Rib

The nicest way of casting on for reversible patterns is kitchener rib. The back is the opposite of the front from the very first row.

Knot the 2 yarns together and cast on the required number of stitches with a needle that is 1 or 2 sizes smaller (see also pages 24 and 25). Hold the yarn in your left hand. Hold the short end pieces with your right hand, bring the needle under the front yarn for the first stitch, and pull the back yarn to the front from top to bottom. Then continue as described above. You need twice as many stitches for the desired width, since the "knit" and "purl" casting-on stitches are each needed for 1 side.

In the next row, work according to the jacquard technique, alternately knittung 1 stitch with the first color and purling 1 stitch with the second color, keeping to the color of the casting-on stitches.

1 For open casting on, undo the row of chain stitches and put the stitches onto a cable needle.

2 Alternately knit the stitches from the front needle with the first color and purl the stitches from the back needle with the second color.

3 A "facing" of the same length appears on both sides.

Open Cast On

If you want to have the same color facing on both sides at the bottom edge, an open cast on (page 20) is the best and easiest solution. If this facing is supposed to hold the knitted piece in a little, like ribbing, the first few rows until the facing is joined together can be worked with thinner needles.

Crochet a loose row of chain stitches in a contrast yarn in the length as the number of stitches required for 1 side. Now pick up the stitches from the horizontal parts of the chain stitches, on the back, and work in stockinette stitch to a length of twice the facing length, ending with a purl row.

Undo the chain stitches and catch the open stitches with a thinner cable needle. Make sure that you have the same number of stitches. Fold the piece together wrong side on wrong side. Now continue according to the jacquard technique, with 2 colors of yarn, and alternately knit 1 stitch from the front needle in the first color and purl 1 stitch from the back needle in the second color.

Double Cast On

The simplest way of casting on is with both yarns, but this is less attractive. The only time this method is good is if you are working a double scarf, for example, and the edge will be hidden between fringes later. In the first row, for every double cast-on stitch, always knit 1 stitch in the first color and purl 1 stitch in the second color.

Chain stitch selvedges are worked on both sides. To do this, knit both selvedge stitches at the beginning of every row together, but slip them at the end of every row.

In the binding-off row, the stitches of the front and back are knitted together.

Selvedge Stitches

No matter if you are knitting a double scarf or a reversible jacket in which the pieces have to be joined seamlessly and attractively, you should always work seam selvedge stitches—i.e., selvedge stitches worked in stockinette stitch. To do this, knit the selvedge stitch for the front—in other words, the first stitch on the needle—and purl the selvedge stitch for the back—i.e., the

second stitch. Then knit the next-to-last stitch—i.e., the selvedge stitch for the front—and purl the last stitch. Work the selvedge stitches this way in every row.

Important: Make sure when you turn the work that the yarn in the color of the first stitch on the needle is at the front—i.e., that it does not cross the yarn for the second stitch. Only in this way will you get the open edge (see photo 1, below) with which you can later sew both sides using invisible stitch (photo 2, below).

You cannot avoid crossing the yarns at those places where the main color changes, or in the case of small patterns that reach all the way to the edge (such as the zigzag pattern in the bottom part of the knitted piece). For very attractive edges, you should try to lay the patterns out so that they begin and end approximately 2 to 3 stitches after and before the selvedge stitch. In our sample, they are the diamond pattern and checkered pattern.

A double cast on and cast off, and chain selvedge stitches, are not as attractive.

1 If the knitted piece is turned at every new row so that the yarn of the first selvedge stitch is on the outside, the edges can be opened up to the first pattern stitches.

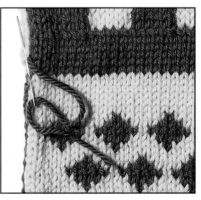

2 Then you can either sew both sides of the knitted piece together (such as for a scarf) or you can sew the pieces of a cardigan together using invisible stitch.

Using Jacquard Technique

Reversible patterns are usually worked with the jacquard technique—i.e., you work with two colors of yarn at the same time. You can use a yarn holder or hold both yarns over your left forefinger as explained for jacquard patterns (starting on page 142).

In reversible pattern, there is no yarn carried on the back of the work within the knitted piece, since you alternately work 1 stitch in each color. If you don't work any patterns, but rather work 2 sides, each in 1 color, the piece can be opened up if it is put onto 2 needles (see photos on pages 22–25 for casting on in kitchener rib). If you work patterns, the stitches cross within the piece every time the color changes (see photo 1, page 161).

At first glance, the stitches on the needle, which are very close to one another, seem rather confusing. But if you think about the stitches in pairs, this way of working is easier to understand. A knit stitch on the front and the next purl stitch on the back belong together. Before the first

stitch of a pair—i.e., the stitch on the front—put both yarns behind the work, then knit this stitch in the appropriate color. Then put both yarns at the front of the work and purl the second stitch in the appropriate color.

In order to make the purl stitch easier to work, hold the yarn not being used with your left thumb. Or work the stitch "the wrong way," pulling the yarn through the stitch from top to bottom. Then the stitch in the next row must be knit twisted, since it is on the needle "the wrong way" (see also page 134, bottom).

Working a pattern is also simple if you think of the stitches as being in pairs. When you make a color change of 1 stitch, first knit the knit stitch in the second color, then purl the purl stitch in the first color. The next knit stitch is knit in the first color again, the next purl stitch is purled in the second color. The examples in the drawings show how the stitches are worked for plain knitting and reversible knitting.

1 Before a knit stitch, put both yarns at the back of the work and knit the stitch in the appropriate color.

2 Before a purl stitch, put both yarns at the front of the work and purl the stitch in the second color.

Using One Yarn at a Time

If you don't like working with 2 colors of yarn at the same time, you have the option of working each row in only 1 color at a time—i.e., working each row twice. However, this is harder and takes longer.

To do this, use a circular knitting needle so that you can push the stitches to the end of the needle, where the yarn in the color you need is located.

Now work 1 row on the right side of the work, for example, with the blue yarn. If you are not working a 2-color pattern, knit all the knit

Drawings 1 and 2 show a square and a small diamond with the stitches for 1 side. The numbers on the right side stand for a row on the right side of the work, those on the left side stand for a row on the wrong side of the work.

Drawing 1

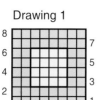

Drawing 2

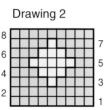

Drawing 3

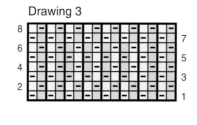

Drawing 4

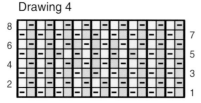

Drawings 3 and 4 show the same color sequence for a reversible pattern. The darker vertical lines separate the pairs of stitches. The short horizontal lines show the purl

stitches of the individual rows. Read the stitches—i.e., colors of the rows on the right side of the work from right to left, those on the wrong side of the work from left to right.

stitches and slip all the purl stitches purlwise. Before you slip the purl stitches, the yarn has to be placed at the front of the work every time. At the end of the row, push the stitches back to the other end of the needle and now work all the purl stitches with the yellow yarn. Now slip the knit stitches—i.e., the blue stitches—as if to knit them. The yarn has to be put at the back of the work each time.

If you are working a pattern, however, you have to pay even more attention. In this case, you are working not only knit stitches but also purl stitches. Sometimes you are working the stitches on the right side of the work, and sometimes those on the wrong side of the work. At every change from the right to the wrong side, 1 knit stitch and 1 purl stitch, or vice versa, have to be worked in the same color or slipped purlwise.

1 Before a knit stitch, put both yarns behind the work and knit the stitch in the appropriate color.

2 If you started a scarf using casting on in kitchener rib, join the stitches of both sides using grafting stitch.

Casting Off

Before casting off normally or in kitchener rib, put all the knit stitches and purl stitches of the knitted piece separately on 2 knitting needles.

If you started a scarf using casting on in kitchener rib, you can now join the stitches from both needles using grafting stitch.

If you started with an open cast on, after you separate the knit and purl stitches you should work as many rows in stockinette stitch, over the stitches of 1 side, as you worked for the facing. Only afterwards join them with the stitches from the second needle, using grafting stitch.

If the knitted piece is **part of a cardigan**, such as the back, put the shoulder stitches onto a stitch holder for now. Then work the front and sew the shoulder stitches of both sides together using grafting stitch. Make sure that the stitches on the needles and the seam itself produce an additional row in each instance.

For **necklines and armholes**, the stitches on each side are bound off separately. For neckline facings, you can then pick up the stitches of 1 side "normally," work twice the length of the desired facing, and sew the stitches to the inside using grafting stitch.

For **sleeves**, the 2 sides are also bound off separately. Then each sleeve must be sewn on twice using grafting stitch, once from the inside and once from the outside. The last thing you do is sew the side and sleeve seams using invisible stitch, also twice, once from the outside and once from the inside.

Border

For a reversible blanket, the edges are also finished with a double facing. To do this, pick up 3 stitches every 4 rows from the selvedge stitches, and work about 10 rows in stockinette stitch. Then sew the open stitches onto the other side using grafting stitch (see pages 114–117).

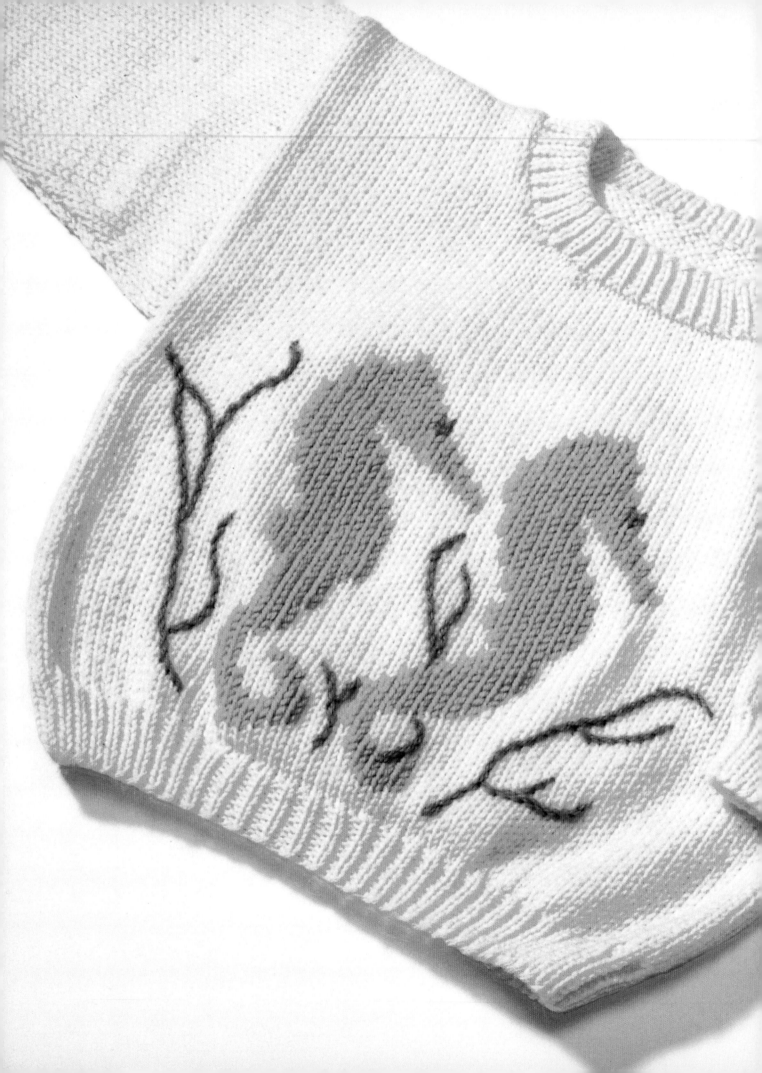

Decorative Details

Knitted pieces are made one of a kind with lovely embroidery, attractive smocking, or bobble embellishments.

Crocheted and Knitted Bobbles

Whether they are worked in lots of colors or tone on tone, you can achieve a unique effect with crocheted or knitted bobbles on stockinette stitch or even on individual patterns.

Crocheted Bobbles

You can crochet bobbles separately and knot them in, or you can crochet them onto the stitches where you want them as you are knitting. The advantage of crocheting them separately is that you can knot the bobbles into the piece later at wherever you want them. On the child's blue sweater, for example, lots of colorful bobbles made from scraps of yarn are irregularly distributed over the entire sweater. For small bobbles, 2 to 3 double crochets are enough. For large bobbles, you can crochet 4 to 6 double crochets. Of course the thickness of the yarn you are using is important too. In the examples shown below, each bobble is made from 4 double crochets.

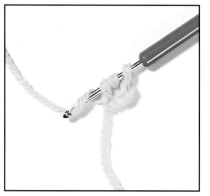

1 Chain 3 and work 4 double crochets into the first of these chains, leaving the last loop of the double crochet on the hook each time.

2 Then draw the yarn through all the loops on the hook, chain 1, and pull the yarn through this stitch.

3 Pull the end of yarn at the beginning and at the end of the bobble through the piece separately, and knot them together well on the back of the work, or sew them in.

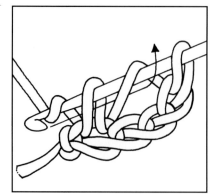

Instead of the first double crochet, work 3 chain stitches. Place the yarn around the hook from back to front, bring it through the chain stitch, and pull it through the stitch and yarn over.

1 If you crochet bobbles directly into the piece, bring the bobble yarn through the desired stitch and continue to work as for a bobble crocheted separately.

2 At the end, go through all the loops on the hook with the yarn of the background color, and put this stitch on the right needle. Then knit to the next bobble.

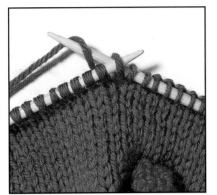

1 From the horizontal thread between 2 stitches, work 5 stitches, alternately k1, k1 twisted. Turn the work.

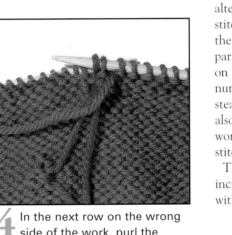

2 Work another 3 rows stockinette stitch, reverse stockinette stitch, or garter stitch over the 5 stitches.

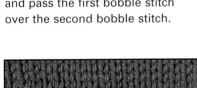

3 In the next row on the right side of the work, k3 tog, k2 tog and pass the first bobble stitch over the second bobble stitch.

4 In the next row on the wrong side of the work, purl the bobble stitch together with the stitch ahead of it.

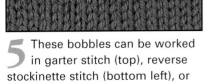

5 These bobbles can be worked in garter stitch (top), reverse stockinette stitch (bottom left), or stockinette stitch (bottom right).

Knit-in Bobbles

Bobbles can be knit different ways. Small bobbles are knit over 3 stitches, large bobbles over 5 to 7 stitches. The number of rows also depends on how big you want the bobbles to be. Of course the size of the bobble is also determined by the thickness and the consistency of the yarn.

Bobbles are knit either over the horizontal thread between 2 stitches, or out of a stitch. The way you work is the same either way.

For bobble increases from a horizontal thread, or out of a stitch, alternately knit 1 stitch and knit 1 stitch twisted (alternately inserting the needle into the front and back part of the stitch). Leave the stitch on the left needle until the desired number of stitches is reached. Instead of knit twisted stitches, you can also work purl stitches. Or you can work a yarn over between the knit stitches.

The steps and photos show the increase from the horizontal thread with the stitches worked twisted.

The instructions for this sweater are on page 201.

Duplicate Stitch and Embroidery

The instructions for this child's sweater are on page 203.

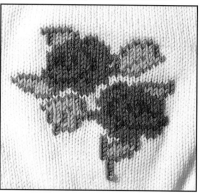

These pretty flowers can be embroidered as a small embellishment at the side of a sweater just above the ribbing.

Embroidery makes plain sweaters unique. Duplicate stitch, outline stitch, and satin stitch are all explained on the following pages.

Duplicate Stitch

Small designs, such as the stylized cat, or designs with many colors, such as the rose, should always be embroidered in duplicate stitch. It is almost impossible to knit such designs in neatly. Larger designs, such as seahorses, can also be worked in duplicate stitch. Here again, the advantage is the neat appearance. You can also put the design exactly where you want it.

Work the embroidery with a tapestry or yarn needle. You can use the original yarn, or you can use an embroidery yarn that matches in thickness.

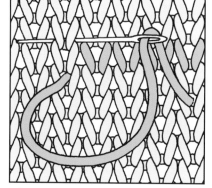

1 Bring needle out below and in the center of the stitch that is to be covered in duplicate stitch, then bring it around the stitch above it. In the first row, work from right to left. If a second row of embroidery is to be worked above that, work this row from left to right.

2 Then put the needle back into the place where it came out, and bring it out again in the center of the stitch next to that. After the last duplicate stitch, bring the yarn to the back through the place where it came out, and sew the ends in.

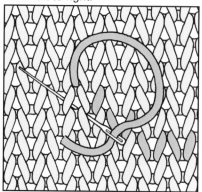

3 For a diagonal shift, put needle in where it came out and bring it out again 1 row higher and 1 stitch over to the left or right, as needed.

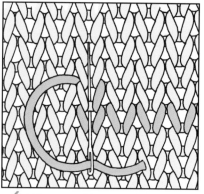

4 When working vertical duplicate stitches, put needle in where it came out and bring it out again 1 horizontal thread higher.

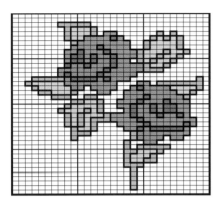

Design chart: Each box on the chart represents 1 stitch.

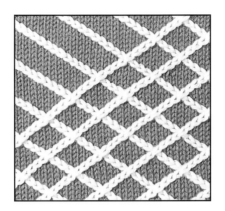

For Vertical or Diagonal Lines

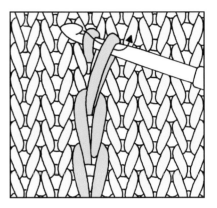

the hook from front to back again, 1 or 2 rows higher. Bring another loop through and draw it through the loop on the hook.

It is easier and faster to work slip stitches with a crochet hook than to embroider duplicate stitches. Hold the yarn under the work. Insert the crochet hook between 2 stitches, from front to back, and bring the yarn to the front. Then insert

Small designs, like this stylized cat face, should be worked in duplicate stitch. Such designs can even turn a purchased sweater into a one-of-a-kind item.

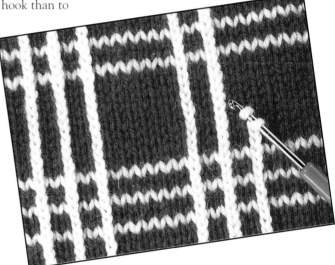

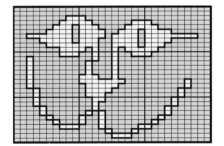

You can embroider the cat face according to this pattern chart.

Tip

At the start of your embroidery, leave the yarn end on the front so that it won't get tangled on the back as you work. When you start a new thread, sew it in first. Then bring it to the front and start embroidering. Of course you should always sew the ends of the yarn in as soon as you have finished with them.

Embroidery on Organza

It is rather difficult to work this embroidery directly onto a knitted background, since the stitches are generally too large and too loose. Small designs should therefore be drawn on organza (a very thin fabric made of silk). Larger ones can also be drawn on somewhat coarser waste canvas. Baste this pattern securely onto the knitted piece using running basting stitch or prick stitch. In the particular case of larger designs, prick stitch is better, because organza and even waste canvas can easily pull out of shape when you are using running basting stitch.

On organza, you should always embroider with a sharp embroidery needle. On waste canvas, you can also work with a tapestry needle. When using waste canvas, the stitches have to be pulled a little tighter so that the embroidery is snug against the background even after the waste canvas is removed.

Outline Stitch

Individual lines are worked in outline stitch, such as those next to the seahorses on page 168. These lines are frequently used to separate different areas of color. Not only does outline stitch accentuate the area, it also hides any irregularities in the appearance of the stitches.

To work outline stitch, bring the needle out at the desired location. Insert it to the right, and bring it out again halfway between the beginning and end of the stitch, always working above the yarn of the previous stitch.

Work outline stitch from left to right. Turn the knitted piece as necessary.

1 Draw the design onto organza or waste canvas, and baste it to the knitted piece with prick stitch.

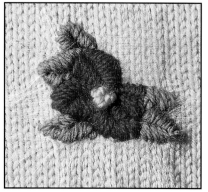

2 After the embroidery is done, pull the threads of the organza or waste canvas out individually.

The larger areas are divided into 2 fields. French knots fill the center.

Full-size pattern for the flower.

Even a delicate butterfly can be embroidered on knitted pieces by using organza.

Outline stitches emphasize color areas and make them look neater.

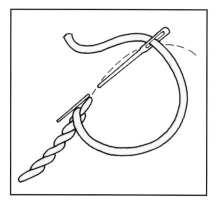

Outline stitch

Lazy Daisy, French Knot, and Multiple French Knot Stitch

For a lazy daisy, bring the needle out at the desired location, then go back down in the same place. Come back out where you want the petal to end. Place the loop around the needle. Go back down in the same place or slightly above it, and come back up in the center of the flower for the next petal.

For a **french knot**, bring the needle out at the desired location, and wrap the yarn around the needle twice. Hold the loops tight with your thumb and pull the needle through. Then go back down just below the place you came out.

For a **multiple french knot**, bring the needle out at the desired location, wrap the yarn around the needle several times, hold the loops tight with your thumb, and pull the needle through. Then go back down right next to the place you came out. The size of the knot is determined by the number of loops.

Satin Stitch

You can fill an area with satin stitch. Work parallel stitches right next to one another. The stitches can lie horizontally or diagonally. They can also be directed in slightly, as for the flower petals above. To achieve this, leave a slightly larger gap between the stitches on the outside edge than between those on the inside edge of the area.

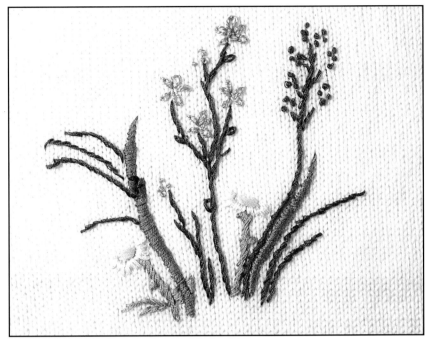

A colorful meadow of outline and satin stitches, lazy daisies, and french knots. Such delicate designs can only be worked over organza.

Lazy daisy stitch

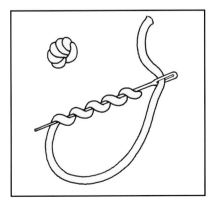

French knot

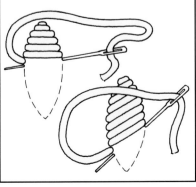

Satin stitch

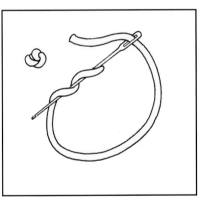

Multiple french knot

Smocking

Smocking can be worked on practically any background. Stockinette stitch, ribbing, and even shaker knitting gets a completely different look.

Please note that the width of the gauge will change significantly. Depending on the pattern, you will need approximately 25% more stitches. That's why it is absolutely necessary to knit a sufficiently large sample for gauge. Finish this sample just like the piece itself: Block the sample, let it dry under a damp cloth, and then do the smocking. Only after you have done all this can you count the stitches and rows.

In smocking, individual stitches are sewn together using back stitch. These stitches have to be marked first, either with knit or purl stitches, or with basting thread.

If you are knitting with tightly twisted wool, cotton, or a synthetic blend, you can use the same yarn for smocking. Normally, it will be strong enough and won't tear. If the yarn is thick and tear-resistant, you can even sew with half the yarn. If you are knitting with a loosely twisted wool or angora, you must use a stronger, but not too heavy, yarn or thread for sewing.

Start smocking in the bottom-left corner and always work 2 horizontal rows at the same time. By alternating the stitches in this way, you get slanted threads on the wrong side of the work, and the knitted piece will remain stretchable.

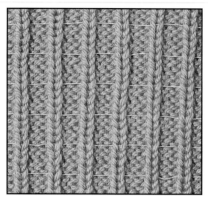

For the ribs, alternately work 3 stitches in reverse stockinette stitch and 1 in stockinette stitch,…

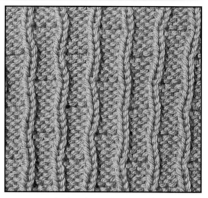

…or mark the locations to be smocked with knit stitches as you are working.

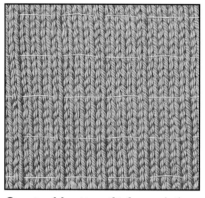

On stockinette stitch, mark the stitches to be smocked with basting thread or…

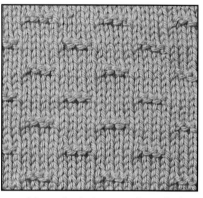

… with purl stitches, and catch the knit stitches next to the marking stitches each time.

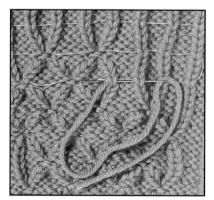

Come out with the needle to the left of the first rib stitch. Then sew around the second and first rib stitch and pull them together. Now go down with the needle to the right of the second rib stitch and bring it out again 4 rows higher to the left, next to the second rib stitch, and…

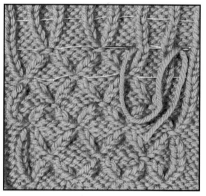

…sew around the third and second rib stitch. Then go down with the needle to the right of the third rib stitch, and bring it out again 4 rows lower to the left, next to the third rib stitch. Keep repeating these steps. At the end of the row, turn the work, and work from left to right again.

The finished smocking piece has a pronounced texture.

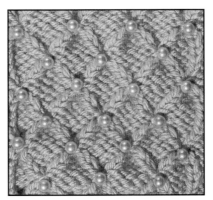

Sewing small beads on top of the smocking stitches makes the piece particularly attractive.

Smocking Stretched-out Sweaters

If a sweater worked in ribbing or shaker knitting has gotten stretched out and too wide because it was worn and washed frequently, you can get it back into shape with smocking. Depending on the desired width of the sweater, you can smock the whole sweater, just the middle or the sides, or even just individual vertical strips.

In shaker knitting, larger intervals between the smocking stitches are more attractive. Here again, the width of the knitted piece will be reduced by about 25%.

Smocking on a stockinette stitch background

In 2 x 2 ribbing, catch only the outer knit stitch with the needle each time.

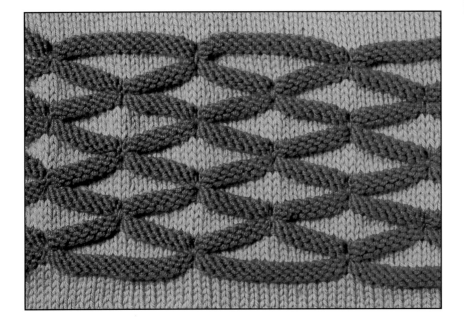

You can even smock **crosswise ribs**: For this pattern, you alternately work 4 rows of stockinette stitch in turquoise as well as 1 row of knit stitches on the right side of the work and 3 rows of reverse stockinette stitch in dark blue. Smock the knitted piece after you have blocked it: At intervals of 16–20 stitches, sew 2 dark blue ribs together and shift the smocking on the ribs above the first two.

Pom-poms, Tassels, Fringes

A pom-pom or tassel looks great on a child's knitted hat, as do fringes on a scarf.

1 Sew yarn around 2 cardboard rings until the inside hole is filled with yarn.

Pom-poms

A large pom-pom, or 2 or 3 small ones, gives a finishing touch to a child's knitted hat. Many little pom-poms at the bottom edge of pullovers without ribbing are also a lot of fun. You can make snakes and other animals out of pom-poms. And a gift package wrapped with wool and decorated with a lot of colorful pom-poms is very original. There are no limits on your imagination!

Cut 2 rings of the same size from sturdy cardboard. The outside diameter of these rings corresponds to about half the diameter of the finished pom-pom. (You can also buy plastic pom-pom makers in needle-work stores.) The inside diameter has to be about 1/3 to 1/2 of the outside diameter. For example, if the outside diameter is 2½", the inside diameter of the circle should be about ¾"–1¼". The bigger the inside diameter, the firmer the pom-pom.

Now place the 2 rings on top of each other. Thread a heavy yarn needle with several long pieces of yarn, and sew around the cardboard rings until the hole in the middle is filled with yarn.

Then cut the yarn along the outside edge. Pull the cardboard circles apart slightly, wind double yarn around the bundle of yarn very

2 Cut the yarn around the edge, and put a knot between the cardboard circles with a strong piece of yarn or thread.

3 Trim the pom-pom into shape with a sharp pair of scissors.

You can use any type of yarn for pom-poms. Even scraps of yarn can be used for a bright and colorful pom-pom.

tight, and knot it securely. This piece of yarn has to be very strong so that it does not tear. For example, if you are using angora or loosely twisted yarn for your pom-pom, it is better to use a piece of synthetic yarn, or even a piece of buttonhole thread in a matching color rather than the yarn of the pom-pom itself.

Remove the cardboard circles and trim the pom-pom into a perfectly round shape.

Tassels

Tassels are even simpler to make than pom-poms. A fat tassel can even replace a pom-pom on a knitted hat. Instead of fringes, you can make many little tassels on a scarf. Tassels are also a traditional and attractive touch on pillows, tablecloths, and table runners.

For tassels, you need scraps of yarn and a rectangular piece of cardboard that is as long as the desired tassel length.

Place a double piece of yarn along the top edge of the cardboard and loosely wind the yarn around both the piece of yarn and the cardboard. Then knot the top threads tight together, and cut the bunch of yarn at the bottom edge. Wrap yarn tight around the bunch of yarn about ½" below the top edge, pull the ends through the wrapped part, and cut them off. Finally, trim the bottom edge of the tassel so that it is straight.

1 Wrap yarn around a rectangular cardboard, and tie the bunch of yarn at the top. Cut it open at the bottom.

2 Wrap the bunch of yarn tightly with some more yarn, and trim the ends to a uniform length.

Whether they're solid or mixed colors, they're always decorative.

Fringes

Hand-knit scarves somehow look incomplete without fringes. Individual fringes can also look very attractive on vests and cardigans.

The pieces of yarn have to be twice as long plus approximately ¾" as the desired length of the fringe. For short fringes, wind the yarn around a rectangular piece of cardboard cut to the right size. For longer fringes, you can even wrap the yarn around a book of the correct size. Then cut the bunch of yarn at the bottom edge.

Now put 2 to 3 pieces of yarn together and fold them in half. Insert a crochet hook through a stitch of the scarf from bottom to top, and pull the pieces of yarn through so that a loop is formed on the bottom. Draw the ends of the yarn through this loop and pull them tight. Leave a space of 1 to 3 stitches between every fringe.

For a fringed edge with multiple knots, the pieces of yarn have to be about 2½" longer than the desired fringe length. Knot the fringes in with a crochet hook, as described above. Then, for the first row of knots, take only half of the bunch of yarn at the beginning and end. In between, always knot half of 2 bunches of yarn together at a distance of about ½" from the edge. Bring the knot to the desired location the same way as for the tailor's knot (page 153). Work the second row of knots the same way. At the beginning and end, knot the first half bunch of yarn together with half of the next one.

1 Pull the bunches of yarn down and through with a crochet hook.

2 Bring the ends of the yarn through the loop and pull them tight. Finally, trim the fringes so they are the same length.

A fringed edge with multiple knots on a scarf is very attractive.

175

Practical Tips

In this chapter, you will find different pattern shapes, a way to convert patterns for different sizes and yarns, as well as information about making pieces shorter or longer, how to fix dropped stitches, and much more.

Measurements and Patterns

If you want to design your own sweater, you first have to decide on the correct pattern. Here are some hints and basic shapes.

Armhole length — Neckline width — Shoulder
Armhole length · Total length · Length to neckline · Armhole length · Side length · Sleeve length · Sleeve width · Sleeve length to armhole · Ribbing width
Ribbing width · Total width

To determine the correct size, the best thing is to measure a sweater that fits well and to transfer the measurements to the pattern. For the patterns on the following pages, only half of the front and back is included in the drawing.

Sweater Width

In general, the following applies for traditional sweaters: ½ body measurement + 3¼" = ½ sweater width. For a relaxed fit, you have to allow a little more. Measure at the widest part of the chest. For very long sweaters, the hip measurement also has to be taken into consideration.

For sweaters that come only to the waist, measure the waist. If the sweater is supposed to be relatively snug, add about 1½" for the front and for the back, starting from the ribbing.

Sweater Length

The length is measured from the neck/shoulder point over the chest to the desired length. Note that depending on the type of yarn and the way you knit, long sweaters usually stretch somewhat in length. For example, you should work a sweater

in single shaker knitting a little shorter than you want it to be, because this patterns tends to stretch in length more than double shaker knitting or textured patterns.

For sweaters that come only to the waist, measure the length from the neck/shoulder point to the waist, and add the ribbing length.

Necklines

For necklines, calculate ⅓ of the back width measured on the body plus approximately 1¼" to 1½"—in other words, about ⅓ of the sweater width for normal sweaters. For V-necks, a little less is enough, since the length of the neckline also influences the width in this case.

To prevent sweaters and cardigans from slipping to the back, you should make a small neckline on the back part too, except when you are making a completely straight boat neck. It should be at least ¾" deep. If you are adding a rather

long neckband, it can also be 1¼" to 1½" deep.

Armholes

If you don't like dropped shoulders, you should always work an armhole. The looser the fit of the sweater, the deeper the armhole can be. Armholes can be straight, slanted, or rounded.

Slanted Shoulders

Slanted shoulders make every sweater fit better, because nobody has straight shoulders. And the wider the sweater, the more important it is to have slanted shoulders, especially if you haven't put in any armholes.

For short shoulder pieces, it is enough to work regular decreases over ¾" to 1¼". Wide, long shoulder seams can be decreased over as much as 3".

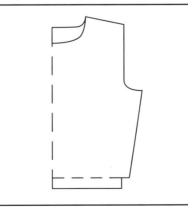

This sweater is a knitted version of Pattern 6. Instructions start on page 198.

also applies to very large chest measurements.

Pattern 2: Slanted shoulders and armholes assure a good fit, particularly for oversize sweaters.

Pattern 3: If a sweater is very long, you can wait to just before the waist to start working the slanted edge.

Pattern 4: A traditional vest has slanted shoulders and very deep armholes. Work a few decreases in the armhole facings at the shoulder seam (see also page 65) so that the facings lie flat. Sleeveless sweaters are worked the same way.

Sleeve Width

For a relatively snug wristband, add about 1¼" to the measured wrist circumference. For the sleeve to drape well, an inch should be added after the wristband ribbing. The sleeve width at the top end is determined by the size of the armhole.

Sleeve Length

First measure from the top vertebra at the neck in the center of the back, over the shoulder, over the arm (which should be bent slightly), to the wrist. Now deduct ½ the width of the

front or back from this measurement, and you have the sleeve length. If you plan to make an armhole, the armhole depth has to be added again. Here's an example: The back/sleeve measurement is 30", ½ the width of the front or back is 12". This means that the sleeve has to be 18" long. If you make the armholes with a depth of 2", the sleeve has to be 20" long.

About the Patterns

Pattern 1: If a sweater is supposed to fit snugly at the waist or hips, slanted side edges are worked in addition to the increases after the ribbing. This

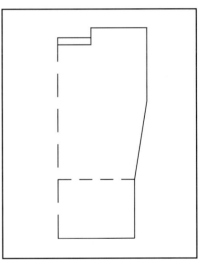

Pattern 3

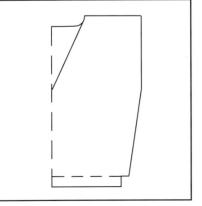

Pattern 1

Pattern 2

Pattern 4

Practical Tips

Pattern 5: If you don't like dropped shoulders, bind stitches off over a width of 1½" to 3", straight across, when the front or back is long enough to start the armhole. Then the sleeve has to be lengthened by the armhole depth.

Pattern 6: This sleeve shape provides a better fit. Here the stitches for the armhole are bound off in several steps. Match the top of the sleeve to this slanted edge.

Pattern 7: A slightly rounded armhole with a matching, slightly rounded shape at the top of the sleeve produces the best fit.

Pattern 8: For a traditional, rounded top of the sleeve, the stitches are bound off in a rounded shape, but the stitches over the last 2¾" or so are bound off straight across. The length of the rounded part varies, but it should be at least 2" less than the armhole length on the front and back. The excess width is evenly distributed over the shoulder area when the sleeve is sewn in.

Pattern 9: For a puffy sleeve, a normal armhole is worked on the front and back. On the sleeve, about ¼ of the stitches, in total, are decreased on both sides, then the other stitches are bound off straight across. When the sleeve is sewn in, the straight bound-off part at the top of the sleeve is gathered and the rest of the sleeve is sewn in normally.

Pattern 10: Shoulder yokes can be worked with or without a rounded shape at the top of the sleeve. The yoke width must be deducted from the front and back, half from each. The neckline is reduced by this length. At the back, no neckline is necessary. Slanted shoulders can also be used with this pattern.

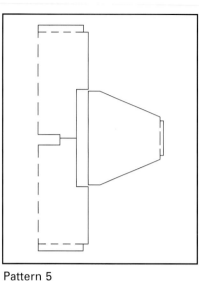

Pattern 5

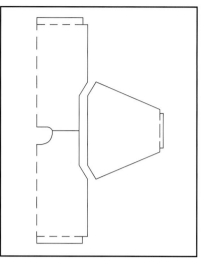

Pattern 6

Pattern 7

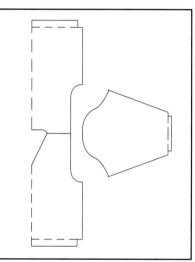

Pattern 8

Pattern 9

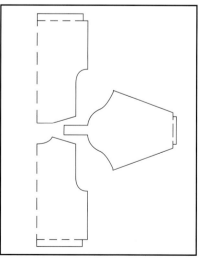

Pattern 10

180

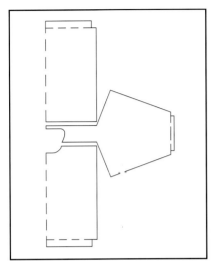

Pattern 11

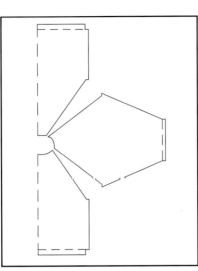

Pattern 12

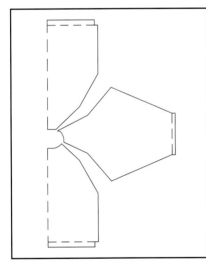

Pattern 13

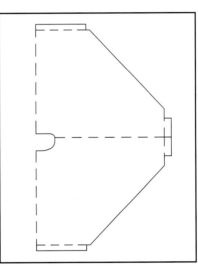

Pattern 14

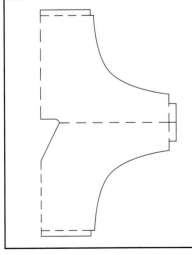

Pattern 15

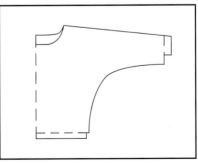

Pattern 16

Pattern 11: If you are working a very wide shoulder yoke and the back neckline is not supposed to be as deep as half the yoke width, the yoke has to be extended over the back to the center of the back.

Pattern 12: In this raglan pattern, the back is bound off straight across at the neckline and the front neckline is rounded slightly. The sleeves end in a rounded part that is deeper towards the front. This means that the second sleeve has to be worked as a reverse of the first. Before starting the slanted edge at the top of the sleeve, bind off a few stitches straight across on both sides so that there isn't "too much material" at the armpit.

Pattern 13: This pattern assures a very good fit. For about ½ the length of the slanted raglan edge, decrease the stitches every other row, then every fourth row. The second sleeve has to be worked as a reverse of the first (see also the sweater, page 202).

Pattern 14: For a dolman sleeve, increase evenly from the waistband ribbing to the wristband ribbing. You can work this sweater in one piece over the shoulder. Or you can put the stitches at the shoulder/arm line on stitch holders and sew the 2 parts together later, using grafting stitch (starting on page 114). Pieces with such a large number of stitches should always be worked on a long circular needle.

Pattern 15: For a kimono pattern, the increases for the slanted edges at the sides and the sleeves are worked in a rounded shape.

Pattern 16: For a kimono pattern with a flattened shoulder/sleeve line, the simplest solution is to bind the stitches off and sew them together later using grafting stitch (page 114).

Converting Patterns

You've found a great sweater in a magazine, but the instructions aren't given in your size. Or you would like to use yarn that works up to a different gauge. Don't worry, the changes are easy to figure out!

The most important thing for converting patterns to a different size or yarn is the gauge. In the following examples, 22 stitches and 30 rows are 4" x 4". This means that .4 square inches contains 2.2 stitches and 3 rows; these are the numbers you use for your calculations. So you have to multiply the inch measurements for the width by 2.2, those for the length by 3.

If you come up with numbers that are not whole numbers, round off. For example, if your calculation gives you 127.6 stitches, that would be 128 stitches; if you come up with 114.4, you can choose either 114 or 115. The 2 selvedge stitches are always added to these numbers; this means that for these parts, you need 130 and 116 or 117 stitches, respectively.

In instructions, patterns are usually shown in only half their width, so that the indicated width has to be doubled. To make the calculations easier to understand, we have shown the patterns in their entire width.

Front and Back

For a size 4 pattern, the calculation is as follows: 54 x 2.2 = 118.8. This means that you need 119 stitches plus 2 selvedge stitches = 121

stitches for the necessary width. (For size 8: 58 x 2.2 = 127.6 + 2 selvedge stitches = 130 stitches.)

If you now calculate the ribbing the same way, 105.6—i.e., 108 stitches including selvedge stitches—would be enough. However, since ribbing patterns tighten, you should use a few more stitches, such as 112 stitches, and add the additional 9 stitches you need either in the last row of ribbing or the first row of the basic pattern, evenly distributed over the row, and twisted. (For size 8: 52 x 2.2 = 114.4 + another 6 stitches = 120 stitches.)

When the piece is 24¾" long, work the neckline. In traditional patterns, the neckline width is approximately ⅓ of the sweater width, deducting the selvedge stitches. For size 4, the calculation would be: 18 x 2.2 = 39.6—i.e., 37 stitches for the neckline. (For size 8: 20 x 2.2 = 44—i.e., 42 stitches.) This leaves 18 x 2.2 = 39.6 + 2 selvedge stitches = 42 stitches for the shoulders. (For size 8: 19 x 2.2 = 41.8 + 2 selvedge stitches = 44 stitches.)

For the back neckline, you need ¾"—i.e., 6 rows. This means that after binding off the center stitches, you can decrease twice. With this gauge, 4 stitches once and 2 stitches once are the best option. Therefore, bind off the center 25 stitches (size 8: 30 stitches) first.

For the front neckline, you have 2½"—i.e., 18 rows. Here the last 4 rows are supposed to be worked on the same number of stitches—i.e., you can decrease 7 times = 14 rows. For an attractive rounded edge, the decreases should become smaller as you go: For size 4, first bind the center 15 stitches off straight across, then, every other row, 3 stitches once, 2 stitches twice, and 1 stitch 4x. (For size 8: the center 16 stitches, then, every other row, 4 stitches once, 3 stitches once, 2 stitches once, and 1 stitch 4x.)

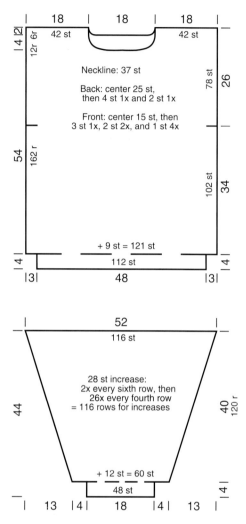

Patterns for Size 10

Neckline: 37 st

Back: center 25 st, then 4 st 1x and 2 st 1x

Front: center 15 st, then 3 st 1x, 2 st 2x, and 1 st 4x

Sleeves

For the sleeves, you do the same calculations: The width after the wristband ribbing is 26 x 2.2 = 57.2 + 2 selvedge stitches = 60 stitches for size 4.

For the ribbing, 7" = 39.6 stitches + 2 selvedge stitches, but 42 stitches in the ribbing pattern might be too tight. Add a few stitches—6 stitches in this case. Increase the missing 12 stitches at the end of the ribbing evenly distributed over the row.

Now first calculate the top sleeve width: 52 x 2.2 = 114.4 + 2 selvedge stitches = 116 stitches.

182

Patterns for Size 14

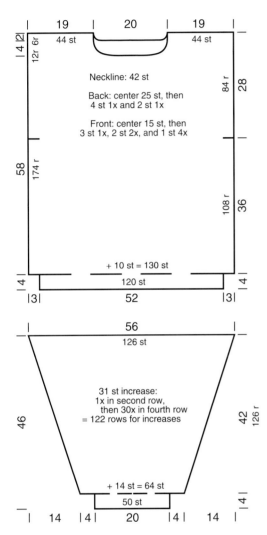

This means 56 stitches in total—i.e., 28 stitches per side—have to be increased.

These increases must be evenly divided over all the rows: 40 x 3 = 120 rows in total. Now divide 120 by 28 = 4.29. This means that you have to increase approximately every fourth row: 28 x 4 = 112. Since the distance from the last increase to binding off is supposed to be approximately the same as that between increases, it is too large here. Divide the extra 4 rows over the beginning of the sleeve. This means that you can increase 1 stitch on both sides every sixth row twice,

and every fourth row 26 times. Or you can divide the first few increases even more evenly: Increase 1 stitch alternately every fourth and sixth row 4 times, then 1 stitch every fourth row 24 times = 116 rows.

In general, increases are spaced farther apart at the bottom end of the sleeve and closer together towards the top of the sleeve. As an example: You want to make the sleeve only 14½" long but still increase 28 stitches. This means: 108 rows divided by 28 = 3.86. Therefore, some increases have to be worked every fourth row, some every third row—i.e., alternately every second and fourth row.

The answer is: Increase 1 stitch every fourth row 20 times = 80 rows, then alternately every second and fourth row 8 times = 24 rows—i.e., 104 rows in total.

Here's a little trick: If you multiply 18 x 4 in the example above, you get 112 rows. You have 108 rows— i.e., 104 rows to the last increase. The difference between 112 and 104 is 8. Therefore, you work 8 increases with a smaller distance between them.

Another example: You want to divide the 28 increases up over 94 rows: 94 ÷ 28 = 3.35. Here you multiply 28 x 3 = 84 rows. The number of rows available for increases is 90 = 6 rows difference. Therefore, you must increase at a greater distance 6 times = 6 x every fourth row and 22 x every third row—i.e., alternately every second and fourth row = 90 rows.

Working in Different Patterns

First of all, you have to knit a sample piece of each pattern for gauge. Then count the number of stitches and rows. Here's an example: You want to knit a sweater that has 3 cables on the front and back, and a center cable on the sleeve. Samples of

stockinette stitch give you 16 stitches for a 4" x 4" square, or 4 stitches per inch. The cable, which is made up of 26 stitches, is 4.8" wide. The sweater you want to make is 24" wide, the sleeve is 11.2" wide after the wristband ribbing, and 23.2" wide at the top.

The calculation for the front and back: 24" – 14.4" for the 3 cables = 9.6". 9.6 x 4 = 38.4 stitches + 2 selvedge stitches = 40 stitches. This means that you need a total of 40 + 78 stitches for the cables = 118 stitches. The 40 stitches in stockinette stitch are divided up between the cables—for example, 8 stitches between each of the cables and 12 stitches at each side.

The calculation for the sleeves is as follows: After the wristband ribbing: 11.2" – 4.8" cable = 6.4" x 4 = 25.6 stitches. Add the 2 selvedge stitches and the 26 stitches for the cable = 54 stitches. At the end of the sleeve: 23.2" – 4.8" = 18.4" x 4 = 73.6. Add 2 selvedge stitches and 26 stitches for the cable = 102 stitches. You must increase 24 stitches on both sides. With a sleeve length of 18", you have 99—i.e., 100 rows to work with. 100 ÷ 24 = 4.17; 4 x 24 = 96. Therefore, you must increase 1 stitch every fourth row 24 times.

Following this principle, you can perform these calculations for any pattern.

This pattern chart is on page 215.

Lengthening and Shortening Pieces

Your sweater came out too short, or a cardigan or vest has "grown" longer, or the ribbing has stretched out of shape or been damaged.

In all these cases, you have to take the piece apart at a certain point and make the changes as seamlessly as possible. This is not a big problem if the basic pattern is simple. Just follow the steps shown here.

Making a sweater or cardigan **longer** is harder than making it shorter. You still have to have enough of the original yarn in the correct dye lot, or be able to buy it. Also, worn pieces are often slightly washed out or discolored, so you might not even be able to use the original yarn. For children's sweaters, this is not always very important; you can use an entirely different color and just work in a few stripes. However, you should always use the same type of yarn, because the gauge must be the same, and the washing instructions should be the same.

When you **shorten** a piece, you don't have these problems. You just have to work carefully!

For Sleeves

If you want to shorten a sleeve, you must put up with a wider sleeve width above the ribbing. If you are making a sleeve longer, you normally can't follow the increase repeats of the slanted edge unless the sleeve was relatively wide above the wristband.

Lengthening sleeves of children's sweaters is usually not a worthwhile thing to do. For one thing, they are generally subject to a lot of wear. Also, the shape changes so much that the work involved in changing them is not much less than that for knitting a whole new sweater. You might be able to save some sweaters by taking the sleeves out entirely, adding facings to the armholes, and making a sleeveless sweater out of them.

If you want to save the ribbing, cut the selvedge stitch about 3 rows above the ribbing. Then you can catch the stitches by undoing the last few rows. Undoing the rows is only necessary if there is no yarn end for sewing when you have cut the selvedge stitch. If you are making a new ribbing, you can cut the selvedge stitch 1 row above the ribbing.

In most cases, wristband ribbing has to be knit on again, since the number of stitches changes both when lengthening or shortening the sleeve.

Undoing the Knitted Piece

Actually, only 1 row of knitting is "undone." After the yarn is pulled out, the open stitches of the top and bottom pieces can be put onto a knitting needle in a straight row. Use a thinner needle to do this so that you don't pull or drop any stitches.

To lengthen a piece, you can then add as many rows as needed with the appropriate-size knitting needle, and join the pieces again, using grafting stitch. If you work the added knitting onto the top piece, the knitting will shift over half a stitch. Within the piece, this cannot be seen. However,

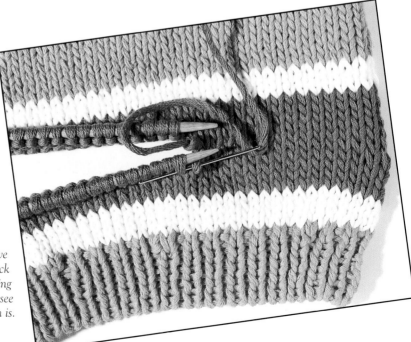

Once the pieces have been sewn back together using grafting stitch, you can't see where the seam is.

184

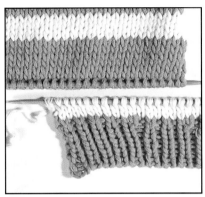

1 First open the seams as far as needed. To lengthen a piece, pull the selvedge stitch out a little—2 to 3 rows above the ribbing. To shorten a piece, pull it out at the point you wish to shorten the piece to and cut it open.

2 Pull on one end of the cut yarn and carefully gather the piece to the end of the row. At the end of the row, watch to see which stitch is being pulled. Put a knitting needle into this stitch and pull the gathering yarn out a little (to sew it in later). Then cut the yarn.

3 Now pull the yarn out all the way. This way, 1 row of knitting is neatly undone. The open stitches of the top and bottom pieces will be in front of you in a straight row. (If the yarn is very fine or tears easily, you will have to undo the yarn 1 stitch at a time.)

you have to be a little careful at the edges: When you sew the seams, pay attention to the line of stitches. At one edge, the seam now has to go along the selvedge stitch. At the other side, it has to go within the first stitch after the selvedge stitch. You should work a seam selvedge edge, because this is the only way you will be able to sew the seam within the selvedge stitch.

To shorten a piece, undo the bottom piece only up to the next-to-last row above the ribbing. That makes it easier to sew the ribbing back on using grafting stitch.

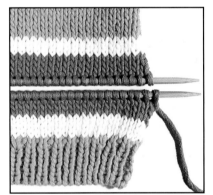

4 Put the open stitches onto a thinner knitting needle. As you pick the stitches up, make sure that they are on the needle correctly. If there is not a long enough yarn end at the sides to be sewn away, you can undo a row as you pick up the stitches and put the stitches onto the needle one at a time.

5 Now you can continue knitting on either the top or bottom piece. If you work on the top piece, the knitting will shift over half a stitch. You have to pay attention to that when you sew the seams again (see text on left). After the piece has been lengthened, you can join the pieces again, using a grafting stitch.

Tips for Ribbings

Ribbing holds knitted pieces in shape. Unless you want a box-shaped sweater, elastic thread or pieces of elastic will help to give stretched-out ribbing its shape back. If the ribbing is damaged, you then have to redo it.

K nitted items made of wool or wool blends are relatively resilient. The ribbing can be pressed into shape after washing and usually does not stretch out of shape. However, cotton and some synthetic fibers are different. Ribbing made of these yarns tends to stretch out of shape easily, so you should always work this ribbing with needles 2 sizes smaller than for the rest of the sweater.

You can get very thin elastic thread (see top photo) that you can knit almost invisibly into the ribbing. But if this thread wears out, the ends will stick out all over, and the pieces are hard to pull out and remove.

Sewing in or Crocheting on Elastic Thread

The best and most durable solution is if you pull a somewhat heavier elastic thread through with a tapestry needle after the ribbing is finished.

Pull the elastic thread through on the wrong side of the work, through part of a knit stitch in each instance, and knot the threads very tightly in the selvedge stitches. If you pull the thread through an entire knit stitch, part of the thread might still show on the right side of the work. Depending on the width of the ribbing, you should put in 4 to 6 rows this way and spaced evenly over the ribbing.

Even more durable is the method of crocheting the elastic thread on with slip stitches. Although 2 to 3 rows are generally enough, you need a lot more material. In addition, you have to sew the ends in very securely, because if the knot comes out, so does the whole row. That's why it's important that you crochet each row individually and sew it in individually.

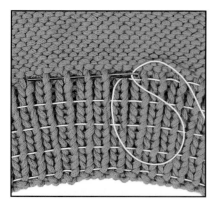

On the wrong side of the work, at regular intervals, pull elastic thread through ½ of all the knit stitches with a tapestry needle, and sew or knot them into the selvedge stitches.

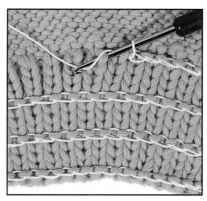

Or crochet slip stitches through ½ of all the knit stitches with the elastic thread, at regular intervals, and sew them securely at the edges.

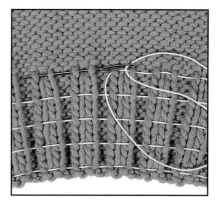

For 2 x 2 ribbing, always put the tapestry needle through the first and last loops of the knit stitches when you sew or crochet the elastic thread in.

Elastic Waistband

For heavy sweaters, skirts, or children's pants, wide elastic can be sewn on or inserted into a double waistband.

For a Single Waistband

Cut the elastic to the required length plus ¾" for the seam. Now put the beginning and end of the elastic on top of each other and sew them together with a few stitches.

Pin the elastic onto the waistband. Using overcast stitches, sew it on with a tapestry needle and the original yarn or a yarn that matches in color and is not too thin. Work from left to right, but keep inserting the needle into the knitted piece from right to left. Alternately put the needle through a knit rib at the top edge, above the elastic, and through the 2 loops of the knit rib just before the basic pattern at the bottom edge, below the elastic, skipping 1 rib each time. Don't pull the yarn too tight.

For a Double Waistband

Double waistbands can be knit together or can be sewn down later (see also hems, pages 58–59).

No matter which way you work, you can leave a few stitches open, insert the elastic, pull it through, sew it together, and then sew the rest of the waistband seam. Or you can knit together or sew the entire waistband seam, and pull the elastic through the narrow opening in the side seam.

Knitting on New Ribbing

Worn-out or damaged ribbing can also be replaced as follows: Open the seams partway. Now pull a marking thread through ½ of all the knit stitches of the second row of the

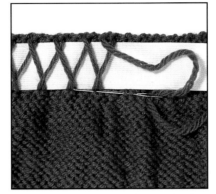

For a single waistband, the elastic is sewn on with overcast stitch.

For a double waistband, cut the elastic to the required length plus about ¾" and pull it through.

1 Pull a marking thread through the second row of the basic pattern. Then pick up the stitches in the first row of the basic pattern on a thin knitting needle.

2 Cut the purl stitches of the ribbing open carefully, below the knitting needle, take the ribbing off the sweater, and remove the small pieces of yarn.

basic pattern. This marker makes your work much easier, because it prevents you from slipping into another row. Then pick up the stitches in the first row of the basic pattern on a thin knitting needle.

Now you can cut all the purl stitches of the ribbing, take off the ribbing, and pull the ends of the yarn out. Now work 1 row of knit stitches on the right side of the work, or 1 row of purl stitches on the wrong side of the work, using the required needle size. In this row, make sure that the stitches are not on the needle twisted.

Then work in the ribbing pattern again. In the first row, work the previous increases as decreases (k2 or p2 tog evenly distributed). Work the ribbing to the desired length and bind off loosely.

Dropped Stitches

Whether your cat or child played with your knitting, or whether you weren't paying attention, dropped stitches are a nuisance, but you can easily fix them with a crochet hook.

For Stockinette Stitch

It is quite easy to fix a mistake here. For knit stitches, put the crochet hook through from the front—i.e., from below—and pull the horizontal thread above it through. Repeat.

For Textured Patterns

For reverse stockinette stitch, the easiest thing to do is to turn the work and crochet the knit stitches. For textured patterns, you have to work differently: knit and purl stitches as required by the pattern.

For purl stitches, insert the crochet hook from behind—i.e., from above—and pull the horizontal thread through. Then take the crochet hook out again.

For knit stitches, pull the horizontal thread directly above the stitch on the crochet hook through that stitch.

For purl stitches, insert the hook into the stitch from behind—i.e., from the top—behind the horizontal thread above it, and pull the horizontal thread through.

For every purl stitch (and also for every first knit stitch), the crochet hook has to be taken out and put into the stitch again.

For garter stitch, you insert the crochet hook into the stitch alternately from the front and back.

For Single Shaker Knitting

Here there is a smooth side and a rough side. Either a dropped stitch on the smooth side (the shaker knit stitch side) or a rough stitch on the other side has to be rescued.

If a stitch was dropped in single shaker knitting, you must first undo the individual threads, as explained for double shaker knitting. In contrast to the double shaker knitting, single shaker knitting always has alternately a short thread and a long thread on both sides.

For a smooth stitch in single shaker knitting, insert the crochet hook into the stitch, put the hook under the short thread above that stitch, catch the long thread, and pull it through.

On the rough side, catch the stitch with the crochet hook. If there is still a short thread above that stitch, pull it through first. Then put the hook under the next short thread,...

...crochet the long thread, and then also crochet the short thread. Repeat these steps.

For Double Shaker Knitting

It's a little more complicated to fix dropped stitches in double shaker knitting with a crochet hook. However, the repairing idea can be seen with the example of two-color double shaker knitting:

First stretch the piece sideways and untangle the threads as much as possible. Crochet with the very long pieces of yarn (the green ones, in this instance). The threads between them (the white ones, in this instance) are the "yarn overs." First pull the particularly loose green threads up and then work as described in the photos. Keep repeating this process and put the last stitch back onto the left needle together with the last short thread—i.e., the yarn over.

For single-color double shaker knitting, the idea is the same. Here the long threads can only be easily distinguished from the short ones if they are pulled through to the top.

Undoing Your Work

If you've made a really big mistake over many stitches, the only solution is to undo your work. Undo the knitted piece to the row before the mistake. To pick up the stitches, use a needle that is about 1 size smaller than the one you used for knitting. This makes it easy to pick up the stitches, even if you knit tightly.

Before you undo a stitch, always put the needle into the stitch underneath it from back to front. Pull the yarn out carefully. Continue working this way, 1 stitch at a time. Hold the yarn in your left hand and keep winding it around your forefinger as you undo the stitches. At the end of each row, turn your work and continue working with the appropriate needles.

In the case of shaker knitting, picking the stitches up is slightly more difficult. In order for the

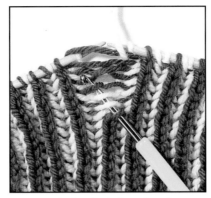

Double shaker knitting: Put the crochet hook through the last (green) stitch. Bring the needle under the 2 short (white) threads above it. Catch the long (green) thread and pull it through the stitch on the hook under the 2 short threads. The lower one of the 2 short threads is the "yarn over" of the stitch you just crocheted. Now put the crochet hook under the top one of the 2 threads and the next short thread, catch the next long thread, etc.

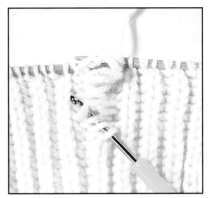

In single-color double shaker knitting, the long threads have to lie on top. Catch the next long thread with the crochet hook, under 2 short threads, and pull it through the stitch under the short threads.

stitches not to be pulled too tightly, it is very important to use a thin knitting needle. Put the needle through the purl stitches and the yarn over from back to front. Then carefully undo the yarn and catch

the next knit stitch. If the knit stitch continues to drop, catch the horizontal thread of the knit stitch underneath it. Then undo another row. At the stitch in question, simply transfer it to the right needle.

When undoing knitted pieces, pick up 1 stitch at a time from back to front.

When undoing shaker knitting, catch the yarn over along with the purl stitches, and carefully pick the knit stitches up onto the needle.

Pattern Charts

Pattern charts have the great advantage that you can easily imagine what a pattern will look like.

Written instructions for individual stitches are often complicated and more difficult to understand because of the long text. Here is some information about the width and the length of a pattern, then about how to read a pattern chart.

Pattern Width

The width of the pattern repeat is given under each pattern chart. for the textured pattern shown, it is 10 stitches. These 10 stitches are constantly repeated. The last stitch of the pattern is only worked at the end of the piece to complete the pattern. To calculate the number of stitches needed, the number of stitches must be divisible by 10 + 1 stitch + 2 selvedge stitches—for example, 43 stitches.

On some patterns, several stitches are shown on both sides of the pattern repeat to complete the pattern. In this case, you start with the first stitches of the chart after the selvedge stitch, then repeat the pattern repeat as indicated. At the end, work the last stitches on the chart and the selvedge stitch.

Pattern Length

Many charts show only the rows on the right side of the work. That is practically always the case if the stitches are simply purled in the rows on the wrong side of the work. Or it

is usually also the case if all the stitches are worked as they lie—i.e., the purl stitches are purled, the knit stitches are knit.

This can be clearly seen using the example of a simple textured pattern. **Chart 1** shows the pattern in the rows on the right side of the work; the row numbers are given only on the right side of the chart. **Chart 2**, on the other hand, is more confusing, although it shows the same pattern. Here the rows on the right and wrong side of the work are shown the way they are worked; the numbers for the rows on the right side of the work are on the right, the number for the rows on the wrong side of the work are on the left.

Chart 3 shows another possible way of representing the stitches. Here the stitches are shown in the rows on the right and wrong side of the work the way they appear on the right side. The chart explanation would then have to say: Open box = knit stitch on right side of work, purl stitch on wrong side of work. Box with horizontal line = purl stitch on right side of work, knit stitch on wrong side of work.

Reading a Pattern Chart

On all pattern charts, the rows on the right side of the work read from right to left, the rows on the wrong side of the work from left to right, always in the knitting direction. The selvedge stitches are not shown, unless otherwise indicated.

For a textured pattern, the text for the first 3 rows would read:
Row 1: selv st, * k2, p7, k1, * k1, selv st.
Row 2 and all subsequent rows on WS: work the st as they lie. (Or:
Row 2: selv st, p1, * p1, k7, p2, rep from *, selv st.)
Row 3: selv st, * k3, p5, k2, rep from *, k1, selv st.

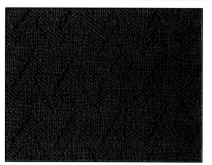

Textured pattern

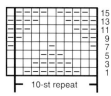

Chart 1: Only the rows on the right side of the work are shown.

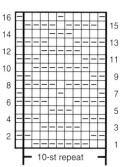

Chart 2: The same pattern with the rows on the right and wrong side shown as they are worked.

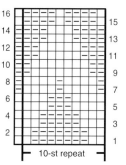

Chart 3: The stitches on the right and wrong sides are shown as they appear on the right side of the work.

The pattern repeats between the asterisks. This means in the first row, for example, that after the first 3 stitches, you alternately p7 and k3 (the last stitch before the asterisk and the first 2 stitches after the asterisk).

Reading patterns in words might seem easier to some knitters than reading pattern charts. But the complicated length of the text becomes clear when you read the instructions for the little openwork pattern according to **Chart 4**:

Row 1: selv st, * p2, k5, k2 tog, yo, p1, rep from *, p1, selv st.

Row 2 and all WS row: work the st as they lie.

Row 3: selv st, * p2, k4, k2 tog, k1, yo, p1, rep from *, p1, selv st.

Row 5: selv st, * p2, k3, k2 tog, k2, yo, p1, rep from *, p1, selv st.

Row 7: selv st, * p2, k2, k2 tog, k3, yo, p1, rep from *, p1, selv st.

Row 9: selv st, * p2, yo, single dec (slip 1 st knitwise, k1, psso), k5, p1,

rep from *, p1, selv st.

R 11: selv st, * p 2, yo, k 1, single dec, k 4, p 1, rep from *, p 1, selv st.

Row 13: selv st, * p2, yo, k2, single dec, k3, p 1, rep from *, p1, selv st.

Row 15: selv st, * p2, yo, k3, single dec, k2, p1, rep from *, p1, selv st.

Repeat **Rows 1 to 16.**

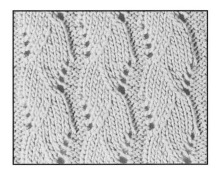

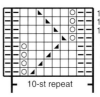

Chart 4: Pattern chart for openwork pattern

10-st repeat

Intarsia Pattern Chart

On pattern charts for intarsia work, the rows on the right side of the work also read from right to left, while the rows on the wrong side of the work read from left to right.

Large areas of color are often worked in reverse on the back as compared with the front, so that the same areas of color come together at the side seams and shoulders. For this purpose, you read the first row and all other odd rows as rows on the wrong side of the work even though you are knitting these rows. And you read

Intarsia is sometimes worked in reverse,...

or the same way as the chart.

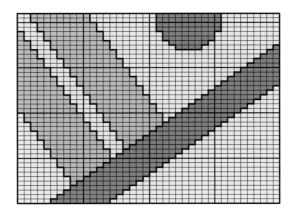

Chart 5: For intarsia patterns, every row is shown on the chart. Each box represents 1 stitch.

the rows on the wrong side of the work from right to left.

In the example shown, **on the front** you work 26 stitches in yellow, 9 stitches in red, and 5 stitches in yellow. That is the sequence in which you cast the stitches on, too.

If you are not working any ribbing, you cast the stitches on the same way, but start with a purl row on the wrong side of the work, and read the first row of the chart from left to right, the second from right to left, etc.

If you are working **the back** in reverse, cast on 5 stitches in yellow, 9 stitches in red, and 26 stitches in yellow. Then, after the ribbing, read the first row of the chart from left to right, the second from right to left, etc.

TIP

Sometimes the stitches on pattern charts look as if they don't fit on top of each other. This could be because of increases, decreases, and yarn overs. Just put a ruler under the row you are working on so that the previous row doesn't confuse you. On pattern charts for intarsia work, put the ruler on top of the row you are working on so you can compare the color sequence more easily.

Sleeve Increases in Openwork Patterns

In complicated openwork patterns, increasing with yarn overs can sometimes create not-so-easy-to-solve problems. Here are some tips to make it easier.

W orking openwork patterns on straight pieces is easy for most knitters. The problems start with increases in the sleeve.

Here is the simplest solution: Draw the slanted edges of the sleeves on graph paper. For symmetrical patterns like the diamond pattern shown here, it is very helpful if you draw at least the right side of the sleeve. Then the pattern repeat is repeated as often as necessary, and the pattern is widened in reverse on the left side.

Adding an Extra Stockinette Stitch at the Edges

You will get especially neat-looking sleeve seams if you work an extra stitch in stockinette stitch next to the selvedge stitches, and work the pattern and increases next to that stitch. That is how this sleeve was calculated and is shown in the drawing. It is always easier to sew a seam between a selvedge stitch and a knit stitch than between a selvedge stitch and a pattern with confusing increases. In the pattern, the horizontal threads are difficult to see, and it is almost impossible to make an invisible seam. The additional stitch at the sleeve seam does not affect the pattern and practically disappears into it.

Adjusting the Pattern to the Slanted Edge of the Sleeve

When working the slanted edge of a sleeve, a pattern might call for a yarn over after the selvedge stitch—i.e., after the selvedge stitch and the additional knit stitch—but there are no stitches available to knit together, which is also called for. This happens in Rows 31 and 45 of the example shown. At these points, the number of stitches is increased with the yarn over, and you do without the knitting together.

Vice versa, it can happen that after the selvedge stitch, 2 stitches have to be knit together. However, a yarn over right next to the seam doesn't look nice (as in Rows 55 or 77 of the chart). Instead of the decrease, simply work 2 knit stitches and 1 twisted increase. The rule of thumb for slanted edges of sleeves is that

In an openwork pattern, it is easier to sew the sleeve seams using invisible stitch if an additional stockinette stitch is worked on both sides next to the selvedge stitch.

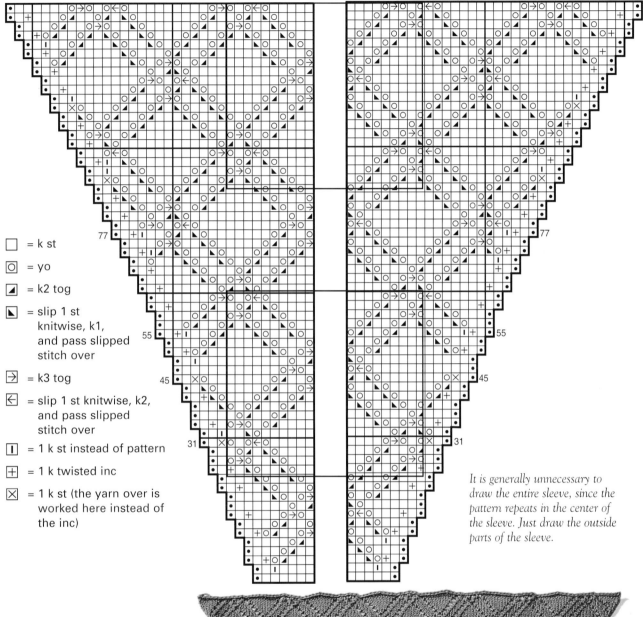

- □ = k st
- Ⓞ = yo
- ◢ = k2 tog
- ◣ = slip 1 st knitwise, k1, and pass slipped stitch over
- → = k3 tog
- ← = slip 1 st knitwise, k2, and pass slipped stitch over
- Ⅰ = 1 k st instead of pattern
- ⊞ = 1 k twisted inc
- ⊠ = 1 k st (the yarn over is worked here instead of the inc)

It is generally unnecessary to draw the entire sleeve, since the pattern repeats in the center of the sleeve. Just draw the outside parts of the sleeve.

always, at difficult points, it is better to increase a few more stitches in stockinette stitch and start working the pattern afterwards. In the case of very small openwork patterns, you can even wait until you have enough increases in stockinette stitch to start an entire new pattern repeat. That always looks better than messy sleeve edges.

The complete instruction for the sweater shown here is on page 199.

Basic Patterns

This section includes the instructions for all the designs in this book. It also has socks and gloves, which are explained in detail with tables for all sizes.

Sweaters

Here are the instructions for all the designs in this book—from intarsia work to embroidered children's sweaters.

The paper patterns show only half the width. Only for the raglan sweater worked in shaker knitting is the entire left sleeve shown.

The instructions ask for a normal cast on with 1 needle. However, you can cast on in kitchener rib (starting on page 22).

The number of stitches indicated always includes selvedge stitches.

According to the instructions, stitches at the shoulder seams are always bound off. However, shoulder seams in grafting stitch or knit seams generally look better. To finish the seams this way, put the stitches temporarily on a stitch holder and finish the shoulders after you are done with the second piece.

The symbols and abbreviations used in the instructions are explained on page 237.

Sweater with Intarsia Pattern

Size: 8/10

Yarn: virgin wool yarn approx. 125 m (137½ yds)/50 g (1¾ oz); 450 g (15¾ oz) of black, 50 g (1¾ oz) each of turquoise, red, green, yellow, orange, pistachio, and plum

Basic pattern: Stockinette stitch on size 6 needles.

Gauge: 21 st and 29 rows = 4" × 4"

Ribbing: Alternately k1, p1 on size 3 needles.

Back: Cast on 128 st with black and work ribbing for 1½" starting on WS. Continue in stockinette stitch with black. When the piece is 26½" long, bind off the center 26 st, then 4 st 1x and 3 st 1x, every other row, on both sides, for the neckline. When the piece is 27¼" long, bind off the shoulder stitches.

Front: Cast on 5 st with plum, 30 st with orange, 17 st with yellow, 17 st with plum, and 59 st with black (128 st). Work in ribbing for 1½", keeping the color pattern the same. Continue in stockinette stitch, following the pattern chart. Every row is shown; 1 box corresponds to 1 stitch.

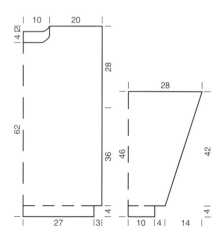

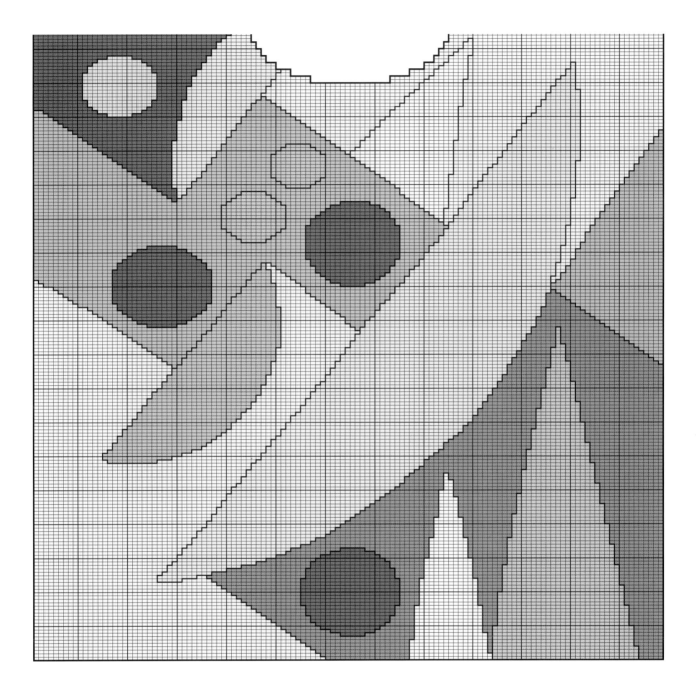

When the piece is 24¾" long, bind off the center 16 st, then 4 st 1x, 3 st 1x, 2 st 1x, and 1 st 3x, every other row, on both sides, for the neckline.

When the piece is 27¼" long, bind off the shoulder stitches.

Sleeves: Cast on 50 st with black and work ribbing for 1½". In the last row, increase 12 st evenly distributed over the row (62 st).

Continue in stockinette stitch with black, and increase 1 st every fourth row 29x (120 st).

When the piece is 18½" long, bind off all stitches.

Finishing: Correct the color changes on the front, if necessary (see page 147).

Sew the shoulder seams, sew the sleeves on, then sew the side seams and sleeve seams.

For the neckband, cast on 116 st with black on a short size 3 circular needle, and work in round ribbing for 1¼", then k 2 rounds. Sew stitches of the neckband to the neckline using back stitch, undoing the 2 knit rounds as you sew it on (see pages 70–72).

Jacquard and Textured Pattern Sweater

Size: 8/10

Yarn: Cotton yarn approx. 85 m (93½ yds)/50 g (1¾ oz); 600 g (21 oz.) of rust, 150 g (5½ oz) of black, 50 g (1¾ oz) each of red, curry, natural, brown, and yellow

Basic pattern I: Work the jacquard pattern in stockinette stitch on size 6 needles. The pattern chart shows every row. Read RS rows from right to left, WS rows from left to right. Work all selvedge stitches with both color yarns.

Gauge I: 22 st and 27 rows = 4" x 4"

Basic pattern II: Work the textured pattern on size 6 needles. Only the RS rows are shown; on WS rows, work all stitches as they lie.

Gauge II: 22 st and 30 rows = 4" x 4"

Ribbing: Alternately k1, p1 on size 3 needles.

Back: Cast on 124 st with black and work ribbing for 1½" starting on WS. In the last WS row, inc 11 st evenly distributed over row (135 st).
Now work the 56 rows in basic pattern I as follows: selv st, pattern repeat 5x, st 1 to 13 of pattern repeat, selv st.
Then work in basic pattern II as follows: selv st, pattern repeat 11x, last st of chart, selv st.
When the piece is 17½" long, bind off 1 st every other row on both sides 12x for the armholes (111 st).
When the piece is 28" long, bind off the center 29 st, then 3 st 1x and 2 st 1x, every other row, on both sides, for the neckline.
When the piece is 28¾" long, bind off the shoulder stitches.

Front: Work like the back, but when the piece is 25½" long, bind off the center 15 st, then 3 st 1x, 2 st 2x, and 1 st 5x, every other row, on both sides, for the neckline.

Sleeves: Cast on 46 st with black and work ribbing for ¾". Purl the last row on WS, inc 9 st evenly distributed over the row (55 st).
Now work Rows 1 to 31 of basic pattern I, then continue in basic pattern II. Center the patterns on the middle of the sleeve. In the jacquard pattern, stitch 13 is the center st. For the slanted edges of the sleeve, on both sides, inc 1 st every fourth row 15x, then inc 1 st alternately every second and every fourth row another 20x (125 st). When the piece is 18" long, bind off 3 st every other row 4x, and 2 st every other row 3x. Then bind off the remaining stitches in a straight line.

Finishing: Sew the shoulder seams, sew on the sleeves, and then sew the side seams and sleeve seams. For the neckband, cast on 124 st with rust

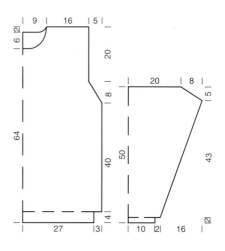

on a short size 3 circular needle, and work round in ribbing for 1¼", then k 2 rounds. Sew the st of the neckband to the neckline using back stitch, undoing the 2 knit rounds as you sew it on.

Textured pattern

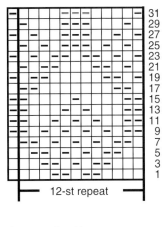

12-st repeat

Jacquard pattern

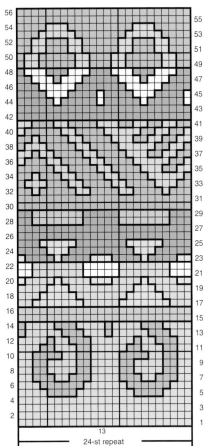

13
24-st repeat

Openwork Pattern Sweater

Size: 8/10

Yarn: Approx. 550 g (19¼oz) smooth, mercerized cotton yarn approx. 115 m (126½ yds)/50 g (1¾ oz)

Basic pattern: Work the openwork pattern on size 5 needles. Only the RS rows are shown; on WS rows, purl all st and yo.

Gauge: 20 st and 30 rows = 4" x 4"

Ribbing: Alternately k1, p1 on size 3 needles.

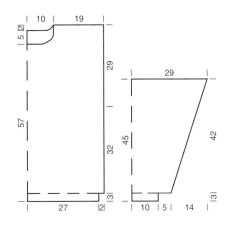

Back: Cast on 110 st and work ribbing for 1¼" starting on WS. In last row on WS, inc 8 st evenly distributed over row (118 st). Then work in basic pattern as follows: selv st, first st of chart, pattern repeat of 16 st 7x, last st of chart, selv st. When the piece is 24¾" long, bind off the center 28 st, then 3 st 1x and 2 st 1x, every other row, on both sides, for the neckline. When the piece is 25½" long, bind off the shoulder stitches.

Front: Work like the back, but when the piece is 24¾" long, bind off the center 16 st, then 3 st 1x, 2 st 2x, and 1 st 4x, every other row, on both sides, for the neckline.

Sleeves (see increasing in openwork patterns, page 181): Cast on 52 st and work in ribbing for 1¼". In the last row on WS, inc 9 st evenly distributed over the row (61 st). Then work in basic pattern as follows: selv st, st 12 to 16 of the pattern repeat, pattern repeat of 16 st 3x, st 1 to 6 of pattern repeat, selv st.

For the slanted edges of the sleeve, on both sides, inc 1 st alternately every fourth and sixth row 12x, then inc 1 st every fourth row 16x (117 st).

When the piece is 18" long, bind off all st straight across = 4 pattern repeats (128 rows).

Finishing: Sew the shoulder seams, sew on the sleeves, then sew the side seams and sleeve seams.

For the neckband, pick up 116 st on a short size 3 circular needle, and work in round ribbing for 1¼". Bind off normally or in kitchener rib.

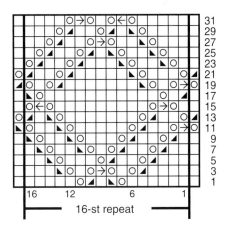

16   12   6   1
16-st repeat

Cardigan with Cables

Size: 12/14

Yarn: 1200 g (42 oz) Shetland wool yarn approx. 166 m (182½ yds)/50 g (1¾ oz)

Basic pattern: Work the cable pattern according to the chart on size 8 needles. The chart shows half of the back, which is the same as the left front, not including selvedge stitches. In addition, 1 row of ribbing, and above it the increases in the last row of the ribbing, on the wrong side of the work, are shown in yellow. For the narrow cables, repeat Rows 1 to 6. For the wide cables, repeat Rows 1 to 32 (the pattern repeat of the basic patterns is shown in yellow).

Gauge: The 44 st with the wide cables (pocket width) are 7" wide. In the ribbing/cable pattern, 20 st and 25 rows = 4" x 4"

Ribbing: Alternately k2, p2 on size 6 needles.

Back: Cast on 122 st and work in ribbing for 1½" (the first row of the pattern chart). The row on WS starts with selv st, p1. In last row on WS (second row in yellow), inc 44 st purl twisted as shown (166 st).

Now continue working in the basic pattern with cables. Here, too, reverse the pattern from the center of the back part, but continue crossing the narrow cables to the left.

When the piece is 18" long, bind off 3 st 2x, 2 st 2x, 1 st 5x, every other row, then 1 st 1x after 4 rows, on both sides, for the armholes = 134 st.

When the piece is 28¾" long, bind off the center 24 st, then 5 st 1x and 3 st 1x, every other row, on both sides, for the neckline.

Put the stitches for the shoulders on a holder and bind them off later by knitting them together with the stitches of the front parts. Work firmly.

Right front: Cast on 60 st, working in ribbing for 1½", begin the first row on WS with selv st, k1 (front edge). In the last row on WS, inc 21 st as shown (81 st).

When the piece is 9½" long, 17 st in from the side edge, put the next 44 st on a holder for the pocket opening (see also pattern chart). Cast on 34 st for the inside pocket and work in stockinette stitch for 6", then continue in pattern for 2", increasing 10 st (44 st).

When the piece is 8" long, join the stitch into the work and continue working the entire front. (The pocket is shown in detail on page 95.)

When the piece is 17½" long, start binding off 1 st every fourth row on the right edge for the neckline by purling the last 2 st before the selv st together.

At the same time, when the piece is 18" long, work the armhole at the left edge the same way as for the back. Knit the shoulder stitches together with the shoulder stitches of the back part, RS on RS, and bind off firmly.

Work the **left front** in reverse, read the inc from left to right. The narrow cables are still crossed the same way.

Sleeves: Cast on 54 st and work in ribbing for 1½". Begin the first row on WS with selv st, k1; the beginning of the sleeve (without selv st) is shown on the pattern chart. In the last row on WS, inc 18 st as shown (72 st).

For the slanted edges of the sleeves, inc 1 st alternately every second and fourth row on both sides 31x (134 st). Above the increases, first p1, then alternately k4 and p2. Alternately work the 4 knit st as a rib and as a cable.

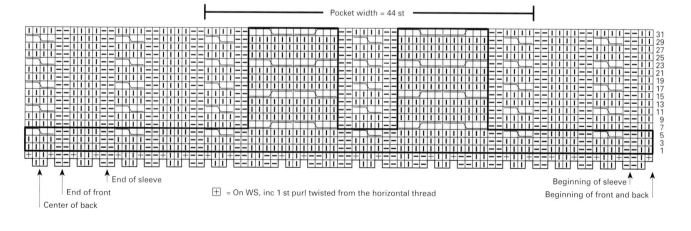

Pocket width = 44 st

End of sleeve
End of front
Center of back

⊞ = On WS, inc 1 st purl twisted from the horizontal thread

Beginning of sleeve
Beginning of front and back

When the piece is 17" long, bind off on both sides every other row 4 st 1x, 3 st 1x, 2 st 3x, 3 st 1x, 4 st 1x, and 5 st 1x. Then bind off the remaining st straight across. When binding off over a narrow cable, k2 tog 1x. When binding off over a wide cable, k2 tog 3x.

Finishing: Work a double facing above the pocket stitch as follows: First cast on new selv st with needle size 6, * work the next 4 st in cable pattern, 14 st in ribbing, starting with 2 purl st, over the wide cable, p2 tog 2x, rep from *, then after the last 4 st in cable pattern, cast on another selv st (42 st).

When the piece is 1¼" long, work another 1¼" in stockinette stitch with size 4 needle. In the first row, k2 tog 1x above each of the narrow cables.

Turn the stockinette stitch part of the facing in and sew it down. Sew the narrow sides on, using invisible stitch.

Sew the sleeves on, then sew the side seams and sleeve seams.

Pick up 356 st from the front edges and the neckline edges, and work 1¼" in ribbing. The first row on RS starts with selv st, 2 knit st (see also photo on page 60). On the right front, evenly distributed along the straight edge, work in 5 round buttonholes over 2 purl st, in each instance (page 100). Sew buttons on.

Child's Sweater with Bobbles

Size: 4

Yarn: 200 g (7 oz) light mohair yarn approx. 150 m (165 yds)/50 g (1¾ oz) and small amounts of cotton yarn in different colors for the bobbles

Basic pattern: Stockinette stitch on size 6 needles

Gauge: 22 st and 30 rows = 4" x 4"

Ribbing: Alternately k1, p1 on size 3 needles.

Back: Cast on 80 st and work in ribbing for 1¼", starting with a WS row. In the last row on WS, inc 6 st evenly distributed (86 st). Continue in stockinette stitch.

When the piece is 14½" long, bind off the center 20 st straight across, then 3 st 1x and 2 st 1x, every other row, on both sides, for the neckline.

When the piece is 15¼" long, bind off the shoulder stitches.

Front: Work the same way as the back, but for the neckline, when the piece is 12¾" long, bind off the center 10 st, then 3 st 1x, 2 st 2x, and 1 st 3x, every other row, on both sides.

Sleeves: Cast on 36 st and work in ribbing for 1¼". In the last row on

WS, increase 6 st evenly distributed over the row (42 st).

Continue in stockinette stitch and increase on both sides 1 st every fourth row 17x (76 st).

When the piece is 10 ¾" long, bind off all stitches.

Finishing: Crochet approximately 80 bobbles and knot them evenly distributed onto the front and sleeves (see page 166).

Sew the shoulder seams, sew on the sleeves, then sew the side seams and sleeve seams.

For the neckband, pick up approximately 80 st from the neckline with a short size 3 circular knitting needle, and work in ribbing for 2". Bind stitches off very loosely, turn the neckband in, and sew it on.

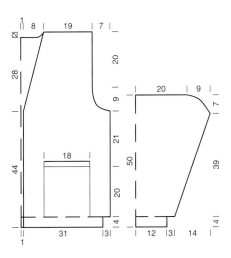

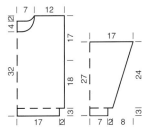

Raglan Sweater in Shaker Knitting

Size: 8/10

Yarn: Approx. 800 g (28 oz) tweed-colored virgin wool/alpaca yarn approx. 110 m (121 yds)/50 g (1¾ oz)

Basic pattern: Single shaker knitting worked on size 5 needles

Row 1 (WS): Selv st, * k1 st, slip 1 st purlwise with yo *, k1, selv st

Row 2 (RS): Selv st, p1, * k the st tog with the yo, p1 *, selv st

Repeat Rows 1 and 2.

Gauge: 16 st and 34 rows = 4" x 4"

Ribbing: Alternately k1, p1 on size 3 needles

Back: Cast on 99 st and work in ribbing for 1¼". Start the first row on WS with selv st, k1.
Continue in single shaker knitting. When the piece is 14¾" long, start decreasing for the raglan sleeve edges, on both sides, 2 st 1x, then 2 st every eighth row 8x, and 2 st

every fourth row 11x. Work these dec 4 st in from the edge in each case: At the right edge, slip the fifth st = k st with the yo purlwise, k the next 2 st tog with the yo, and pass the slipped st over with the yo. On the left side, 7 st before the end of the row, k the next 3 st with the yo (= 5 loops) tog.
When the piece is 28" long, 4 rows after the last dec, bind off the remaining 19 st.

Front: Work like the back, but when the piece is 25½" long (with the seventh dec in the fourth row; before these dec, there are still 39 st on the needle), bind off the center 19 st, then 2 st 2x and 1 st 1x, every other row, on both sides, for the neckline.

Left sleeve: Cast on 38 st and work in ribbing for 1¼". Start the first row on WS with selv st, k1.
Continue in single shaker

knitting, and in the first row, inc 1 st purl twisted after the selv st, then 2 st 5x evenly distributed (49 st). For the double inc, work 1 st purl twisted from the horizontal thread after a knit st, k the next st, then inc 1 st purl twisted from the horizontal thread.
For the slanted edges of the sleeve, on both sides inc 1 st every sixth row 12x, then inc 1 st alternately every fourth and sixth row 8x (89 st). If you work double increases, 2 st have to be inc every twelfth row 6x, then 2 st every tenth row 4x (see also page 131).
When the piece is 15¼" long, dec 2 st 1x for the raglan seam, then 2 st every fourth row 12x, as described for the back. Continue decreasing as follows: On the right side, dec 2 st every eighth row 7x. On the left side, dec 2 st every eighth row 5x, after another 8 rows, 4 st every other row 2x, and 2 st 1x. Then bind off the remaining 3 st.
Work the **right sleeve** in reverse.
Finishing: Sew the raglan seams, then sew the side seams and sleeve seams (see sewing seams, page 113). For the neckband, pick up 70 st on a short size 3 circular needle, and work in round in ribbing for 2½". Bind the stitches off loosely. Turn the neckband in and sew it on.

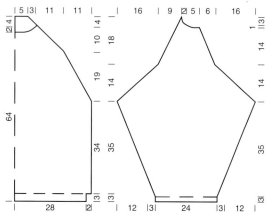

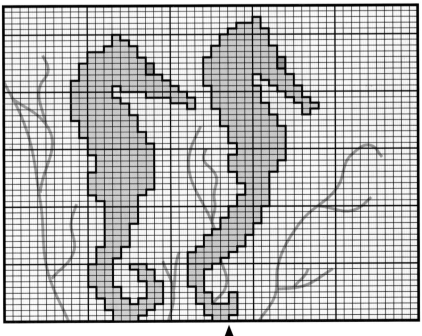

Child's Sweater with Seahorses

Size: 2

Yarn: 200 g (7 oz) natural-color virgin wool yarn approx. 125 m (137½ yds)/50 g (1¾ oz), and small amounts of light green and green for embroidery

Basic pattern: Stockinette stitch on size 6 needles

Gauge: 22 st and 30 rows = 4" x 4"

Ribbing: Alternately k1, p1 on size 3 needles

Back: Cast on 68 st and work in ribbing for 1¼". In the last row on WS, inc 4 st evenly distributed (72 st). Continue in stockinette stitch. When the piece is 12¾" long, bind off the center 20 st straight across, then 3 st 1x and 2 st 1x, every other row, on both sides, for the neckline. When the piece is 13½" long, bind off the shoulder stitches at the left shoulder, continue in ribbing for another ¾" at the right shoulder, then bind off the stitches.

Front: Work the same way as the back. But for the neckline, when the piece is 11½" long, bind off the center 14 st, then 4 st 1x, 2 st 1x, and 1 st 2x, every other row, on both sides. Also, when the piece is 12¾" long, work ¾" of ribbing on the right side for the left shoulder, making a buttonhole 1½" and 2¾" in from the side edge. To make the buttonholes, in a row on RS, yo in front of a purl st, and k the next 2 st tog. When the piece is 13½" long, bind off the shoulder stitches at the right shoulder.

Sleeves: Cast on 36 st and work in ribbing for 1¼". In the last row on WS, increase 6 st evenly distributed over the row (42 st).

Continue in stockinette stitch and increase on both sides 1 st every sixth row 2x, then 1 st every fourth row 11x (68 st). When the piece is 10¾" long, bind off all the stitches.

Finishing: Embroider the seahorses on the front in duplicate stitch and the lines in outline stitch. The center of the front is indicated on the chart, every box =1 st.

Sew the right shoulder seam. On the left shoulder attach the front facing over the back facing. Then sew the sleeves on and sew the side seams and sleeve seams.

For the neckband, pick up approximately 90 st from the neckline and work in ribbing for ¾". After ½" make the third buttonhole 4 st in from the front edge. Sew the buttons on.

Center of front

Socks

Now we'll making the rounds, because socks are knit with a set of needles in the round. Once you have the hang of it, it's really very simple. And since you need at most 50 g (1¾ oz) of yarn per sock, you'll be done in no time.

Y ou should always use a yarn that is machine washable and very durable, such as Regia 4-fädig made of 75% virgin wool and 25% polyamide, which we have used here. This yarn is about 210 m (231 yds) per 50 g (1¾ oz) and is done on size 2 double pointed needles.

If you prefer cotton, try Schoeller Esslinger's Fortissima Cotton, which is 75% cotton. This yarn is also reinforced with 25% nylon. It is approximately 209 m (230 yds) per 50 g (1¾ oz), and is worked with the same size needles.

Reinforcing the heel and the toe is a good idea, because these parts are particularly subject to wear. Reinforcement yarns are available in many different colors.

Socks should be knit as tightly as possible with an even gauge. Normally, size 2 needles are the right size, but if you knit very loosely, size 0 might be better. That is why you should definitely knit a sample for gauge.

Double pointed needles usually come in a set of 5 needles. Divide the stitches evenly onto 4 needles. Change rounds at the center in the back: The heel is worked

over the first and fourth needles. The arch—the top of the foot—is worked over the second and third needles.

Ribbing

Cuff

Heel

This sock was knit with Regia 4-fädig. You can find the number of stitches and rows for different sizes in the table.

Toe

Gusset

Turn

← Length from gusset pickup to toe →

Size calculation													
Total length of foot in inches	5.8	6.2	6.8	7.2	7.8	8.4	8.8	9.4	10	10.6	11	11.4	12
Stitches to cast on	44	48	48	52	52	56	56	60	60	64	64	68	72
Stitches for heel width	22	24	24	26	26	28	28	30	30	32	32	34	36
Rows for heel length	20	22	22	24	24	26	26	28	28	30	30	32	34
Stitches for turn	7/8/7	8/8/8	8/8/8	8/10/8	8/10/8	9/10/9	9/10/9	10/10/10	10/10/10	10/12/10	10/12/10	11/12/11	12/12/12
Stitches picked up on both sides	11	12	12	13	13	14	14	15	15	16	16	17	18
Length of foot from gusset pickup to toe	2.6	2.8	3.4	3.6	4.2	4.6	5	5.4	6	6.2	6.6	6.8	7.2

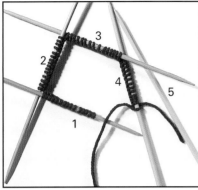

The cast-on stitches are divided up among the 4 needles of the set. The round starts in the center, at the back, between the first and fourth needle.

Great for knee-high socks: A rubber band can be inserted into the band worked in stockinette stitch.

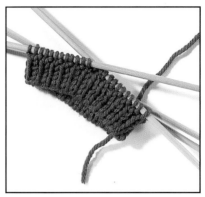

The kitchener rib method of casting on is also very good for socks (see also page 207).

Ribbing

Work the ribbing either in 1 x 1 or 2 x 2 ribbing. Cast the stitches on with 2 needles so that the edge is stretchable and wide enough.

Casting on in kitchener rib (see page 207) gives you a more stretchable edge. First cast on all the stitches on 1 needle and then divide the stitches up among the needles in the first row, closing them into a round in the second row. It might be easier to cast on with yarn in a different color: In the first row, alternately knit 1 stitch out of the crochet chain, then work 1 yarn over. At the same time, divide the stitches up onto the 4 needles.

For knee-high socks, I also recommend a double band with picot edge (pages 58–59) into which you can put an elastic later. To make this band, work about 8 to 10 rounds in stockinette stitch on size 0 needles, then an openwork round (alternately knit 2 stitches together, yarn over), then another 8 to 10 rounds in stockinette stitch (in the first round, knit all stitches and yarn overs). In the next round, knit 1 stitch from the needle together with 1 stitch of the casting on, on the fourth needle;

leave the last 3 stitches open. Or you can turn the band in later and sew it on. Then continue with size 2 needles.

Cuff

If the cuff is going to be worked in stockinette stitch, you can continue working with the same number of stitches as for the ribbing. If you are going to work in a pattern, any change in the gauge has to be taken into consideration. For cables, stitches have to be added, and fewer stitches might be enough for openwork patterns.

The width of the pattern repeat is also important. If, for example, you have selected a pattern repeat of 6 stitches, and have cast on 60 stitches, the pattern repeat is worked 10 times. If you have 64 stitches, you must increase 2 stitches for the cuff, then decrease 2 stitches before you start the heel.

TIP

In order not to have any loose stitches at the transition from 1 needle to another, the first 2 stitches on every needle have to be knit especially tight (see also Tip for more attractive edges, page 29). Place the needles so that the end of the used needle lies on top of the next one, and work underneath the previous needle with the new needle. Hold the needle on which you are working between your thumb and forefinger in such a way that the needle in front lies in between.

For a reinforced heel, every other stitch on the right side of the work is slipped rather than worked.

Heel and turn are worked with the first and fourth needles on the right and wrong side of the work.

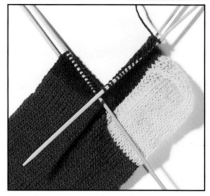

For the gusset, pick stitches up from the heel edges, then continue working in rounds.

Heel

The heel and turn are worked with the first and fourth needles. Temporarily put aside the stitches on the second and third needle. The heel and turn will wear better if you add a reinforcement yarn.

The heel is worked in stockinette stitch. If you wish, you can work the first and last 2 or 3 stitches in garter stitch. You can also work the turn and heel on only 2 needles.

The heel length proportion is always 2 rows less than the number of stitches. For example, if you have 30 stitches, you will have 28 rows.

An additionally reinforced heel is worked with slipped stitches. On the right side of the work, alternately knit 1 stitch and slip 1 stitch purlwise. On the wrong side of the work, purl all the stitches.

Turn

For the turn, the heel stitches are divided evenly onto 3 needles. For example, if you have 30 stitches, put 10 stitches on each needle. You can also leave all the stitches on 1 needle, but you won't work the outer stitches. If the number of stitches is not divisible by 3, put the extra stitches on the center needle.

Continue working back and forth: In the first row, slip the last stitch on the second needle knitwise, knit the first stitch on the third needle, and pass the slipped stitch over. Turn the work. In the second row (WS), slip the first stitch purlwise, purl the following stitches, then purl the last stitch on the second needle together with the first stitch on the third needle. Turn the work. In the third row, slip the first stitch purlwise, work a single decrease over the last stitch on the needle and the first stitch of the third needle. Keep repeating Rows 2 and 3 until all the stitches on the first and third needles have been used up. Put the remaining stitches (here there are 10) onto 2 needles, at 5 stitches each on the fourth and first needles.

Gusset

Knit the stitches on the fourth and first needles, then pick up 1 stitch every other row on the heel edge (in the example, 28 rows were worked, so 14 stitches will be picked up). To prevent a hole from forming between the heel and the cuff, increase 1 stitch knit twisted out of the horizontal thread in the corner between the edge of the heel and the cuff (15 stitches in total). Then work the

stitches on the second and third needles. For the fourth needle, first increase 1 stitch in the corner, knit twisted, then pick up 1 stitch every other row along the heel edge. Then work the remaining 5 stitches. There are now more stitches on the first and fourth needles (20, in this case), which will be reduced again as the gusset decreases are made.

Now work 1 round using all the stitches. The stitches on the first and fourth needles should always be worked in stockinette stitch, while the stitches on the second and third needles can be worked in a pattern.

In the next row, knit the second and third to last stitches on the first needle together for the decreases, then knit the last stitch. On the fourth needle, knit the first stitch, slip the second stitch knitwise, knit the third stitch, and pass the slipped stitch over. Then work 2 rounds without decreasing. Repeat these 3 rows until the original number of stitches (here it is 15) on the first and fourth needles has been reached again. Work the desired length of the foot.

Toe

For a banded toe, the decreases are worked at the end of the first and third needles and at the beginning of the second and fourth needles:

On the first and third needles, work to within 3 stitches from the end, then knit 2 stitches together and knit the last stitch. On the second and fourth needles, knit 1 stitch, slip the next stitch knitwise, knit the third stitch, and pass the slipped stitch over the third stitch.

In order to make the rounded part as attractive as possible, evenly reduce the number of rows: Work the decreases, as described, 1x in the fourth round, then 2x in every third round, 3x in every second round and then in every round. Pull the last 8 stitches together with the working yarn or place the stitches from the top onto the bottom stitches and sew them together using grafting stitch.

For children's socks, it is usually enough if between decreases, 2 rounds using all the stitches are worked 1x and 1 round 2x to 4x. Then decrease in every round.

A banded toe is the most attractive finish.

Even nicer when you cast on in kitchener rib

Just as with neckbands, ribbing for gloves, mittens, or socks can be started by casting on in kitchener rib (page 22). You can either start with a chain of crochet stitches in a contrasting yarn, or you can start with the yarn you are going to use.

Using the actual yarn, you cast on the required number of stitches on 1 needle. Here, don't use a smaller needle size; otherwise, the ribbing edge becomes too tight. In the first row, the stitches are then divided up among the 4 needles. Alternately knit 1 stitch and slip the next stitch purlwise. Each time you have worked one-fourth of the stitches, start a new needle.

Now work in rounds. In the first round, all the knit stitches are slipped purlwise, all the purl stitches are purled. In the second round, the knit stitches are knit and the purl stitches are slipped.

Then repeat the first round once more. Now continue in the ribbing pattern.

If you start with a row of crocheted chain stitches in a different color, you already divide the stitches up among the 4 needles in the first row: Alternately knit 1 stitch out of the horizontal back part of a chain stitch, and work 1 yarn over. Then continue with the actual yarn.

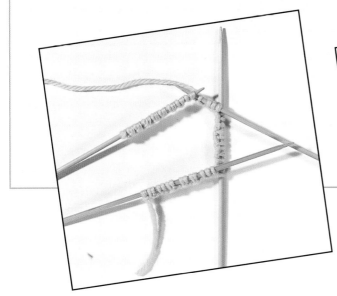

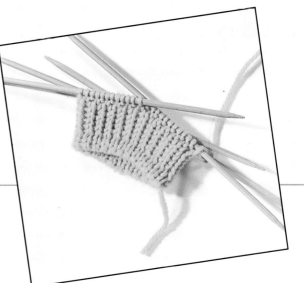

Gloves and Mittens

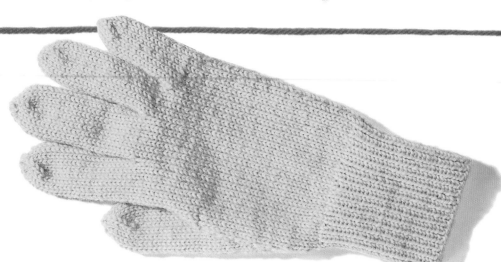

You need a little dexterity for knitting gloves, because even the few stitches for the fingers have to be worked in rounds.

Just like socks, gloves should be knit relatively tightly. These gloves were worked in pure virgin wool of approximately 125 m (137½ yds)/ 50 g (1¾ oz), on size 4 double pointed needles. The gauge is 26 stitches and 38 rows for a 4" square.

For the right glove, work the palm with the first and second needles, the back of the hand with the third and fourth needles. Reverse this for the left glove. Since all the fingers are worked symmetrically, only the position of the thumb has to be changed. Everything else is worked the same way.

	5/6/7/8		4/5/6/7		5/6/7/8		6/7/8/9	
	Pinkie finger	3	Ring finger	3	Middle finger	3	Fore-finger	
	5/6/7/8		4/5/6/7		5/6/7/8		6/7/8/9	

The gloves are described in size 7. All information for sizes 6, 7, 8, and 9 (for yarns with a gauge of 26 stitches and 38 rows = 4") is contained in the table.

Glove size	6	7	8	9
Hand circumference in inches	6.8	7.6	8.8	9.6
Stitches to cast on	40	48	56	64
Stitches for thumb gusset	13	13	15	17
Stitches for thumb fourchette	7	7	9	9
Length of pinkie finger	2	2.4	2.8	3.2
Length of ring finger	2.4	2.8	3.2	3.6
Length of middle finger	2.6	3	3.4	3.8
Length of forefinger	2.4	2.8	3.2	3.6
Length of thumb	2	2.2	2.4	2.6

Ribbed Cuff

Cast on 48 st with size 3 needles (see also casting on in kitchener rib, page 207) and divide the stitches evenly among the 4 needles of the set (12 st per needle). Work the cuff to the desired length. However, it should be at least 2½" long. If you tend to knit ribbing very tightly, or if you want to turn the cuff over, you can also cast on a few stitches more and knit 2 stitches together several times in the first row of stockinette stitch.

Then continue in stockinette stitch on size 4 needles.

Thumb Gusset

After 2 rounds, start with the increases for the thumb gusset. On the first needle, knit 2 stitches. Before and after the third stitch, inc 1 stitch knit twisted out of the horizontal thread. Then work 3 rounds without increasing. In the fourth round, inc 1 stitch on both sides of the increased stitch. Repeat these increases every fourth round 4 more times (13 stitches for the thumb gusset). After the last round of increasing, work another 3 round, then put the 13 thumb stitches onto a stitch holder.

For the left glove, work to within 3 stitches before the end of the fourth needle for the thumb gusset, then work the increases before and after the third to last stitch.

Thumb Fourchette

Above the thumb stitch on the stitch holder, cast on a fourchette of 7 stitches. End the round and work another round over all the stitches.

In the next round, work decreases over the 7-st fourchette as follows: Slip the first fourchette stitch knitwise, knit the second fourchette stitch, and pass the slipped stitch over. Knit the next 3 stitches and knit the last 2 stitches together. In the next round, repeat the decreases. Then work 1 round without decreases and in the next round, slip the first of the last 3 fourchette stitches knitwise, knit the next 2 stitches together, and pass the slipped stitch over. Now you have the original 12 st on the first needle again.

Continue evenly up to the little finger.

Pinkie Finger

When the glove is long enough for the pinkie finger, work to within 6 stitches from the end of the second needle. Now work the last 6 stitches on the second needle and the first 6 stitches on the third needle on extra needle with a new piece of yarn. Cast on 3 stitches as the fourchette from the back of the glove to the palm. Divide these 15 stitches among 3 needles, 5 stitches on each, and work in the round in stockinette stitch.

When the finger is about 2" long, try the glove on. Starting about ½" before the fingertip, knit the last 2 stitches on each needle together. Work these decreases until only 6 stitches are left in total. Cut off the yarn and draw the 6 stitches together with the yarn.

Now, using the previous yarn, work 3 stitches out of the fourchette, then work about 3 rounds over all the stitches to the ring finger.

Ring Finger

Work to within 5 stitches from the end of the second needle. With a new piece of yarn, work the last 5 stitches on the second needle, the 3 stitches of the fourchette, and the first 5 stitches on the third needle on extra needle with a new piece of yarn. Cast on 3 stitches as the next fourchette. Divide these 16 stitches among 3 needles, (5/5/6 stitches), and work in round in stockinette stitch for about 2½". Slip the last stitch from the second and third needles onto the first and fourth needles, respectively.

Work the tip as for the pinkie finger. Since there is 1 stitch less on 2 needles, don't knit any stitches together on these needles in the first dec round. Draw the last 6 stitches together with the working yarn.

Middle Finger

Put the first 7 stitches from the first needle and the last 7 stitches from the fourth needle on a stitch holder for the forefinger.

Knit the 6 stitches on the back of the glove, knit 3 stitches from the fourchette of the ring finger, knit the next 6 stitches on the palm, and cast on 3 stitches for the next fourchette. Divide these 18 stitches among 3 needles and end the middle finger like the pinkie finger.

Forefinger

Knit 3 stitches from the fourchette, then knit the remaining 14 stitches. Divide these 17 stitches among 3 needles (5/6/6 stitches), and finish the forefinger like the other fingers.

Thumb

In addition to the 13 thumb stitches from the stitch holder, knit another 7 stitches from the fourchette. To prevent a hole from forming, knit the first and last stitches twisted from the horizontal thread next to the thumb stitch. Divide these 20 stitches among 3 needles (6/7/7 stitches). Knit in round over all the stitches. When the thumb is 2" long, work the tip as for the other fingers.

Mittens

Mittens are started just like gloves. After the thumb fourchette, continue working over the 48 stitches to the end of the pinkie finger. Then start the decreases for the banded tip.

For the banded tip, knit 1 stitch on the first needle, slip the second stitch knitwise, knit the third stitch, and pass the second stitch over it. Work to within 3 stitches before the end of the second needle, then knit 2 stitches together and knit the last stitch. Work the decrease on the third needle as on the first needle, and on the fourth needle as on the second needle. Repeat these decreases every other round until only half the stitches are left on the needle, then work the decreases in every round until only 8 stitches in total are left.

Place the remaining stitches of the right band flat onto those of the left band and sew them together using grafting stitch.

TIP

Since the last 6 stitches of the fingertips are drawn together using the working yarn, the stitches should not be too large. For this reason, work the last round of decreases with a needle one size smaller than that used for the other rounds.

Stitch Patterns

This chapter contains the pattern charts for all the patterns in this book as well as a great many other beautiful patterns.

Shaker Knitting

On WS, work all stitches as they lie.
Repeat Rows 1 to 40.

26-st repeat

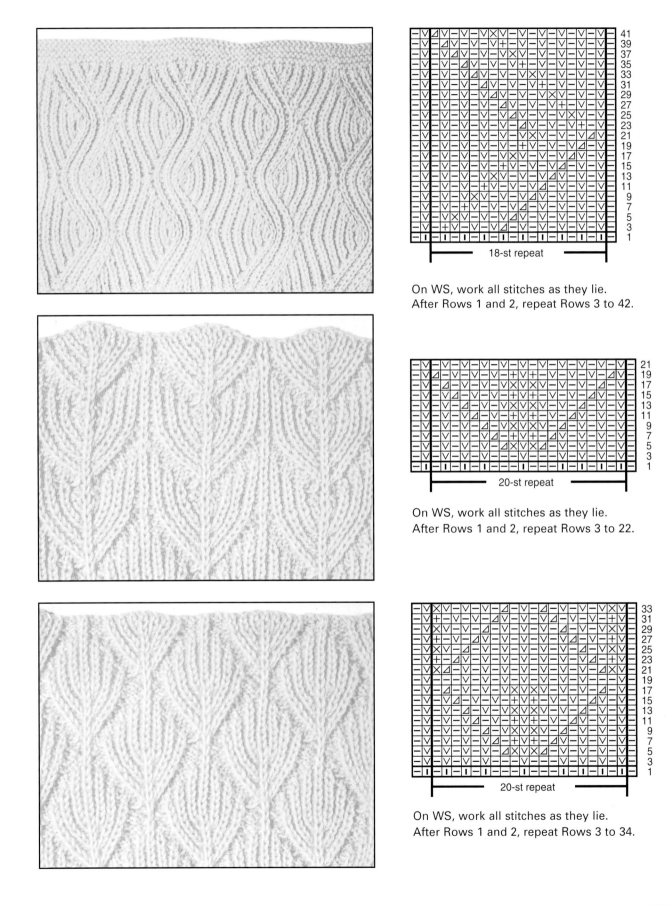

On WS, work all stitches as they lie.
After Rows 1 and 2, repeat Rows 3 to 42.

On WS, work all stitches as they lie.
After Rows 1 and 2, repeat Rows 3 to 22.

On WS, work all stitches as they lie.
After Rows 1 and 2, repeat Rows 3 to 34.

Cables

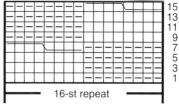

On WS, work all stitches as they lie.
Repeat Rows 1 to 16.

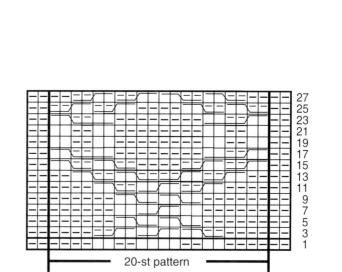

On WS, work all stitches as they lie.
Repeat Rows 1 to 24.

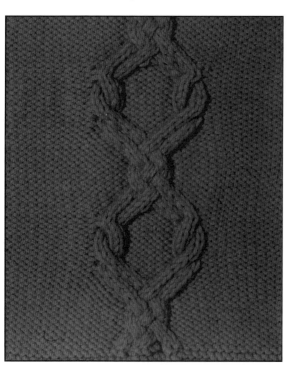

On WS, work all stitches as they lie.
After first 2 rows, repeat Rows 3 to 28.

= put 2 st on 1 cable needle in back, 2 st on second cable needle in back, k2, purl the 2 purl st on the second cable needle and knit the 2 st on the first cable needle.

= put 2 st on 1 cable needle in front, 2 st on second cable needle in front, k2, purl the 2 purl st on the second cable needle and knit the 2 st on the first cable needle.

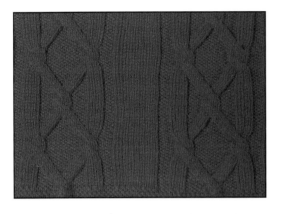

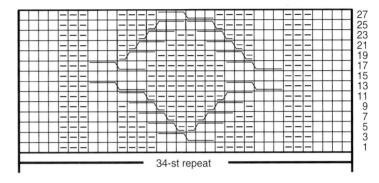

On WS, work all stitches as they lie.
Repeat Rows 1 to 28.

On WS, work all stitches as they lie.
Repeat Rows 1 to 8.

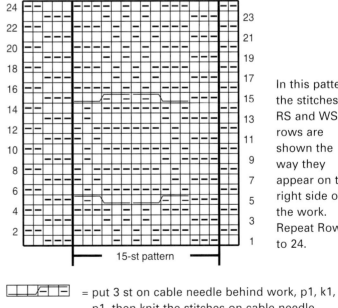

In this pattern, the stitches on RS and WS rows are shown the way they appear on the right side of the work. Repeat Rows 1 to 24.

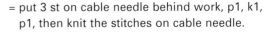 = put 3 st on cable needle behind work, p1, k1, p1, then knit the stitches on cable needle.

= put 3 st on cable needle in front of work, k1, p1, k1, then knit the stitches on cable needle.

Stitch Patterns

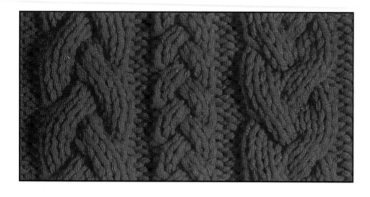

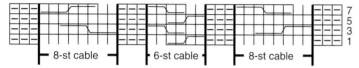

On WS, work all stitches as they lie.
Repeat Rows 1 to 8.

Pattern on page 132.

On WS, work all stitches as they lie.
Repeat Rows 1 to 6.

Pattern on page 135.

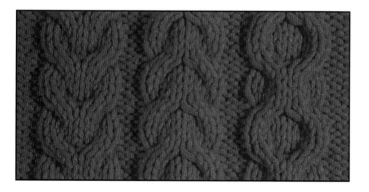

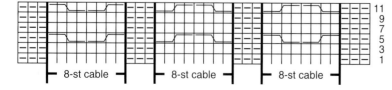

On WS, work all stitches as they lie.
Repeat Rows 1 to 12.

Pattern on page 132.

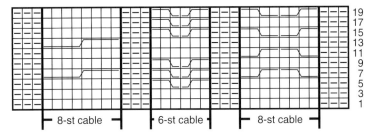

19
17
15
13
11
9
7
5
3
1

├─ 8-st cable ─┤ ├─ 6-st cable ─┤ ├─ 8-st cable ─┤

On WS, work all stitches as they lie.
Repeat Rows 1 to 20.

Pattern on page 132.

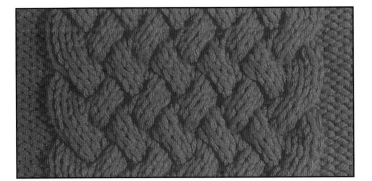

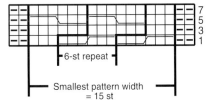

7
5
3
1

├─ 6-st repeat ─┤

├──── Smallest pattern width ────┤
= 15 st

On WS, work all stitches as they lie.
Repeat Rows 1 to 8.

Pattern on page 135.

11
9
7
5
3
1

├─ 6-st cable ─┤ ├─ 6-st cable ─┤ ├─ 6-st cable ─┤

On WS, work all stitches as they lie.
Repeat Rows 1 to 12.

Pattern on page 132.

Openwork Patterns

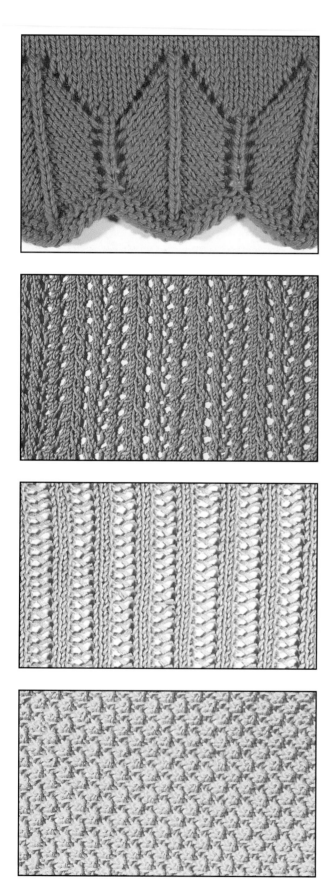

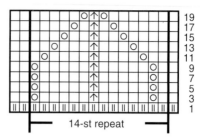

On WS, work all stitches as they lie, knit the garter stitches and purl the yarn overs.
Repeat Rows 1 to 20.

Openwork pattern with points on page 57.

On WS, work all stitches as they lie, purl yarn overs.
Repeat Rows 1 to 4.

On RS and WS, the stitches are shown in the pattern chart the way they are worked.
Repeat Rows 1 and 2.

On WS, purl all stitches.
After the first 2 rows, repeat Rows 3 to 6.

= work 3 stitches over 1 st: k1, p1, k1.

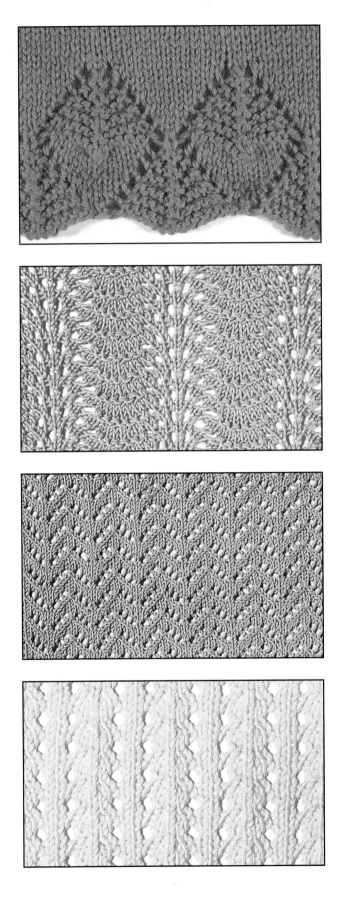

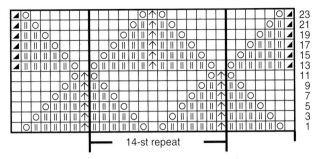

On WS, work all stitches as they lie, knit the garter stitches, and purl the yarn overs.
Repeat Rows 1 to 24.

Openwork pattern with garter stitch on page 57.

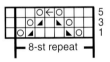

On WS, purl all stitches and yarn overs.
Repeat Rows 1 to 4.

On WS, purl all stitches and yarn overs.
Repeat Rows 1 to 6.

Arrowhead lace pattern on page 136.

On WS, purl all stitches and yarn overs.
Repeat Rows 1 to 4.

Vertical openwork stripes on page 137.

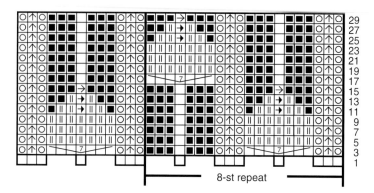

On WS, work all stitches as they lie, purl the yarn overs, and knit the garter stitches.
After the first 2 rows, repeat Rows 3 to 30.

= work 7 stitches in 1 st: alternately k1, yo, end with k1. On WS, knit all stitches.

→ = k3 tog, on WS k1.

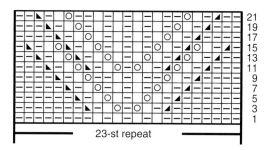

On WS, work all stitches as they lie, purl the yarn overs.
Repeat Rows 1 to 22.

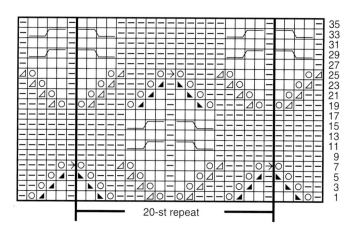

On WS, work all stitches as they lie, purl the yarn overs.
Repeat Rows 1 to 36.

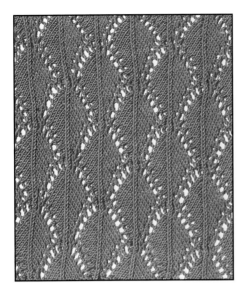

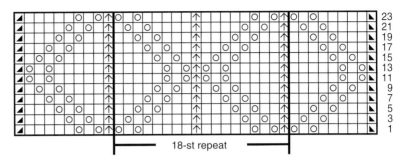

On WS, purl all stitches and yarn overs.
Repeat Rows 1 to 24.

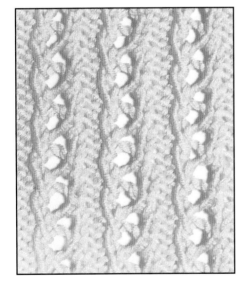

On WS, purl all stitches and yarn overs.
Repeat Rows 1 to 4.

Openwork stripe on page 137.

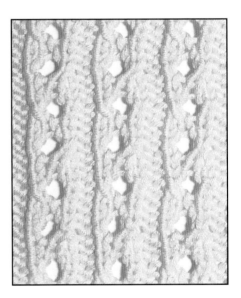

On WS, purl all stitches and yarn overs.
Repeat Rows 1 to 4.

Openwork stripe on page 137.

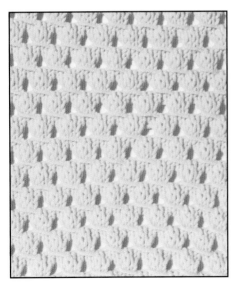

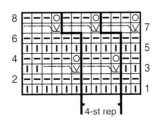

On RS and WS, the stitches are shown in the pattern chart the way they are worked.
Repeat Rows 1 to 8.

= slip 1 st knitwise, knit the next 3 st, and pass the slipped st over.

221

Twisted Stitches

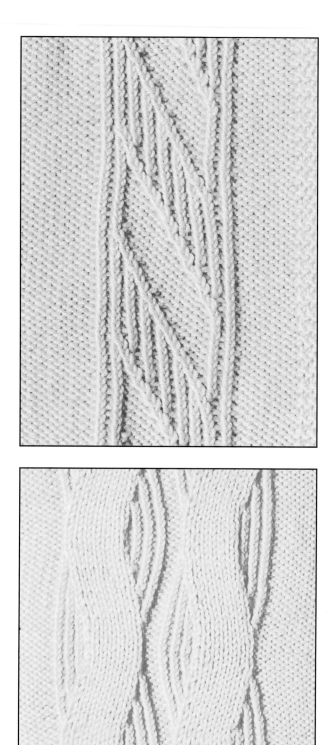

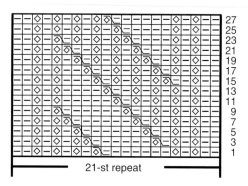

21-st repeat

On WS, work all stitches as they lie, work the twisted stitch twisted again.
Repeat Rows 1 to 28.

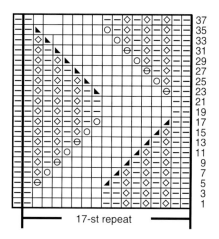

17-st repeat

On WS, work all stitches as they lie. Work the twisted stitches and the yarn overs with left diagonal line with twisted purl; knit the normal yarn over.
Repeat Rows 1 to 38.

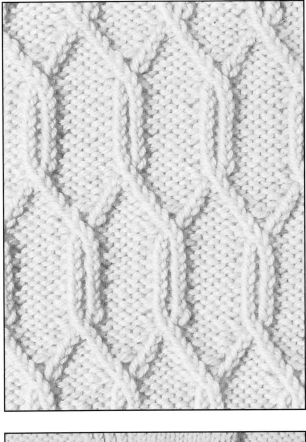

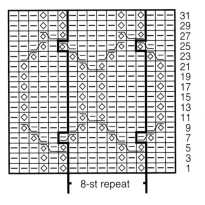

8-st repeat

On WS, work all stitches as they lie and work the twisted stitches twisted again. Repeat Rows 1 to 28.

= put 1 st on cable needle in front of work, knit the next st twisted, purl the next st, knit the st from cable needle twisted.

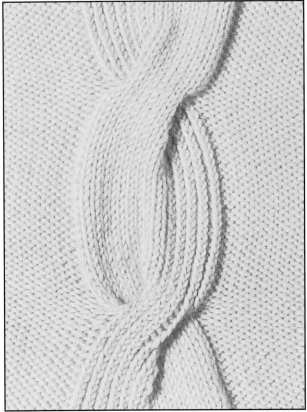

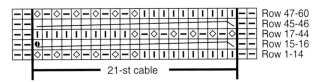

	Row 47-60
	Row 45-46
	Row 17-44
	Row 15-16
	Row 1-14

21-st cable

On WS, work all stitches as they lie and work the twisted stitches twisted again. Work Rows 1 and 2 7x, then Rows 15 and 16. Work Rows 17 and 18 14x, then Rows 45 and 46. Now work Rows 47 and 48 7x (60 rows). Repeat these 60 rows.

= put 10 st behind the work on cable needle, work 10 st in ribbing pattern, then knit st from cable needle.

= put 11 st behind the work on cable needle, k10, then work st from cable needle in ribbing pattern.

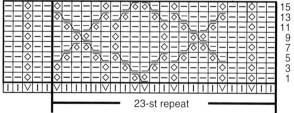

On WS, work all stitches as they lie and work the twisted stitches twisted again.
Repeat Rows 1 to 16.

Pattern on page 139.

15-st repeat

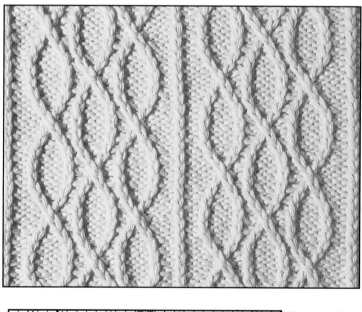

On WS, knit all knit stitches, slip all purl st purlwise.
After the first row (WS) on the chart, repeat Rows 1 to 16.

◇ = On RS, knit 1 twisted. On WS, slip 1 purlwise with yarn in front of the work.

Pattern on page 139.

23-st repeat

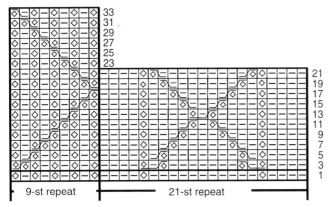

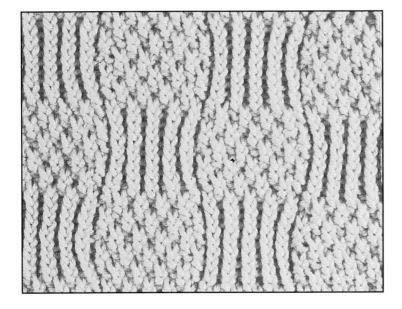

On WS, work all stitches as they lie.
After the first 2 rows, repeat Rows 3 to 22 for 9-st pattern, Rows 3 to 34 for 21-st pattern.

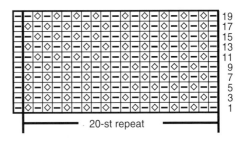

= put 2 st behind work on cable needle, k1 twisted, purl the first st from cable needle and knit the second st twisted.

= put 1 st in front of work on cable needle, k1 twisted, p1, then knit the st from cable needle twisted.

= put 1 st in front of work on cable needle, k1 twisted, then knit the st from cable needle twisted.

= put 1 st behind work on cable needle, k1 twisted, then knit the st from cable needle twisted.

Pattern on page 139.

On WS, work all stitches as they lie and work the twisted stitches twisted again. Repeat Rows 1 to 20.

Pattern on page 139.

Leaf Patterns

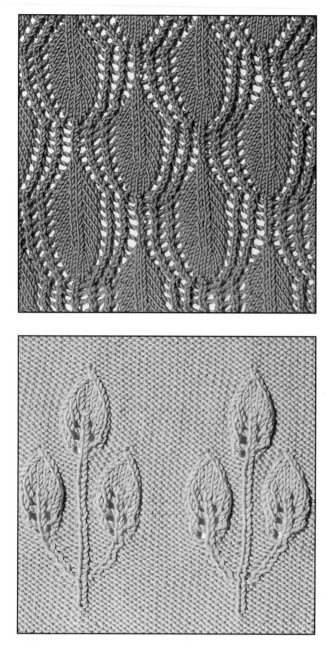

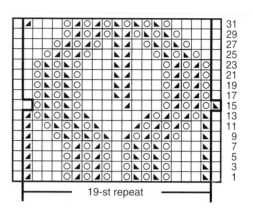

On WS, work all stitches as they lie,
purl all yarn overs.
Repeat Rows 1 to 32.

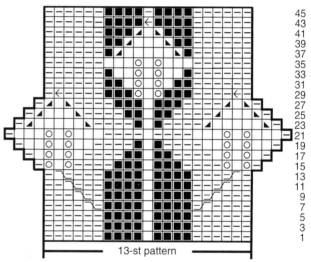

The black boxes have no meaning. They're only
intended for a better overview. On WS, work all
stitches as they lie and purl all yarn overs.
Repeat Rows 1 to 46.

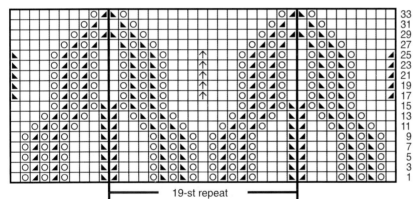

19-st repeat

On WS, purl all stitches
and yarn overs.
After the first 32 rows,
repeat Rows 33 and 34.

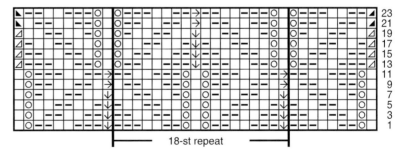

18-st repeat

On WS, work all stitches as they lie and purl all yarn overs.
Repeat Rows 1 to 24.

Aran Isle Patterns

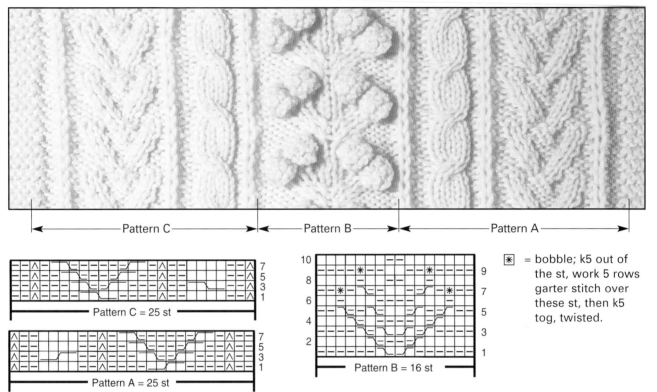

Pattern C ◄————————► Pattern B ◄————► Pattern A

Pattern C = 25 st

Pattern A = 25 st

Pattern B = 16 st

✳ = bobble; k5 out of the st, work 5 rows garter stitch over these st, then k5 tog, twisted.

Work pattern A, pattern B, and pattern C next to one another widthwise. Only the rows on RS are shown for patterns A and C. On WS, work stitches as they lie.
For patterns A and C, repeat Rows 1 to 8. For pattern B, repeat Rows 1 to 10.

28-st pattern   22-st pattern

On WS, work all stitches as they lie. Repeat Rows 1 to 24.

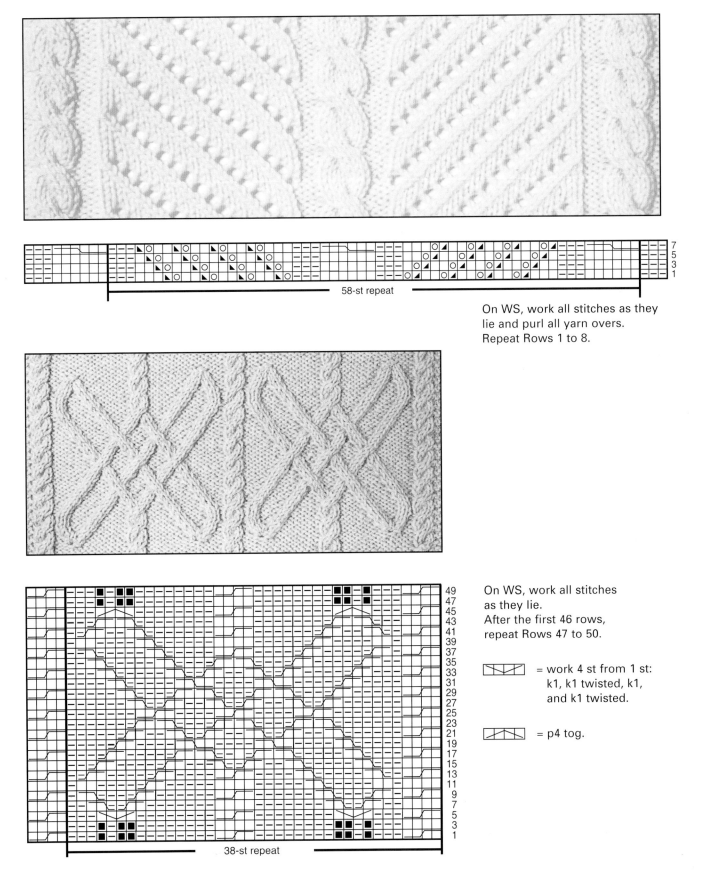

On WS, work all stitches as they lie and purl all yarn overs.
Repeat Rows 1 to 8.

On WS, work all stitches as they lie.
After the first 46 rows, repeat Rows 47 to 50.

= work 4 st from 1 st: k1, k1 twisted, k1, and k1 twisted.

= p4 tog.

Slipped Stitches

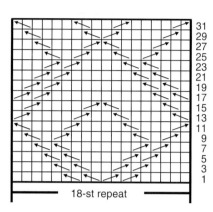

On WS, purl
all stitches.
Repeat Rows
1 to 32.

18-st repeat

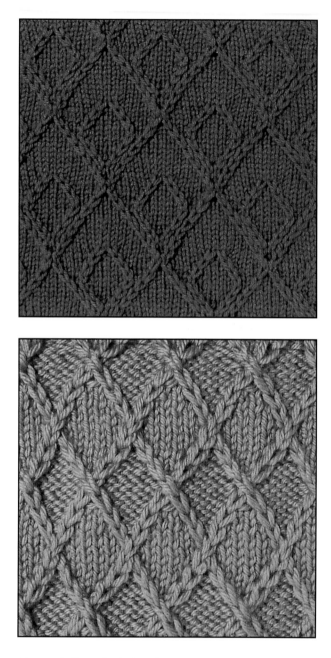

Crossed slipped stitches from page 140.

= put 1 st on cable needle behind work, slip 1 st purlwise (yarn will be behind work), then k st from cable needle.

= put 1 st on cable needle in front of work, k1, then slip st from cable needle purlwise (yarn will be behind work).

On WS, work all stitches as they lie.
Repeat Rows 1 to 6.

8-st repeat

= put 1 st on cable needle behind work, slip 1 st purlwise (yarn will be behind work), then k st from cable needle.

= put 1 st on cable needle in front of work, k1, then slip st from cable needle purlwise (yarn will be behind work).

= put 1 st on cable needle behind work, slip 1 st purlwise (yarn will be behind work), then purl st from cable needle.

= put 1 st on cable needle in front of work, p1, then slip st from cable needle purlwise (yarn will be behind work).

= put 1 st on cable needle behind work, slip 1 st purlwise (yarn will be behind work), then slip st from cable needle purlwise.

= put 1 st on cable needle in front of work, slip 1 st purlwise, then slip st from cable needle purlwise (yarn will be behind work).

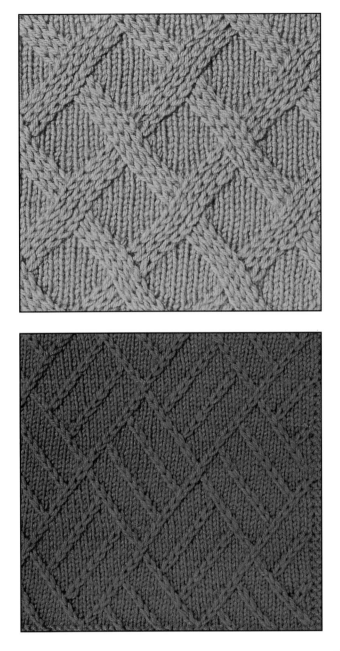

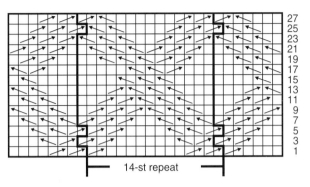

14-st repeat

On WS, purl all stitches.
Repeat Rows 1 to 28.

= put 1 st on cable needle behind work, slip 1 st purlwise (yarn will be behind work), then k st from cable needle.

= put 1 st on cable needle in front of work, k1, then slip st from cable needle purlwise (yarn will be behind work).

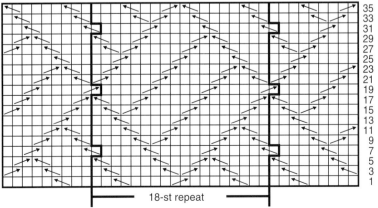

18-st repeat

On WS, purl all stitches.
Repeat Rows 1 to 36.

= put 1 st on cable needle behind work, slip 1 st purlwise (yarn will be behind work), then k st from cable needle.

= put 1 st on cable needle in front of work, k1, then slip st from cable needle purlwise (yarn will be behind work).

Textured Patterns

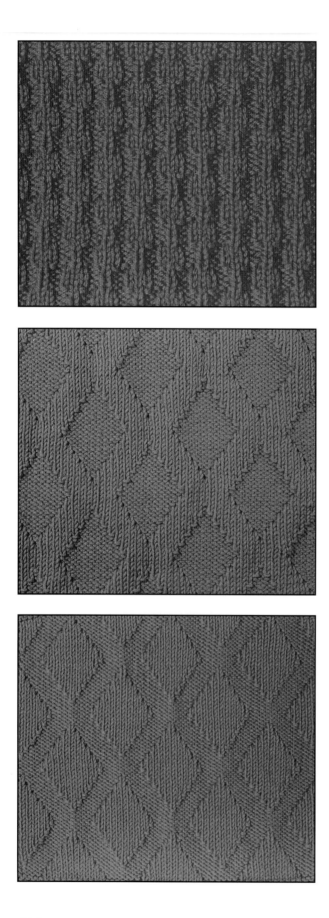

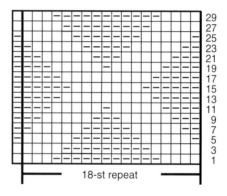

7
5
3
1

8-st repeat

On WS, work all stitches as they lie.
Repeat Rows 1 to 8.

29
27
25
23
21
19
17
15
13
11
9
7
5
3
1

18-st repeat

On WS, work all stitches as they lie.
Repeat Rows 1 to 30.

The same pattern from the back.

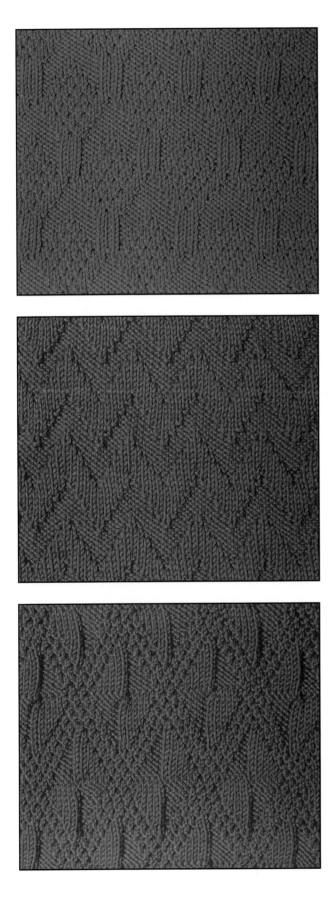

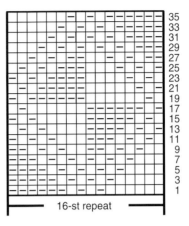

On WS, work all stitches as they lie.
Repeat Rows 1 to 36.

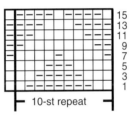

On WS, work all stitches as they lie.
Repeat Rows 1 to 16.

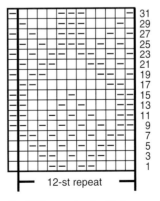

On WS, work all stitches as they lie.
Repeat Rows 1 to 32.

Jacquard Patterns

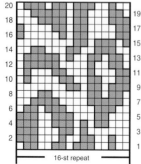

Repeat Rows 1 to 40.

Repeat Rows 1 to 20.

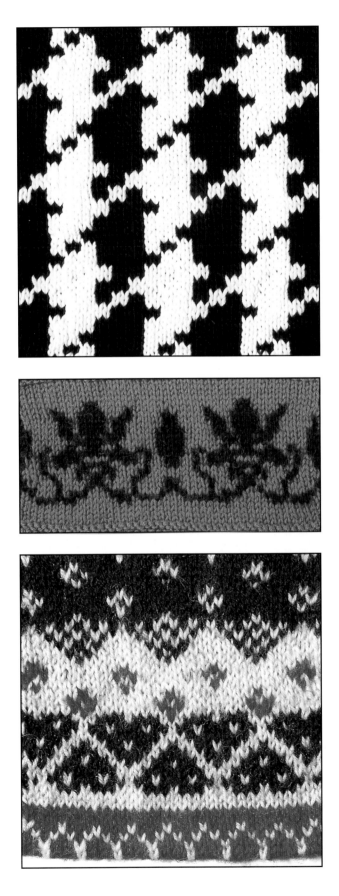

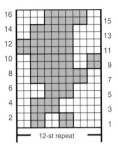

Repeat Rows 1 to 16.

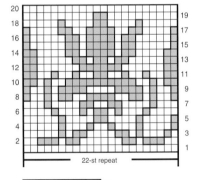

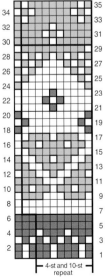

After the first 29 rows,
repeat Rows 30 to 35.

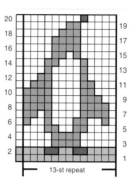

13-st repeat

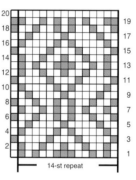

14-st repeat

The second pattern from the top was worked as shown in this pattern chart; in the pattern below it, the colors were switched.
Repeat Rows 1 to 20.

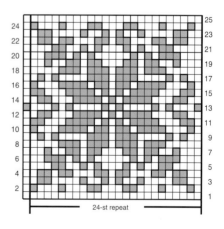

24-st repeat

Symbols and Abbreviations

☐ or □ = RS: k1; WS: p1

⊟ = RS: p1; WS: k1

⊞ = RS: k1; WS: k1 (garter st)

⊗ = RS: k1 twisted; WS: p1 twisted

◉ = RS: p1 twisted; WS: k1 twisted

◎ = 1 yo; on WS p1

⊖ = 1 yo; on WS k1

◢ = k2 tog

◣ = single dec: slip 1 knitwise, k1, and pass slipped st over

◿ = p2 tog

◺ = p2 tog twisted

→ = k3 tog

↑ = double dec: slip 2 st knitwise, k1, and pass slipped st over

← = slip 1 st knitwise, k2 tog, and pass slipped st over

↓ = p3 tog

✳ = bobble: work 5 st in 1 st (alternately k1, yo). Work 3 to 5 rows of stockinette stitch over these 5 st; in the next row on WS k5 tog twisted

⊞ = inc 1 k st, twisted, from horiz. thread between stitches

⊠ = inc 1 p st, twisted, from horiz. thread between stitches

■ = box not defined (no stitch)

▽ = 1 st worked in st of previous row: k1, but insert needle 1 row lower

△ = shaker knitting st: RS: slip st purlwise with 1 yo; WS: purl st tog with yo

⬛ = cross 2 st to left: place 1 st in front of work with cable needle, knit next st, then knit st on cable needle

⬛ = cross 2 st to right: place 1 st behind work with cable needle, knit next st, then knit st on cable needle

⬛ = cross 2 st to left: place 1 st in front of work with cable needle, purl next st, then knit st on cable needle

⬛ = cross 2 st to right: place 1 st behind work with cable needle, knit next st, then purl st on cable needle

⬛ = cross 3 st to left: place 2 st in front of work with cable needle, k1, then knit st on cable needle

⬛ = cross 3 st to right: place 1 st behind work with cable needle, k2, then knit st on cable needle

⬛ = cross 3 st to left: place 2 st in front of work with cable needle, p1, then knit st on cable needle

⬛ = cross 3 st to right: place 1 st behind work with cable needle, k2, then purl st on cable needle

⬛ = cross 4 st to left: place 2 st in front of work with cable needle, k2, then knit st on cable needle

⬛ = cross 4 st to right: place 2 st behind work with cable needle, k2, then knit st on cable needle

⬛ = cross 4 st to left: place 2 st in front of work with cable needle, p2, then knit st on cable needle

⬛ = cross 4 st to right: place 2 st behind work with cable needle, k2, then purl st on cable needle

⬛ = cross 4 st to left: place 3 st in front of work with cable needle, p1, then knit st on cable needle

⬛ = cross 4 st to right: place 1 st behind work with cable needle, k3, then purl st on cable needle

⬛ = cross 6 st to left: place 3 st in front of work with cable needle, k3, then knit st on cable needle

⬛ = cross 6 st to right: place 3 st behind work with cable needle, k3, then knit st on cable needle

⬛ = cross 8 st to left: place 4 st in front of work with cable needle, k4, then knit st on cable needle

⬛ = cross 8 st to right: place 4 st behind work with cable needle, k4, then knit st on cable needle

⬛ = cross 2 st to left: place 1 st in front of work with cable needle, p1, then knit st on cable needle twisted

⬛ = cross 2 st to right: place 1 st behind work with cable needle, k1 twisted, then purl st on cable needle

Abbreviations

dec = decrease, decreases
inc = increase, increases
k = knit
k tog = knit together
p = purl
p tog = purl together
psso = pass slipped stitch over
rep = repeat
RS = right side of work
selv st = selvedge stitch
single dec = slip 1 stitch knitwise, knit next stitch, and pass slipped stitch over it
st = stitch, stitches
tog = together
WS = wrong side of work
yo = yarn over

Index